E. St. C

D

DAY

D
DAY

JOHN GUNTHER

HARPER & BROTHERS
PUBLISHERS
New York and London

For

M. H. and Her Typewriter

with Love

CONTENTS

D
DAY

Chapter I

To Africa Through the Ice

WHEN I arrived at the airport near New York that hot morning I had no idea by what route I was traveling. All I knew was that I wanted to get to Africa quickly and that the Air Transport Command had arranged my passage. The young captain, who had been a lawyer on Long Island a couple of months before, seemed a trifle puzzled that I had no ticket, no travel orders. He looked up my name on a flimsy typewritten list. "Well," he said dubiously, "your priority is here, so I guess it must be all right." He reached for a ticket. "U.K. or M.K.?"

I looked at him.

"United Kingdom or Marakesh?" He was scribbling now.

"I thought I was going to Algiers."

"Yes, but the plane flies via the United Kingdom and we only run you as far as Marakesh, Morocco."

It was Sunday, and I had no British visa. The consulate would be closed. I didn't say anything.

"Well, we'll push you right through to Marakesh, and you can pick up something to Algiers when you get there."

"What's this about United Kingdom?"

"You'll lay over a few hours in Scotland . . ." he squinted at a clock . . . "sometime tomorrow morning."

But we didn't get off till that evening. We waited at the New York airport from about 10:30 in the morning—a fine hot Sunday morning—until almost ten at night, awaiting our ship which began its journey in Washington.

The wait did not seem too interminable. I was busy, interested, and curious, talking to the officers in charge, and listening with glue in my ears to what they said. I have spent a good many hours of my life hanging around airports, and never begrudged a moment of it. The shoptalk is always wonderful.

"Your ship is the one that took Davies to Moscow," said the dispatching officer. He pointed to the apron just outside the hangar, where the largest airplane I have ever seen was squatting. "That one is going off to China with Madame Chiang late this afternoon." (But as it turned out, Madame Chiang did not get off that day, and I missed seeing her.) Later I found that our ship had also taken Mr. Churchill and General Marshall to Gibraltar a few weeks before—and here was I—going to Africa via Scotland!

I was fascinated by the fuss-less mechanics of everything. The passport inspection was so cursory that no one noticed I had no British visa. I didn't even have to show my brand-new vaccination certificate. As a matter of fact I was never asked to produce that supposedly precious document during the whole trip. I never quite caught up with all the vaccinations I should have had, largely because I never stayed in one place long enough. Before I left New York I had three typhoid shots, yellow fever, smallpox, and the preliminary shot for tetanus. I didn't get around to getting cholera and typhus till Cairo, and I had to wait till Turkey for the rest.

A junior officer took charge of me, with the utmost casualness, and weighed my bags. I had two: an officer's kit bag weighing 38 pounds, and a typewriter weighing 17. The typewriter I had borrowed, at the last moment, from a friend the night before, because it was a few pounds lighter than my own. Then I had dragged bag and typewriter to a near-by drugstore to check their weight on a penny scale. I was far over the 55 pounds allowed. So

I had spent two or three hours closely winnowing through my things, discarding what I hoped were nonessentials. Now I approached the big airport scales. I was exactly 55 pounds, to the ounce. This was good guessing and a good omen, I thought. Then the officer said, "Oh hell, we don't count your typewriter." Thus I suddenly found myself with 17 pounds extra. But I had foreseen this possibility, and had carried a suitcase with me to the airport, containing some additional stuff. I piled these things into the kit bag, and sent the taxi driver home with the empty suitcase. Perhaps this all sounds trivial. But you don't think of it as trivial having to make a last-second choice between an extra pair of shoes, a flask, a flashlight, and a book.

This was Sunday, June 27, 1943. For about six weeks I had been working on this trip. I had my credentials as an accredited war correspondent, and after considerable delay I received permission to visit any of three separate theaters, London, Algiers, and Middle East. It was extremely difficult to get approved for Algiers, since General Eisenhower didn't want any more correspondents there. I had been hung up for several weeks on this, and I was only squeezed in after some pretty fancy headwork for which I have to thank my broadcasting employers, the Blue Network. Then I had to get permission to fly—at that time almost all correspondents were being shipped by boat—and a priority. This had been arranged through the efficient courtesy of Major General Harold L. George, Chief of Air Transport Command, United States Army Air Forces, and his special assistant, Lieutenant Colonel Rex Smith, my friend who was formerly managing editor of *Newsweek* and editor of the Chicago *Sun.* Above all, I had to decide where to go.

In Washington and New York, during May and June, I talked to the following people among others, asking them all one question: "If you were going abroad this summer and hoped to see some action, where would you go?"

Harry Hopkins
Sumner Welles, then Under Secretary of State
Wendell Willkie
Dean Acheson ⎤
Thomas K. Finletter ⎦ of the Department of State
Elmer Davis ⎤
Robert E. Sherwood │
Nicholas Roosevelt ⎬ of the O.W.I.
Gardner Cowles, Jr. │
Joseph Barnes ⎦
Brigadier General William J. Donovan ⎤
John C. Wiley │
Edmond L. Taylor ⎬ of O.S.S.
Frederick Oechsner ⎦
John J. McCloy, Assistant Secretary of War
Major General Alexander D. Surles, Chief of Public
    Relations, U. S. Army
William C. Bullitt, then Personal Assistant to the Secre-
    tary of the Navy
Archibald MacLeish, Librarian of Congress
Hanson W. Baldwin, military expert of the New York
    Times
Major George Fielding Eliot, military expert, New
    York *Herald Tribune*
Raymond Gram Swing
Henry R. Luce
Such colleagues as William L. Shirer, Jay Allen, M. W.
    Fodor, Barnet Nover, Walter Duranty, Junius B.
    Wood, Edgar Ansel Mowrer
Hamilton Fish Armstrong, editor of *Foreign Affairs*
Several British officials

Not one of these persons told me exactly where to go. There are at least three men on this list who, at that time, knew where and probably when, to the minute, the invasion of Europe would begin; but none of them were indiscreet enough to tell. In plain fact, I got an astonishing variety of answers to my question, though I don't think anybody tried deliberately to mislead me. I heard everything from a brusque "Gunther, get as far *north* as you can as quickly as you can," to a friendly, "Listen, John, it's an open and shut proposition; be in Istanbul by August first." Two people on my list, very high people, answered with a single succinct monosyllable, "Russia"; one Englishman said, "All you have to do is go where Tedder happens to be"*; two or three folk talked vaguely of the Far East; one said, "Hell, you'll see action *any-where*." I think the soundest advice I got was from Sumner Welles, but he didn't tell me anything specific. The British were very knowing too. In the last analysis, I made up my mind mostly on hunch. I looked at a map, thought about the more obvious strategic possibilities, glanced at a map again, and asked General George to send me to Algiers.

It kept getting hotter and hotter at the airport, with the sun streaming down on the roof of our hangar. There was no place to sit except the metal customs benches. I felt somewhat self-conscious in my new uniform; I bulged in all wrong places; I couldn't figure out what to put in what pockets; I was envious of a group of officers, my traveling companions, who seemingly didn't sweat. By noon, I looked as if I had been dragged heels first through a Turkish bath, and then bounced up and down in a fountain.

I had had about two hours' sleep the night before, which may predispose one to introspection. And as we waited, hour after hour, I wondered why I was taking this trip. There were several valid reasons, certainly. Mainly I wanted to see the war. In 1939 I had seen it start. But I had not been to Europe again since a visit to England in the grim Pearl Harbor winter of 1941. I felt the need to be refurbished and replenished by the gift of action. I

* Air Chief Marshal Sir Arthur Tedder, then commander-in-chief of the RAF in the Mediterranean, and now deputy supreme commander of allied invasion forces under Eisenhower.

was becoming sharply dissatisfied with the life of a broad-caster, who sits comfortably in New York and talks about what he thinks other people may be doing. Also I wanted to write a short book. I was timid, however, about the difficulties of doing just the kind of book I hoped to do. I wanted to write a simple, concrete, personal record of what I saw, nothing more, but nothing less. Oddly enough I have never written a personal book before. The three *Insides* scarcely contain the First Person Singular, except in isolated chapters. I am a professional reporter, but I have always written political books, never a "reportage." Altogether the idea of writing a simple, straightforward account of what I might run into became more appealing and, in fact, irresistible, as I continued to think about it. I knew perfectly well that eyewitness stories were often trite, evanescent, and a burden to the market. And I had no idea of how much I would be lucky enough to see. But anyway, I thought that, come what may, I would add my word about what I saw. And this is it.

Little by little that hot and deliquescent afternoon I began to learn something about the A.T.C.; I learned a good deal more before the summer was over and the trip was done. The Air Transport Command is the division of the Army Air Forces, the successor to the old Ferrying Command, which flies planes, cargo, and human beings from the United States to every battle front, from New York and San Francisco and Miami to the extreme ends of the earth. We have, I believe, garrisons or task forces at not less than seventy outposts scattered through the world. The A.T.C. not only serves them all; it is the in-dispensable and in some cases the only link between these outposts and home. As such, it is incomparably the largest and at the same time the most closely articulated aerial transportation system in existence. Yet very little is known publicly about the stupendous network of the A.T.C., largely for reasons of military censorship. It flies to

Alaska, Australia, the South Seas, Great Britain, various posts in the far north, the Caribbean, Brazil, across Africa, and to India and across the Himalayas and beyond. Its total routes amount to more than ten times those of all the domestic airlines of the world combined before the war. It flies an average of three million miles per day, and in one season it carted more than fifty thousand people across the Atlantic Ocean without losing a passenger or a ship.

One thing that astonished me is that the passenger and cargo ships flown by the A.T.C. are "civilian" planes. I had thought I was going to cross the Atlantic in a bomber. Not so. The A.T.C. planes are not armed; they don't carry weapons either for attack or protection. Of course they are run by the Army, and they carry Army Air Force markings. And the great majority are stripped for military purposes, with "bucket" seats. The ship in which I left New York had regular seats—and very comfortable they were too—but I learned plenty about bucket seats later. Another point: a large number of pilots on many A.T.C. trans-ocean runs are not army officers; they are civilian pilots. They wear uniforms, with special insignia, but they retain the status of civilians; on some routes you seem to be flying an extension of the services of TWA, American Airlines, or Pan-American. This is because— although the planes and equipment belong to the A.T.C. —airlines personnel fly them under contract to the A.T.C. and its operational control.

A young lieutenant who was a traffic manager in Los Angeles last year took me through the hangar. Here were two ships being "cannibalized." This odd expression means that these ships are being torn apart to provide spare parts for other aircraft. Of one, little was left except a skeleton. And wandering between piles of boxes I learned something about the cargo the A.T.C. carries. Some "hot" cargo has priority over that of any passenger;

emergency equipment for grounded planes, for instance.
In its lifetime the A.T.C. has carried almost everything,
including much material that people thought could never
be transported in an airplane. I saw the carefully packed
boxes, bales, and crates, marked blue for the Air Corps,
orange for the Signal Corps, bright red for medical supplies. Inside were spare parts for other planes, a couple
of frigidaires, a teletype machine, oxygen equipment,
small electrical gadgets, bales of felt and twine. Once the
A.T.C. shipped a whole hospital to Alaska. It has carried
the religious equipment a chaplain needs; $2,875,000 in
cash to troops in Iceland; serum, blood plasma, and vac-
cines which must be kept at constant temperatures; radio
equipment for Dakar and Casablanca; and a great deal of
the anti-tank ammunition that helped win the Battle of
El Alamein. I looked at one packing case 24 feet long,
containing the leading edge of a wing assembly; it seemed
inconceivable that it could be shipped by plane. My guide
said, "They'll have to cut it in half to get it out, but we'll
get it in, all right." Loading the ships is a formidable
problem. The cargo must be secured in place without
prejudice to the center of gravity, and yet with nice cal-
culation of what that center will be as gasoline is expended
and the ship thus lightened.

At about 6 P.M.—it was still steamingly hot—we were
told that our ship would take off from Washington soon,
and at eight we learned that it was on the way. The airport took on a new flavor now, compounded of suspense,
satisfaction, and a sense of imminence. Also it was getting
dark, and no airport looks the same at night. The widely
sweeping beacons; the shadows lurking along the runways; the lopsided winking of smaller lights: everything
now had a note of mystery. Inside the hangar, dim illumination came from bluish fluorescent lights, which turned
hands and faces purple. Our passengers knotted together,
and talked in whispers.

Then we saw our ship land, and it taxied up. It was enormous. Looking at it with part of the view obstructed, so that only the huge uplifted nose could be seen, it was like a monstrous kind of electric locomotive; then, fully revealed, it resembled nothing so much as an insanely magnified and streamlined locust. The pilot jumped out and walked briskly across the apron. He has one of the most American-looking faces I ever saw, I thought. I began to analyze what I meant by the adjective "American." He had a clean hooked profile and sandy reddish hair, and in that phosphorescent light, his eyes looked exactly the same color. The passengers from Washington stepped out to stretch their legs and smoke. Two were two-star generals; the A.T.C. officials treated them very soberly.

I felt an intense emotion of pleasure and excitement; I had not even had a ticket that morning and now I had a ticket to the world. We waited a few seconds in what seemed a pond of artificial moonlight and then climbed an exceptionally tall ladder into the ship. The interior was like that of a DC-3 but with double tiers of reclining seats, and much bigger. A young captain, the aide to one of the generals, offered me his window seat. There was only the minimum of delay; we taxied to the end of the runway, and took off at 9:51 P.M.

I found that curtains need not be lifted in a military ship—apparently all the passengers are considered trustworthy—and as we circled slowly over New York, circling and rising with the same motion while the four motors made a honking sound like none I ever heard in an airplane, I saw the lights of the city draw one design after another of incomparable brilliance and beauty. Maybe New York was supposed to be dimmed out, but it certainly didn't seem dim from up there. I wanted to smoke, but fell asleep before the No Smoking sign was switched off. At about two in the morning I woke up, and found that we were flying over water the color of slate. Then the sunrise started pushing through the clouds, turning them into something that looked like corn meal mush. We saw land presently—rough dark green country sharply cut by gullies—and the captain next to me (he was a tank officer) smiled as he looked down, "This isn't tank country; guess we'll leave it to the Air Corps." We circled low over thin greenish scrub, with dark blue lakes melting into it, and then saw an asphalt runway. The lakes, of every shape, spilled like mercury into the fields. We slipped down to land.

This was Gander, Newfoundland. The ground crew in New York had said we would hit Gander at 3:15 A.M. We were just seven minutes late.

Only after breakfast did I begin to realize how remarkable all this was. Here I was, in a tropical uniform, half-freezing in Newfoundland on the way to Africa. Yet the most remarkable thing about the whole flight was, in a way, that it was so *un*remarkable. The most extraordinary thing about it was that it was so ordinary.

Gander was—and doubtless still is—prunes for breakfast and a thin soup of chipped beef; barracks on stilts; a thin icing of frost on mud; a couple of R.A.F. ferry planes; a ping-pong table and the Encyclopaedia Britannica in the officers' mess; broad wooden walks over slimy puddles; the atmosphere of a western frontier town still in construction; Lend Lease; and German foresight. Because, strange as it may seem, this spot was a Nazi project many years ago; it was to have been the Atlantic terminus of a German airline. The United States took over the Gander area as part of the arrangement with Great Britain in 1940, whereby we acquired eight bases on British territory for fifty overage destroyers.

From this point on, for reasons of military security, I cannot name the stops we made. We left Gander shortly after breakfast. We arrived at a northerly airport in the British Isles ten hours later. It was dusk in Europe when we pulled in; of course British time is six hours ahead of ours. We had left New York at 9:51 P.M. Sunday and we had a comfortable dinner in Scotland Monday evening, not quite eighteen hours later.

Twenty minutes out of Gander the sunlight was intense and luminous over a solid sapphire ocean. I saw a stretch of beach, some cottages, and a fishing boat. Then I stared. There were bits of white stuff in the water. But the sea was too calm for waves. Then it dawned on me—ice! The last thing I saw in the Western Hemisphere was an iceberg as big as an aircraft carrier. Surrounding it were hundreds of small ice floes, nuzzling it like dinghies around a boat.

We didn't see a cloud all the way across. Our captain— Budd Merrill of Washington, D.C.—told me he had never seen a more perfect day. As a matter of fact though he had flown the Atlantic twenty or thirty times, he had never before crossed it by daylight. Pilots much prefer a night crossing because it is easier to get bearings from the stars than from the sun. "I've never seen so much ocean in all my life," Merrill exclaimed. Although the weather was perfect, it was clear, from their tight-lipped, uncommunicative white faces, that several of our passengers were nervous; they twitched every time the plane banked or when the motors changed tune. Captain Merrill kept saying, "Hell, you don't need a compass on a day like this; all you need is patience." The navigator told me later that never in his experience of thirty-one trips had they caught the Scotland beam so far out, and that we hit landfall only two hundred yards off course.

Captain Merrill said, "You fellows, anybody who wants to, you can come up here a couple at a time." I wondered how often two-star generals were called "fellows."

Priorities make strange bedfellows. We had two generals; also we had a brace of sergeants, technicians, who can be much more indispensable than generals. Ahead of me sat an astoundingly young full colonel, Air Corps of course. Next to him was a second lieutenant aged at least fifty, bald and gray. . . . Our civilians were laboratory men devoted to some secret process; they kept strictly to themselves. Several had never flown before.

It was very cold at first. The luggage racks on one side were loaded with white bags. I thought they were parachutes; and wondered what good a parachute could possibly do if you had to drop into the water. But the bags were Arctic outfits, for use in case of a forced landing on islands in this area. We unpacked several, and one or two officers put on the white furry parkas they contained. . . . In the other racks were orange Mae Wests and in the rear of the plane five yellow life rafts. A colonel, a medical officer, shrugged. "Almost useless, I'd say. In water this cold, nobody could stay alive more than thirty minutes."

We were running into a thinnish mist, and Captain Merrill let the ship down slightly. Instantly he had to run his wipers over the windshield, because a film of ice formed at once. Whoosh, whish, whoosh, whish. I looked at all the charts. The last lateral rubric is marked DEGREE OF CONFIDENCE. The little boxes were filled with the letter *U*. "What's *U*?" I asked. The navigator replied, "Unknown." . . . I looked at the heavily printed instructions for "ditching," that is crash-landing in the water. I had not known before that you must loosen your collar, otherwise your neck will be broken.

After two or three hours the forward tanks—installed in what had been designed as the bridal suite—were empty, and we were allowed to smoke. And presently the Gulf Stream, far below, reached up to us and it got much warmer. We shed our parkas. One of the generals said, "See if you can see a sign out there. We're going down hill."

I began to ask questions about the ship. We were traveling in what is known as a DC-4 in civilian parlance, but which the Army calls a C-54. This means that it was built by Douglas, under the name Skymaster; it is a huge big brother to the DC-3, and was originally designed for superfast civilian traffic at home. The war came; the Army took all the DC-4's over, and ordered many more. These are splendid ships. I got so fond of them I want to put the statistics down. They are 117 feet 10 inches from wing tip to wing tip, and 94 feet long, which is bigger than a Flying Fortress. They carry 28 passengers and a crew of 8, plus cargo; they are smooth to ride in, and extremely quiet. On the route we flew, with a brisk tail wind, we did 230 miles an hour, that is, almost 4 miles a minute. But what I was most interested in was the weight these ships carry. A C-54 empty weighs 41,729 pounds, including its "winterization" equipment, de-icers and so on; planes on the southern run are lighter. Loaded, on this trip of ours, we weighed 65,000 pounds, well over 30 tons. From Gander across the ocean you need about 2,700 gallons of high-octane fuel. A gallon of gas weighs 6 pounds, so your gas weight for the transatlantic run is 16,200 pounds. Add this to the weight of the craft empty and you have 57,929 pounds, which leaves 7,071 for passengers, crew, and cargo. Our total cargo weight was about 3,000 pounds. The planes are loaded so as to utilize every available ounce. For instance they use 50 gallons of gas (= 300 pounds) in the "run-up" and in taking off. So they are customarily *over*loaded these 300 pounds on departure, since the 300 pounds will be consumed before the plane actually leaves the ground. The ships are almost always loaded 300 pounds heavy. Pilots don't particularly like this. Additionally, as a rule, a plane is loaded 12 pounds heavy over the 300. This is because it is calculated that if a pilot ever ran out of gas, his last two gallons would be useless, since they would burn in a split second. A pilot can do nothing with two gallons. So the minuscule weight of those two gallons is also added to the gross weight of the load; usually it is filled at the final moment with special courier mail, just 12 pounds of it. Of course a plane gets lighter as it flies. A C-54 uses approximately 180 gallons of gas per hour. So at the end of three hours' flight, say 660 miles in normal circumstances, it is 3,240 pounds lighter than when it began.

I began to reflect about this ship, this flight. A C-54 costs half a million dollars. It represents between 25,000 and 50,000 man-hours of work in the Douglas plant at Santa Monica. There must have been technicians, experts in metallurgy, electrical engineers, aviation architects, from a dozen states, a hundred cities and towns and villages, who had done work on this one aircraft. I thought of these people—the draughtsmen, the riveters, the upholsterers, the executives, the men of brawn, the wireless men, the cool-minded laboratory scientists, who had helped to create what I was riding in so comfortably must represent a fairly representative cross-section of the people of the United States. We were riding in what Wichita Falls, Texas, and the tenements of the Bronx had helped to make.

The brash test pilot who was a barnstormer in Georgia twenty years ago contributed something to this plane, and so did the Negro boy in felt slippers who swept out the Pittsburgh aluminum mills, to say nothing of the radio expert with sensitive fingers who went to M.I.T. And I began to think of the materials, the physical components of existence, that go into every American airplane. Zinc from Michigan, bauxite from Nevada, copper from Montana, leather, wool, asbestos, molybdenum, silver foil, paint, wire thinner than a hair—the whole inordinately complex mosaic of an industrial civilization, was somehow assembled, concentrated, knit together, polished, adjusted, in the body of this single plane. Nuts and bolts and manpower; delicate metal tubing and sturdy human beings—they were all *in* this ship, essential parts of it. In fact this plane was America, flying into the air age.

Our cargo was in the main urgently needed spare parts for other aircraft. Because we were flying across the broad ribbon of the Atlantic, other planes would be enabled to fly. We were not merely one airplane. We were many airplanes.

We lay over twenty-four hours at an airport near one of the most famous golf courses in the world. This was because we missed the regular night plane to Morocco by half an hour. But as always when these enforced delays occurred I was delighted. It was refreshing to be in Europe once again; it was exhilarating to taste the cool atmosphere of northern Great Britain; I telephoned friends in London; I had Spam for four successive meals; I appreciated the infinite but wary politeness, the adroit good humor and good manners of the British.

There was a wonderful view as we circled in. I watched a covey of Liberators and wondered how any plane that can be so beautiful in the air can be so duck-bellied ugly on the ground. The weather was still perfect, and someone told us that these were the first four days without rain for a year. Yet weather can be a formidably variegated and dangerous obstruction. For instance we learned that New York had closed in half an hour after we left. And a westward flight had to turn back out of Newfoundland today because sudden adhesive fog settled over Gander two hours after we took off.

A courteous immigration official passed me in even though I had no visa. (But the next day there was a minor complication getting out since officially I had not arrived.) In twenty minutes, by utter fortuitousness, I met four people I knew: the manager of the hotel, whom I had last seen in Bogotá; a British lieutenant colonel who talked admiringly of Eisenhower; an American consul whom I had met in Damascus in 1927; and a young officer who was a traffic agent for the French Line a couple of years ago. As idly as if he were stamping a postcard, this good officer noticed that my ticket read "Marakesh" and he changed it to Algiers so that I would have no complications on arrival south. We went in to dinner. Two of the crew of our ship had never been abroad before. They were bewildered by English money. I felt both shocked and touched at this unsophistication. It seemed extraordinary to have to explain to a grown man who had just navigated a thirty-ton aircraft across the Atlantic what a shilling was. One of our passengers said with an air of thrilled self-discovery, "I've been in forty-six states, but never outside the United States before!" He was proud of himself and excited.

It would be more than absurd to write even a paragraph of generalization about England on the basis of a twenty-four-hour stopover at one airport. I can only describe what I saw. And this, I repeat, is a book which is purely a personal narrative, a report on things seen and heard. But certainly this part of England was eating better than when I had left it a year and a half before. The fecund stream of Lend Lease was obviously telling. I saw neat rows of half grapefruit on the buffet, something that would have been inconceivable before Pearl Harbor; the barman had orange juice and a fair supply of both gin and whisky; matches were of course scarce, but there seemed to be plenty of cigarettes. I noticed that women were at work everywhere, that doors were not locked in the hotel (all keys had long since disappeared), and that there were no towels or sheets. But in a curious way this airport gave less sense of war than New York. I saw no air raid shelters or alert signs.

We sat on the terrace almost all the next day and watched the planes come in. This will be one of the great international airports of the world after the war. Indeed it is all of that now. The ferry planes bank up in adjacent areas and then wait for a break in the weather to come in. Sometimes you see twenty or thirty B-17's fly their way in at once. Sometimes they are escorted by fighters which have no long-range instruments and must slow down so that they barely wallow through the air, in order not to outpace the bombers. We watched four A.T.C. ships take off, one after another; each was setting out on an ocean journey of about 2,200 miles, but it all seemed simpler than a subway ride from Times Square to Brooklyn. Queerly enough the stupendous proximity of the entire world from the point of view of time made the emotional distances greater. I said to a mechanic that I had left New York the day before. He looked up, grinned in a strange way, and then swore softly. "Oh, boy," he muttered, "New York . . . oh, boy!" He was servicing ships that went to America every day. But he hadn't been home in nineteen months. The fact that he was so close, in point of time, made him doubly homesick. On his face was an almost animal envy.

We took off from this northerly British airport at 10:01 P.M. Tuesday. The ship was the same. But our crew was new; the pilot was Captain Virgil Elliott. We struck out over water at once. The water, in that strange northern dusk, was the color of an officer's pink pants. We circled far out in the Atlantic and after midnight it became very cold. I dozed a little, smoked in the can, and at about five in the morning went up front. We were carrying a load of RAF boys; they were shy; they did not mix with the Americans, but kept tentatively smiling our way. We arrived at Marakesh at 8:31 A.M. Africa at first sight looked like a lion's skin stretched out tight and getting threadbare. I knew I was in an Arab country when I saw a blind boy sitting sideways on a mule.

There was a terrific breakfast waiting. I began to

understand why some things were short at home. We saw enormous yellow mounds of butter, giant cans of every known condiment and juice, slices of bacon a quarter inch thick, eggs by the dozen, and coffee enough to made a pool. I wanted badly to see something of Marakesh. But also I wanted to get on to Algiers. We were herded into a DC-3 at about ten. One of our generals said, "First DC-3 I've ever seen in Africa with seats." But already we could see that our flying was going to be rougher from now on.

This plane was an express ship going straight through instead of making the "milk run" via Casablanca and Oran. The earth was tawny, buff, puce. Occasionally came puddles of green, and I was startled to think that it all *looked* camouflaged; nature itself seemed to be a copy of something, a work of applied art. People began to lean toward the windows and shout when we reached the sea. Here was the dazzling and incredible Mediterranean at last. We passed curved shelves of white beach, break-waters that looked made of matches, and tiny harbors at the mouths of rivers the color of pus. The yellowish water made small lateral spouts into the radiant belt of deep purple lining the indented shore.

So we got to Algiers a little after lunch. We had come from New York to Africa, via Scotland, in less than three days overall, and in an elapsed flying time of thirty hours, fifty-eight minutes—without a bump.

Chapter II

Behind the Front

THE first thing I saw outside Maison Blanche, the airport, was a sign TEXAS STREET. Nearby was the A.T.C. office. Everything looked like an American army camp; which indeed it was. And everybody was co-operative and friendly, though seemingly confused and overworked; it took almost as long to arrange transportation into town, a half hour's ride, as it had taken to arrange the whole trip across the Atlantic.

I dumped my bags in the "Yank" office at the bottom of the building that houses Public Relations, and walked straight into two friends, Dick Mowrer of the Chicago *Daily News*, and Irwin Shaw, the playwright. Upstairs I had a brief talk with Lieutenant Colonel Joseph B. Phillips, the Public Relations chief and a friend of long standing. "We thought you'd be dropping in," he said. Joe offered to put me up temporarily at his villa, which is a tremendous boon. Most correspondents cannot get decent quarters here; many are squeezed three or four in a room in a hotel, the Aletti, where accommodations are somewhat primitive—so everybody says.

I went over to have drinks with John Whitaker, another of my oldest friends, who is here working for O.S.S. With him were Samuel Reber (Robert Murphy's assistant) and Raymond Clapper who is passing through on a trip like mine. The drinks were explosive: a combination of ersatz brandy and Algerian champagne. I returned to the villa, and found that it is the residence not only of

Joe Phillips but of Major General J. S. M. Whitley, Eisenhower's British chief of staff, and Brigadier General Robert A. McClure, the American head of political warfare in this area. A British colonel is out in the field for a day or two, and I can have his room until he returns. We talked till midnight. I mentioned De Gaulle and almost everybody in the room started to twitch. Obviously people are sensitive about what is called the political "situation."

My first radio show will be Friday. But I cannot do it "live" because the O.W.I. channel doesn't operate here at 4 A.M., which is the equivalent of my regular time in New York, 10 P.M. So I will have to try to talk New York into letting me do a recording, which can be transmitted at any time and then released at home when convenient.

Water is scarce, and the harbor is pack-jammed with ships. Obviously something quite big is impending.

Now let me tell as much of this story as I can in diary form.

Algiers. Thursday July 1.—Yesterday I asked no questions. I wanted to feel my way along. This morning after breakfast I took Joe Phillips aside and said that I didn't want to be indiscreet, I didn't want to pry, but that if something *was* going to happen soon, could I see it, could I go along? Cool, patient, competent, Joe did not commit himself. He told me nothing beyond what other correspondents had heard off the record a few days before from Eisenhower. But he was encouraging and he concluded that he might be able to dig up an "interesting" short assignment for me soon.

The press room at Public Relations is like so many press rooms I have seen. They have a generic similarity whether they are full of spittoons in the Criminal Courts Building in Chicago, or chaste and splendid as at the old League of Nations in Geneva. Crude desks wedged together; correspondents clutching precious typewriters and lugging them back and forth; bulletin boards containing handouts that no one ever reads plus a couple of mildly dirty cartoons; a peculiar kind of bored animation; everybody talking while everybody else works. I ran into Reynolds Packard of the U.P. whom I had not seen since Austria years before and Drew Middleton of the *Times*, whose work I have admired enormously and whom I had never met. Red Mueller of *Newsweek* and NBC spooned me out into the corridor. He told me that the correspondents were already beginning to thin out; that is, they were leaving town in preparation for what was coming. Did I want to represent the radio "pool" at what he described tactfully as a "forthcoming" operation? I would have to be incommunicado from Saturday on, and I would not be able to do any broadcasting until I got back. I might go in with an assault wave, or I might go in a day or so later. Did I want to take it on? Sure, I agreed.

Then Joe Phillips vetoed the idea. He had something else, he said, talking to me alone. "Excuse me, Sergeant," he told his Wac secretary, and she left the room. Joe asked me if I had ever met Harry Butcher, formerly a Columbia radio executive, now a commander in the Navy, and Eisenhower's chief personal assistant. Joe did not say much more but I gathered that if Butcher approved me, I might be assigned to go with Eisenhower on what would indeed be an "interesting" trip. Phillips didn't need to tell me to keep my mouth shut. I hopped a ride in a jeep and went over to see Butcher.

Today is the first day I have not worn a blouse. It was hot, though not nearly so hot as in New York. I kept experimenting to see how I could get notebook, passport, credentials, cash, a comb, pen and pencil, cigarettes, a lighter, and God knows what else, in two shirt pockets. I knew that I was on trial, as it were, before Butcher, and I wished there could be some magical transformation whereby I would look at least semimilitary. Butcher was

calm, acute, and very friendly, and after half an hour I
felt that everything was going to come out all right. It
took me a long time to find my way out of his headquarters and back to my jeep, which had strayed. In the
courtyard I walked straight into Butcher again, in company with a general bursting with stars. I was so embarrassed at almost knocking them down that I took off
my hat instead of saluting. I was that green.

Lunch at the mess opposite the Aletti, where junior
officers and correspondents—also miscellaneous civilians—
eat in this area. It was pretty awful. We have been in
Africa seven months. This is a region—because Algiers
is really France, not Africa at all—which should, and
could, produce both good food and good cooks in reason-
able quantity. I didn't object to eating a nondescript hash
and watery custard, though since the mess was bossed by
a Frenchman it seemed strange that the French were not
allowed to cook in their own way. *Any* Frenchman, if
permitted, could have made something better out of even
those materials if he had followed his own cuisine.

Of course everyone in Algiers has to work under the
most onerous discomforts. Nothing comes easy. The countryside is stripped bare; all the physical amenities of life
have disappeared. The shops are half empty; taxis don't
exist; alcohol and cigarettes are short. . . . And I continue to be appalled at the building that McClure, Phillips,
and the whole combined O.W.I. and O.S.S. setups have
to work in. At least two hundred officers are jammed and
scrambled in a series of tiny cardboard rooms without
adequate light or space, without adequate secretarial as-
sistance; they are insanely overworked, so that every
irritation caused by physical difficulties—for instance not
being able to get through to anyone on the primitive
telephones or find a paper clip or rubber band—is accentu-
ated. Another point is the lack of transport. No one can

get around. Yet almost everybody is good-tempered almost all the time.

I was told that I would need a lot of kit, and Lieutenant Harry Black, one of Phillips' amiable assistants, volunteered to round it up for me. I was staggered. I found that I now possessed a mosquito net; three blankets; a steel helmet; a gas mask; various gadgets which I did not understand; a musette bag; a bedroll; a flashlight; a canteen; and a series of complex belts, straps, and buckles. The only thing missing was a medical kit. I had been told that a small box of bandages and sulfa tablets was issued with every outfit, but I never got one. Then Phillips' orderly helped me to put everything together. I could make nothing fit. I can never do anything like this with my own fingers. The orderly reminisced about his boss as he smoothly, expertly adjusted my web belt, taught me how to wear a gas mask, fitted the lining in the helmet, and packed the bedroll. "I wouldn't change my job for anything in the Army. Lieutenant Colonel Phillips is the best man to work for a man ever had."

Late that afternoon I had a conference with a remarkable British public relations officer, Colonel John V. McCormack. The whole of Eisenhower's command is interlaced between British and Americans. Colonel McCormack is a peppery and idiosyncratic officer not, I should judge, much over five feet in height. He has been in the British army for forty-three years. He is one of very few British officers who has risen from private to full colonel. He told me where I was to go, and what to do. He was tough, shrewd, and vivid. He said he would give me a note to Lord X, the governor of the place where I'm assigned to. "That story ought to be written. Write it. But leave the Air Force out. The bloody Air Force talks too bloody much."

I am to represent the combined American press in Malta. No one actually dares to use the word Malta in conversation. This is security information of the highest order, since Eisenhower is to set up advance headquarters in Malta just before the invasion of Sicily begins. At first the general did not want any correspondents there. He dislikes personal publicity. But Butcher and Phillips apparently persuaded him that a minimum of coverage from Malta was absolutely necessary, if only for the sake of historical record. Joe probably arranged for me to get this billet purely as a personal favor, and I'm duly grateful. Two correspondents are to go to Malta, myself and Ted Gilling for the British press. Only two. We will be working for the newly constituted pool. I will file to the War Department, Washington, and Gilling for the British Ministry of Information.

Of course this means no broadcasting for the duration of the Malta assignment and perhaps longer. There will be no microphones there; besides, the pool arrangement precludes any individual work for a single organization. I cannot inform New York about this, since we are of course forbidden to mention any security matters in service messages. They will not hear from me for some time. I hope they will understand.

Dinner. John Whitaker arranged a party and took us to a French restaurant along the beach. We had drinks that seemed reasonably authentic, and excellent bouillabaisse and fish. Helen Kirkpatrick, H. R. Knickerbocker, Dick Mowrer, Demaree Bess, and an American colonel made up our group. I had last seen Knick in New York, about a month ago; he has come down to this sector from London. There was a lot of fairly sharp talk about the war. Dick Mowrer said with a sigh that he'd like to write about *peace* for a change. He has come all the way from Alamein. I've only come from New York, but I'd like to write about peace too. I was struck by one thing, the acute personal attachment so many war correspondents form for their commanders, the highly stratified loyalties they feel. They identify and personify themselves with one unit and the officer who runs it.

Helen Kirkpatrick talked all the time about De Gaulle. She is wearing a small Cross of Lorraine. She said things about what is going on here politically that make your hair curl. Twice she has been threatened with expulsion from the theater because of the frankness of her dispatches, though in theory no political censorship exists. My impression is that the real political boss in Algiers is Macmillan, the British minister; the British are professionals, they are seasoned at this kind of game. I have letters to almost all the French here, but I won't have time to present them, I'm afraid.

Back home; Joe Phillips and I talked awhile. Everybody knows now what is going to happen. Some of us will go along; some won't. Nobody pries; nobody asks questions. Do the officers here know that I am going? Probably they do. But nobody says a word.

Algiers, Friday, July 2.—I woke up happy; I love all this. During the morning I wrote part of a broadcast; then had lunch with Knick. We shopped at the PX for leggings, towels, soap. Each of us knows perfectly well that each is setting out somewhere, very soon; but we do not ask one another where. Dinner at the villa was full of brigadiers and generals. Then I worked again on my broadcast. An air raid alert warbled; this was the first one I had heard that might mean business since London two years ago. General McClure lent me a jeep, and I rode down to Public Relations to do my show. Two censors were amiable; so was Captain Wharfield, who handles radio for Phillips. It took some time to get a lift home. The driver of this jeep was a bear cat. Without lights, in a black-out city, we did fifty-six miles an hour. As we whipped around curves at insane angles, the driver held a flashlight aloft with one hand: our only illumination. I was delighted when an M.P. stopped us with a lighted red wand. "Aw, I was only doing about eighteen," said the driver. When he dropped me at the villa he grinned. He has been a truck driver for nine years. "I sure would like to have one of these jeeps when I get home again," he said. "I just love the goddamned little things. I could put it in my pocket."

Algiers-Tunis, Saturday, July 3.—Airport at 7:25 A.M. Gilling and I weighed in. With my new kit I am up from 55 to 95 pounds, not including the typewriter. There were draconian signs everywhere to the effect that not an ounce over 55 would be carried. McCormack had suggested calmly that I sneak out on the apron and just toss my bags into the empty ship when nobody was looking. I did not quite have the nerve to do this. Anyway, they let us on, 95 pounds plus typewriter and all. Then it seemed that although our baggage was aboard we would not be able to travel ourselves. The ship was full of No. 2 priorities and we only had No. 3's. But after some cogent tall talk by Gilling, who knows the ropes, they squeezed us in.

Our DC-3 was a somewhat aged-looking ship full of patched bullet holes, and the first stripped plane I have ever seen. There are no seats; cargo, mail sacks, and baggage are piled in the center of the cigar-shaped cabin in a long arched mound, leaving a cramped narrow irregular aisle along each side. Above is the gear for releasing parachutists, and metal braces hang out of the bare metal walls to hold stretchers; this type of plane is used to drop parachutists on outward trips, and to carry wounded on returning. For seats we have the celebrated "buckets"; that is, a folding shelf of aluminum hangs narrowly along each side of the ship, so that it takes only the minimum amount of space; a depression is scalloped out of the shelf every two feet, and in this you sit, strapped in; there are no arm or back rests, and the shelf as a whole looks like a series of shallow biscuit molds. I adjusted myself on this diabolical contrivance, and cast an eye on the pile of parachutes aft where I thought I could stretch out once we were under way.

This was not an A.T.C. ship. We were riding now with the Troop Carrier Command, something different; this was straight Army. It certainly was rough flying. It compared to the velvet luxuriousness of the flight across the Atlantic as a ride in a caboose might compare to one in a drawing room on the Twentieth Century Limited. We got ready to run up. A sergeant tossed a pail into the ship; it banged and clattered. "Hey," he shouted, "this is for anyone who is sick." A redheaded youngster who seemed to be the dispatching officer yelled to the pilot, "You're late as hell. Scram!"

But we didn't get off for a considerable interval. The redhead came back and poked his head into the plane, reading off two names. And two sergeants had to get off. They were being replaced by two nurses—girls on the way to a field hospital at Mateur—with No. 1 priorities. Nurses on duty, like generals, almost always rate No. 1's. I felt terrified that Gilling and I would be taken off next. I was chatting with an American colonel who was accompanying a Belgian officer somewhere. The redhead appeared again. He called out the Belgian's name. Our full colonel froze. He said stiffly to the redhead who was only a sergeant: "If you take this Belgian officer off, you'll have to take me off too."

The redhead (implacable): "That's up to you." Not even a "sir."

The colonel said, "This is a hell of a note," and he and the Belgian got off.

A young captain with a sun shield flapping over the back of his neck meandered up. He asked our pilot, "Going to Casablanca?" "No," the pilot replied. "Buddy, could you tell me where I could pick up a ship to Casablanca?" "Gotta priority?" "No." "Well, run out into the field

there and don't talk too much and one of those ships 'way
off the runway will slip you in, maybe."

Our pilot was D. M. Robertson; his co-pilot W. C.
Hoff. Both were Westerners; both have a rank quite new
in our Army, "flight officers"; they were sergeant pilots
until a month or so ago. Most of our passengers were
privates; I did not understand why they had such high
priority until I was told they were signalmen on an urgent
technical job. And I admired the sensible elasticity of
our system whereby full colonels got tossed off ships while
essential privates stayed. . . . Again the redhead bounced
up. He had another nurse. The pilot said, "My God." She
climbed on. This made fourteen passengers, and we
weighed close to five thousand pounds of load, just about
the maximum permissible. The pilot said, "It's taking a
chance. They shouldn't do it."

We ran up. As we trundled down the field a sergeant
without warning jumped out of his bucket, opened the
clanging metal door, and popped out. One of the nurses
said to the man next to her, "Soldier! Tell the pilot we've
lost a passenger!" Nobody paid any attention. But the
open door kept banging and now we were about to take
off. The co-pilot came back, crawled over the mounds of
baggage, and wrenched the door closed. A major next to
me was reading a *Reader's Digest* and smoking a cigarette
down to the butt, directly under the large sign No SMOK-
ING. GAS FUMES. We took off. The major sighed. "One
becomes accustomed to minor risks," he drawled, still
smoking. I got out of my bucket and slept soundly on
the floor until we got to Telergma, the port for Constantine.

Here a knot of passengers was waiting, struggling with
priorities. One youthful lieutenant colonel had been
stranded here for four days. There wasn't an inch of room
on any ship. He looked exhausted, and Pilot Robertson
let him on. We were four hundred or five hundred pounds

heavier now—what with new cargo we had loaded—and it took an everlastingly long run before we got off the ground.

A chaplain on board turned pointedly to the lieutenant colonel: "How come you were stuck here so long?"

"Don't know."

"Maybe because you're not British."

This was the first anti-British crack I heard in Africa. (During the whole trip I never heard more than two or three.)

The pilot let me sit forward, and I took the co-pilot's seat until we prepared to land at the Tunis airport. This was one of the best hours I ever had. For a time Robertson, coaching me carefully, let me fly the ship myself; it was the first time I had ever "flown" a DC-3. He and Hoff were eager to show me the battlefields. We nosed right down, poking through valleys and across fences. "Cut over that way, Joe," Hoff would say, and we would turn, twisting low and following the marks of battle.

There were burnt areas, looking like tar paper next to the wrapping paper that made wheat fields; bomb craters in a straight line, showing where a quick stick had fallen, with rings like those left by earthworms; perfectly cut aisles of grain, so distinct they looked like separate hairs in a head; Arab villages on hilltops, where the fences made lines like froth on a beach; here and there burnt-out tanks; on one emergency landing strip a wrecked P-38 on its back; irregular lozenge-shaped lines of trenches; then near Tunis immense piles of blasted, gutted, charred German tanks, troop carriers, trucks, planes, equipment of every kind.

We arrived at Tunis just before twelve. We said good-by to our fellow passengers, as we would say good-by to old friends, though we knew we would never see them again. Meeting us was a sturdy British officer, with red-bronze cheeks, a bushy mustache of silvery black, and intensely white teeth. He was Captain F. P. C. Feilmann of the Army Film Photo Section, British North Africa Forces. "I'm most frightfully glad to see you," Feilmann said. "Most frightfully glad. Jolly good show you got here. Come to lunch. Oh but my dear chaps, I'm putting you up. It's all laid on."

I had never heard the expression "laid on" before. Feilmann turned to his corporal with a sudden instruction. "Corporal, if you will be so good, will you lay that on." Feilmann's villa is the temporary headquarters of the British unit that made one of the greatest of all film documentaries, *Desert Victory.* We had lunch, a copious lunch, and discussed our plans. We had orders to put ourselves in Feilmann's hands, and doubtless he knew where we were going. But even our written orders did not specify our destination, and for a time we talked as if blindfolded; nobody wanted to be the first to give anything away.

This morning Feilmann received a Christmas box from his wife. It had followed him all over Africa, and had taken six months to reach him; it contained a book and a photograph of his infant child whom he has never seen. He was vividly, touchingly, and authentically excited by this. All afternoon his friends came in to be told of this magical event and to see and admire the picture. Feilmann had not had leave for several years. He would show his friends the book and the picture with intense swelling pride. "I say, how frightfully bucked I am!"

A corporal came up. Something had gone wrong somewhere. Feilmann looked stern. His words were unintelligible to me: "Colossal raspberry!" In a different tone he turned to the corporal, "Did the engineers give you tea, Corporal?" "No, sir." "Well, bugger them."

Late in the afternoon we heard some ack-ack. Presumably the Germans were raiding Bizerte eighteen miles away. The ack-ack at that distance made you think a skin had been drawn tight across the whole sky, and that drumsticks were beating it sharply, with close rhythm. It was not so much a sound as a sensation. This—and the P-38's constantly patrolling overhead—made us feel that the front was close, that now indeed we were getting near the war.

Four massive meals a day were served in this villa—cooked in the courtyard just outside Feilmann's office—and the best of the four was, of course, tea. After dinner we looked at the blackout. The simplest of all ways to make a blackout in a town is to cut out its entire electricity system, and this is what has happened here in Tunis. But occasionally we saw flares, and near the salt lake—which had glittered in the sun like ice a few hours before—signal lights were flashing.

I made my bed in one of the towers of what Feilmann called his penthouse. I saw that this room had had a recent tenant. Scrawled on the wall I read:

> Gefr. Karl Brunner
> Hat vom 1.4.43 bis
> 4.4.43 die Zelle NR I
> benützt.

Tunis, Sunday, July 4.—Our villa is on the outskirts of town, in La Marsa, and we drove in to see the city. There are more De Gaulle signs here than in Algiers, and —although large sections are bombed out and most shops are either closed or have scaffolding over their windows— more signs of other kinds of life. I saw a playbill: *La Folle Revue*—Crazy Show. *Chansons et Skechs (sic) en Français et en Anglais.*

We visited the hot dusty field where a big public relations camp has just been built. Sentries; cabalistic signs; barbed wire; great motor pools marked KENTUCKY ASSEMBLY, ARIZONA ASSEMBLY, and the like. I talked to as many of our G.I.'s as I could find. Most of them were so busy and worn out they did not even know it was Independence Day.

In the afternoon something happened that mystified me: it was totally outside the orbit of the war, but I was fascinated. We went swimming. The beach is just behind the ruins of Carthage. When I crawled out of the water an Arab boy, about twelve, who spoke good French, cried out, "A big fish has taken my brother." I could not understand what he meant. Patiently, with tears in his eyes, he explained. His seven-year-old brother had been wading off the rocks. A large fish coasted in, seized the child, and swam out with him; the child disappeared. "The big fish has eaten my brother," the boy repeated. Of course this story could not be true. Yet why should the boy have made it up? But we could not wait to investigate.

I have been observing with careful attention the manner of British officers to their men. It differs radically from ours. The British are more professional. British privates are not nearly so cocky as ours, but they have a peculiar kind of self-sufficiency we have not learned yet. American officers are often somewhat green; they are unused to handling men, and whereas I would not say that the men don't respect them, there is a slapdash camaraderie between officers and men that does not exist in the British army. Our men are considerably more independent; yet they seem to need more the cushion, the impersonal support, of officers whom they trust. Of course one trouble is that the American army grew up too fast. A couple of years ago you could put every American officer in the Hollywood Bowl, and have plenty of room to spare. Also, you can't fire officers, which is a rule in every army; all you can do is shuffle and shift them, and so a lot of dead wood stays at the top.

I listened to Feilmann closely. No American officer would talk as he did. Yet obviously his men respected him to the uttermost—and would do anything for him—

while recognizing absolutely that he was a class apart. Feilmann said to me, "And I'd do anything for my men; I *adore* them. My function is, after all, to take care of them. But they never forget that I'm an officer."

I overheard him rebuking one of his sergeants: "Aren't you being rather temperamental, Smithson?" That was all. The sergeant replied, "No, sir." But he will not be temperamental again.

When Helen Kirkpatrick was here the men were warned that, a lady being present, they must be on their best behavior. But late one evening, when they thought she was safely asleep, a private told off his corporal in loud and bawdy language. When Feilmann investigated, the private's excuse was that in the darkness he did not know it was a corporal whom he was addressing. Feilmann said, "The implication of that is that you would have said what you said if it had been *I*, an officer, who approached you instead of the corporal. And if that had been the case you would now be in a pretty predicament indeed." As it was, the private got off with seven days' C.B.

I have credentials from the North American Newspaper Alliance as well as the Blue Network, and after tea I wrote a brief story about the trip yesterday and filed it to New York. Then we talked shop. That is, we discussed where "it" was going to happen, and in how many different places, and, above all, when. Gilling, an old campaigner, guesses that D Day will be the seventh. (D Day is, of course, the day set in advance for the opening of an operation, and then is the term used for description of the day itself. If Gilling is right, today is D Minus 3.)

This evening a group of British signalers came over to play darts with our photo unit, and Feilmann asked me if I would speak to them. Afterward they asked questions. These gnarled troops with their fabulous Lancashire, Scottish, and West of England voices, were polite, stubborn, very reserved at first, and then bursting with a hard, suspicious curiosity. Was it true that Malayan landlords deliberately did not apply the scorched earth policy? Why did the Russians abolish the Comintern and what did this signify? Why did the Luftwaffe walk out on the German army during the attack of Cap Bon? I kept wondering what kind of questions a similar American group would have asked. Maybe they would be more politically conscious, but I somehow doubt it.

Feilmann typed out his orders of the day. In this small camp, no one reads them but himself. But day by day he prepares them meticulously and posts them. "Two atabrine tablets will be taken after the evening meal at 1900 hours Thursday." And so on. Atabrine is supposed to ward off malaria. The men hate it because it gives them what they call the squitters, or gyppy tummy.

I was scribbling. Feilmann said, "You take more notes than anybody I ever heard of." "It's the way I work," I said.

Chapter III

Maltese Diary—Sans Origine

Tunis-Malta, Monday, July 5.—Up at 5:45 A.M., and off at about eight thirty in a stripped DC-3 decorated with yellow griffins and flown by New Zealanders. Our most conspicuous cargo was an enormous consignment of maps; they were packed in cases weighing fifty pounds each. We skirted Lampedusa, flew over smooth blue water, and arrived in Malta at 10:50. We are here at last.

Then came three somewhat tedious and frustrating hours; it took longer to get to where we wanted to be than to fly from Tunis. Our orders were to report to a certain Major C. S. Lock, Press Liaison Officer to a headquarters known only by a code number. Let me for convenience call this number 947. That number 947 dominated our lives for the next few weeks—not to mention the next three hours. The essence of a military operation of the kind we are about to witness is surprise. Surprise depends on secrecy. Gilling and I stood in the hot dust at the airport, loaded down with kit, and thumbed a lift. It was no small job to move us, but an RAF car courteously took us into what is called the Ditch, RAF headquarters. This car could go no further. The RAF officer said lightly, "Oh, you'll catch a ride somewhere." All around us were white buildings half destroyed, and a thin white dust rose chokingly at every step; ahead we saw a tunnel, and walked in. Apparently this was an army headquarters. In the tunnel—and Malta is, of course, built on tunnels—it was moist, slippery, cold, and dark. We penetrated cautiously into the office of a young British captain, and asked where Major Lock was to be found. He looked carefully through the provisional telephone list and said that no such person was indexed. We were utterly helpless without Lock, and our faces fell. He was the essential next figure in the chain. We asked then, rather timidly, where 947 was. The officer's face changed instantly. "947! You want 947? My dear fellow, this is Fourteenth Army!"

Apparently we had made a grievous error. We had mixed up a couple of armies in a way no well-informed correspondent should be guilty of doing. Both Gilling and I were tired and hungry; we walked out into the glistening sun, and sat for awhile where our great mound of gear was piled up. Then we called the motor pool. No cars. "You see I'm quite helpless in the matter, quite," said a young captain. "If I could get through to another post. . . . But the line is disconnected. Sorry!" Then we tried to get through to 947 itself by telephone. But the existence of this new and major headquarters was so secret that no one would give us the number; people seemed astonished and even resentful that we had heard of it. Patiently we tried to explain that we had *orders* to report to Major Lock at 947. Finally someone said, "Oh yes . . . Lock. . . . He has no office. He just flits around. Where does he sleep? Where does anyone sleep? *Sleep!* Oh, my!"

After an hour during which we must have talked vainly to twenty people we discovered that the secret headquarters of 947 were at a place called P. Mansions. By this time we were in the cubicle of an irascible RAF major. "I shall miss my lunch on account of you two," he kept saying. He denied that anything called P. Mansions existed. "I have been on this miserable——— hole of a miserable——— of a dirty island for seven months, and I tell you," he screamed, "there is no such thing as P. Mansions!" He also denied that 947's secret telephone exchange existed— denied it absolutely—until we ourselves rang the number

for him. Finally we were actually on the wire to 947 at
P. Mansions. And a voice said they'd send a car right
over. We sat down.

The "car" was a 1500-weight. It came in about twenty
minutes. And this was the first 1500-weight I ever rode
in. It is a square truck, metallic and uncompromising,
without springs or seats—a kind of flat metal box, say
12 feet by 14, open at the top and suspended on noisy
wheels. We got to P. Mansions—finally—but no one there
had ever heard of Lock. So, getting impatient now, we
crossed a scorching tawny yard and entered a tunnel
where sentries stood. We had no right to get inside this
tunnel because (we found later) it was the inner holy
of holies, the secret citadel, where Eisenhower and Alexander themselves would work. We had no passes and no
one bothered to look at our credentials. We walked in
freely, and a sergeant directed us to rooms where Major
Lock might, or might not, be found. Within the tunnel,
men shivered and worked in overcoats, though it was almost one hundred in the shade outside. Once we thought
we had grounded our man when we saw a sign PR, but it
was the provost marshal's office, not Public Relations.
We gave up. Outside again, we found a mess. "Will they
let us eat here?" I asked Gilling. "Probably not." Then by
great good luck I walked into an American officer, Lieutenant Colonel L. G. Zinneker, whom I had known in
London. We threw our arms around each other. Seldom
have I been so pleased at seeing a friendly face, at running into someone I *knew*. Then Gilling at last found
Lock. He had been in the next room all the time.

By this time it was almost two. There was gin and
orange juice. "Owld boy," said Gilling, "I could do with
a spot of drink."

I tell this story in such detail for a reason. An army is
a machine. An army set to plunge into a secret military
operation of the highest complexity is a machine strictly

under cover. Gilling and I were two tiny cogs not on the blueprints. It was up to us to find out where we belonged. For instance Lock had never received word about us from Algiers. He had no idea we were coming. Maybe the plane with copies of our orders had been shot down. He was the press officer attached to 947 but until we blew in he had no notion who would be there, if anybody. It wasn't his responsibility. Nobody was being inefficient. But war isn't simple. A lot of people had a great deal to worry about without having to chaperone two stray correspondents who had trouble finding 947.

Gilling is a Cockney, who for many years was Exchange Telegraph correspondent at Buckingham Palace; he knows more about the wheels within wheels of British life in that exalted sphere than anybody I ever met. But also he has seen a great deal of military action: for instance he accompanied the Commando raid at St. Nazaire. Lock is, I believe, from the West of England; he is an experienced public relations man, alert, lean, indefatigable. I never met a PR officer with such initiative, such scrupulous standards, who would go out and fight for you no matter what orders were. At lunch we were introduced to another officer, an energetic and capable young Chicagoan, Captain C. G. Duncan Clark. His father was a well-known Middle West newspaperman; he himself, though a chemist by profession, is our censor. The four of us instantly made up a team.

Lock and Duncan took us to a hotel known as the Phoenicia. "I don't think there's a room there," Duncan said. Lock said, "We'll bloody well make a room."

We managed to get in, and promptly met three other correspondents who live across the hall. They are not, however, like Gilling and me, part of 947; they are attached to Montgomery's Eighth Army, which is also using this island as a jumping-off place. One is Ned Russell, a Californian, of the United Press; the others are

British, the veteran Evelyn Montague of the Manchester *Guardian* and Frank Gillard of the BBC. When they were assigned here they had no idea they were en route to Malta. The fact that Malta is a base of operations is still an absolute dead secret. All stuff out of here must be marked *Sans Origine*.

I looked at the desk in their room. Russell was just finishing a book. I marveled. Some people need a sound-proof chamber to write a book in. On the desk at which Russell was working, and which was shared by three men, I counted the following objects:

2 water bottles, which had once contained gin
1 canteen
1 stamped and addressed envelope
old Malta papers
1 steel helmet
1 musette bag, open and strewing contents
1 pile of dirty towels
1 medicine kit
2 tin cups
5 tops of cigarette tins, used as ash trays
1 shaving mirror
2 shaving brushes
toilet paper
1 can of lighter fluid
1 wallet
5 dog-eared library books
2 pairs of khaki socks hung out to dry
2 cigarettes
1 pair of scissors
1 bundle of manuscript
4 old razor blades

We talked about the inevitable first subject of conversation—when D Day was going to be—and when each of us would go in. These veterans said that it was always fine and exciting to go in with the first assault wave, but not much use professionally, since it was almost always impossible to get any copy out until a day or two later. A correspondent is useless without communications. This group was planning to go in with the Eighth on D Plus 2. (As it turned out they were held up—waiting incommunicado on a landing craft—for several days beyond that, I learned later in Sicily.)

The above parentheses require an explanation. I am writing this book, in New York, several months after the events I describe took place. I am transcribing as carefully as I can the diary I took on the spot. Every day during my trip, I tried to make an accurate record of what I heard and saw; later, in the evenings, I would transcribe these notes into a diary. Now, I am making use of this diary, line by line and page by page, adding nothing. But at times it is convenient to finish off a paragraph like the one above, by describing what I learned later though I could not have known it when I put my first notes down. This is simply a device to make for smoother narrative. Otherwise I would be unendingly repetitious or would have to use footnotes or some other system of salting the tail of events.

We talked about the "pool." Russell and his friends belong to Eighth Army and we are strictly headquarters, but we all work for the pool. That is, anything sent by anybody from D Day up to a period that may be ten days or may stretch to three weeks, anything sent by any accredited correspondent, is to be automatically made available—through release by the great press services—to *every* newspaper and radio chain in Great Britain and the United States. Editors naturally do not like this system. It ends exclusivity. Nor do some of the correspondents, though I don't feel they have a real kick; all it means is that our audience is enormously magnified. The reason Eisenhower set up this pool system was to avoid unfairness. Suppose one correspondent lands with one beach party and through great good luck his stuff gets through right away. Another correspondent ten miles away may, on the contrary, be unable to transmit copy for days. During the African campaign in November "flash" stories of landings finally drifted to a cable head as much as a week late. They were useless of course. Now Eisenhower is trying to prevent fortuitous discrimination. Everything is going to belong to everybody from now on.

In the evening Duncan Clark took me down the street to an officers' bar called the Monico. You have a choice of two things to drink, a pink abomination that was alleged to resemble Pimms No. 1, and Scotch painted across the bottom of a glass at 3s per drink. I watched the crowds storming the small hot room—RAF, Navy with black beards, American technicians, Australians, Tank Corps men in black berets, Eighth Army.

The British kid us a good deal about how generous we are with decorations. An American private who has never seen action may, nevertheless, be wearing two or even three service bars. And apparently we give out Purple Hearts by the bucketful.

Malta, Tuesday, July 6.—What is discretion? Or rather, what is the greatest enormity of indiscretion I ever heard of? An American officer whom I had never met before told me today when D Day was and even mentioned the exact moment that I should be in a certain place.

The Hotel Phoenicia is the weirdest place I have ever lived in. Gilling and I are lucky: we have a room alone. He, a prudent soul, brought his own camp bed with him; I did not. I sleep on an iron frame on which I fold my blankets, underneath a sand fly net. My overcoat, the most indispensable article I have brought with me except a cigarette lighter, is of course my pillow. There are no hooks, hangers, closets, or mirrors. But how quickly, smoothly, one gets adjusted to such minor inconveniences. We have one flat wooden table, like the desk in Russell's room; on this we work. Unfortunately there are no chairs. I slipped into a room that seemed reasonably empty and swiped two. Gilling chuckled, "Oy say, owld boy, you learn fast."

We have to keep the door locked because the traffic is so heavy that someone will steal the room or just pitch camp in it. A covey of brigadiers and full colonels are wandering with hungry eyes down the corridor. When one of us forgets the key, we have to crawl in through the window, along a narrow ledge partly destroyed by bombing. Over this window hangs a very heavy sheet of tar paper half an inch thick. This makes our blackout.

The hotel commands a fine sight of the town; it was built for the luxury trade, but never, I believe, completed. One cannot tell, however, what parts were not finished and what the bombing has obliterated. About one-quarter of the structure is in ruins, and every inch is permeated with the heavy white limestone dust. We live four flights up. There are no elevators of course, the stairs are crumbling, half worn or bombed away, and dangerous in the dark. You can climb right up to the roof where most of the top floor has been blown off. All of it is like living in a transparent filing case, or in scaffolding made of stone.

The first problem every morning, for everbody, is to satisfy the call of nature. There are long lines of officers— almost all of considerable rank—in front of the window-less toilets which are inserted between every three or four rooms. These toilets and bathrooms are somewhat on the filthy side. This is strictly an officers' hotel, but several of us prefer to climb down the stairs and get outside, a quarter of a mile away, to the men's latrines. The reason for the ripe and rare amount of dirt is not disregard of sanitation or carelessness. It is that Malta is so short on water. We have water—with luck and if things are going well—from 6 to 8 A.M., and then perhaps for half an hour in the evening, but that's all. Moreover, we never know just when it will be turned on. I have not had a bath since I left Algiers. Bathing is forbidden here, on account of the water shortage. It is hard enough to get a helmet-ful, cold of course, for shaving.

Duncan Clark wanders in—he shares a room with Lock and another censor down the hall—at about seven each morning and, standing barefoot on the stone floor, wakes us up and reads the paper. The Malta *Times* is a four-page sheet filled mostly with Reuter's bulletins, with a streamer across the top, FOR SECURITY REASONS THIS PAPER MUST NOT BE TAKEN OUTSIDE MALTA. Breakfast is pretty grisly. So are the other meals. It is not merely that the food is coarse—and not so plentiful—but that the surroundings are, if you think about them, a bit awful. I do not mind the stew made of bully beef and the chunks of pork fat called bacon; but the dirt and the thick clouds of flies are almost comically troublesome. The mess is on the first floor. A couple of Maltese boys, not too clean, cook over stoves on the other side of a partition. For some reason, a concession perhaps to the elegance that should befit officers, we have tablecloths; these are so encrusted with grime, food stains, and dead insects that they look like contour maps. There is a makeshift bar next to the downstairs toilet which, since there is seldom any water, reeks. The barman has an ulcer on his lip.

Duncan Clark took me out to Government House in the same 1500-weight we use to get from the Phoenicia to headquarters and back. There is a great lack of transport, since so many vehicles are being waterproofed for the landings. For two men to ride alone in a 1500-weight is a little like two rabbits bouncing in a boxcar. My behind is blue. The governor, Lord Gort, was out; and I liked the language of his aide de camp: "Ah, H. E. has gone to visit Cunningham; I don't know what devilment they're up to." Then in the afternoon we went swimming. We had to try to get clean somehow. But the water was gurgling with refuse from a thousand ships.

Meantime I've been **trying** to learn to identify British

military insignia. In Algiers I called McCormack's first
assistant "Lieutenant," since it seemed logical that a man
with only one pip on his shoulder should be a lieutenant;
then I found out of course that this special pip meant
major. In the British army a brigadier has more things
on his shoulder than a field marshal, and I defy anybody
to spot the difference between several kinds of general at
a hundred yards. But the British, I am observing, dress
more comfortably and sensibly than we do. They know
all about hot places. They wear shorts; we never do; they
wear bush shirts open at the neck and made of a soft
absorbent material. . . . The stout Gilling bought a
mirror and I looked at myself. I certainly seem to be a
remarkable object. I haven't been able to get a shirt
pressed since New York and down my pants are enormous
stains and spots. I've broken both shoelaces; one lens of
my sunglasses is cracked, with bits of glass still sticking
to the frame; I can't keep my insignia up the sleeve and
a huge rusty safety pin is showing; above all I lost my
belt, and there is no place to get another one. Half a
dozen times in the past days brisk well-turned-out officers
have seen me suddenly! they stop quite dead in their tracks,
staring. Of course I can never remember to salute.

I have discovered that a British officer is to be called
"sir" and only "sir." To address them as we do is a
solecism. That is, in the American army, one may say,
"Yes, Captain," or "No, Colonel," at least if one is a correspondent. But to address British officers likewise is as
unheard-of as it would be to say "Yes, Architect," or
"No, Lawyer," in American civil life. (Yet we *do* say,
"Yes, Doctor," though we do not say "Yes, Engineer,"
or "Hello, Dentist.") The British are never called by their
rank, but only by the general appellation "sir." I have
found out that if you leave the "sir" out it impresses them
considerably.

Ned Russell, so friendly and well-informed, took me to

the Monico. We had a brief drink and then hurried back to the Phoenicia in order not to miss dinner. This is a city in which there is no single restaurant; also—among other odd shortages—no small change. At the Monico you get paper slips instead, and in the Phoenicia we use ration coupons. The Eighth Army is beginning to move in in force, and our dinner hall is crowded to bursting now. I met Major Bill Warrener, Montgomery's DADPR.* To my intense delight and pride this amiable redhead invited me to join the Eighth Army in Sicily as soon as this present job was done. I told him I had a letter to Montgomery from Wendell Willkie, and he promised that I would get a chance to present it, if all went well.

Frank Gillard is down with sand fly fever, and at least a dozen folk, including Lock, have gyppy tummy. It's no fun to be in bed with 103 temperature without sheets, towels, or sufficient drinking water.

Someone asked me if I knew when D Day was.

"No," I lied.

Malta, Wednesday, July 7.—Today we set up our working quarters at 947 in P. Mansions. We will continue to sleep at the Phoenicia, but 947 is where we work. Lock even promises beds here in case of emergency. The headquarters is a deserted warehouse, partitioned into rooms; the whitewashed ceiling is vaulted, and rises 40 feet over our heads. Outside a motor pool of 1500-weights, bigger trucks, command cars, jeeps, churns the thick dust into hot spouts or dirty cloud. Inside we are cool and comfortable. Lock is a wonderful manipulator. "Laddie," he says, "you just bloody well leave everything to me." He and Duncan Clark sit at a double desk in the center of the room. Gilling and I share a table in the corner. At the far end of the room is Lock's assistant, Corporal Trotter, who was a traveling salesman in Yorkshire not so long ago. The five of us are alone. We feel

* Pardon the initials—Deputy Assistant Director, Public Relations.

wonderfully self-contained, secure and confident. We have the best jobs in the Army. Anything can happen now.

"I have lice," I said.

"Good God, sir, not lice!" Trotter said.

"I have something."

"Fleas, sir, but not lice, good God!"

Everything that the incomparable Lock doesn't do, Trotter does. His desk is hung with bags for the proper routing of dispatches; he runs errands, handles the telephone, sends out our laundry; keeps the log, and brings us tea.

Lock to Trotter: "Have you had your tea, Corporal?"

Trotter to Lock: "When I have time, sir . . ."

Lock: "Go and have a cup of tea, or I'll kick your ———in."

Trotter: "I don't want tea, sir."

Lock: "Get on now. It's a bloody order."

We signed into the 947 mess today. It is incredible that two messes, both Anglo-American, and both within two miles of one another as part of the same general organism, can be so different. The 947 mess is headquarters, the Phoenicia mess is largely Eighth Army. Here at 947 we have, sensibly, no tablecloths; the bare wooden boards are infinitely cleaner. The servants are British, not Maltese; and they cover the waiting food with sand-fly nets. We get a bottle of gin every ninth day, and there are copious buckets of ice water—actual ice water—and orange juice from Palestine, strictly rationed. The food is about the same. But the fact that we eat it in clean surroundings—and in a building where it is moderately cool—makes all the difference.

The early afternoon went like this. First, I thought I ought to gather some material for a story about Malta, the island, and what it has gone through. Second, I had to do some shopping. I need new glasses (but none except rickety things made of celluloid are available), toilet paper, towels above all (how filthy our towels do get!) and a shoeshine outfit. The prices are staggering. I shan't forget a British Tommy in the blinding glare outside a shop selling glasses; price: 9 shillings. The soldier walked away; his eyes were red-rimmed but he didn't have 9 shillings. Third, Lock took us to see a brigadier who will "brief" us about the operation. I was fascinated to observe that the stem of his pipe just fitted the hole left by a missing tooth.

At four Bill Warrener met me outside the Phoenicia, and we went to see Lieutenant Colonel E. T. Williams, who is General Montgomery's intelligence officer. Williams is—or was—an Oxford don, though he cannot be more than twenty-nine or thirty; he specialized, I believe, in medieval history. That he should be an intelligence officer is very typical of the British army. The three of us had a hard walk up hill, across fields filled with boulders, and through the dust, and we reached the villa General Montgomery was living in. The general greeted us in a wide sunny room. Williams sat on the floor, his arms around his bare brown knees. Montgomery's first words to me were, "You look hot. Very hot. I must say, you look very hot."

"I am hot," was all I could think of to answer. But I will describe this interview in detail in Chapter 7.

Back at the hotel (we carry our typewriters back and forth) I wrote a long N.A.N.A. story about Montgomery, and then in the evening we had drinks with a remarkable officer, Geoffrey Keating, who is in charge of the photographic section. Warrener said, "I've been sworn, boys," meaning that he had been told the final secret details of what is coming. I asked Ned Russell, who is very acute about such things, why he thought the Germans were not bombing the immense concentration of stuff they must know is here. His answer was, "Think of what *we* have in the air. That's what air superiority is." This evening, as a matter of fact, we heard a lot of distant noise. The hotel shook; the tremors were like those of an earthquake; I thought of a minor earthquake I had once experienced in Japan. But there was no sound of planes actually coming over. We may have been hearing our own bombardment of Sicily, which is only eighty miles away; more likely (Gilling's theory), our PT boats and destroyers are exploding depth charges against submarines around the island. I went to sleep at about eleven-thirty. In the morning Duncan Clark said that there had been an alert at 3 A.M. and I was angry at myself for not having waked up.

The most extraordinary thing in the world is the way you get used to things. I feel as if I have been in this hotel for months, and I wouldn't trade a minute of it for anything on earth.

Malta, Thursday, July 8.—Our professional problems have become fairly acute. We are so busy thinking about our jobs that we practically forget the war. For one thing we do not know if the local Malta correspondents of various newspapers are, or are not, included in the pool arrangement. Also several men accredited to the Royal Navy work out of here; and navy stuff is not pooled. So we must take precautions to keep the pool inviolate, to avoid being beaten on our special story. What is more serious is the general problem of transmission. So far as we understand it now, all copy from here—also from the beaches when the invasion starts—is to be shipped by courier plane to either Tunis or Algiers. There is also direct wireless communication to both places, but to use this would mean that copy would have to be coded—since to send it in clear by radio would give it away to the enemy—and code takes too long. Joe Phillips has, I believe, moved up to Tunis with an impressive public relations setup. Tunis is to be the big relay point. On the other hand, communiqués are—so far as we know—to be issued in Algiers, though they will be written here, and both briefing and censorship guidance are to take place in Malta. It is all too elaborate for my understanding. Gilling was the first to point out that a solution to these complexities would be to file direct to London and New York (or Washington) from the cable head here in Malta. A cable ensures secrecy. Also Malta can clear an immense amount of wordage. All the facilities are here. Why not use them? The catch is that Tunis and Algiers would not know, in the event we file direct from Malta, what we are sending. But they could get drop-copies by courier. Lock is going to see into all of this, and let us know.

Lunch with Field Marshal Lord Gort, the governor, at his summer palace a few miles out of town. (The town palace has been bombed out.) The ADC said as I came in, "You'll find H.E. in simply wonderful form. He's simply chugging to go." Gort is a stalwart customer. He has blue, humorous, friendly eyes; the way they are set shrewdly underneath pale bushy brows reminded me of Thomas Lamont. He talks with quick animation and a slurred accent. He was almost like a professor, an antiquarian, reveling in a subject that fascinated him inordinately; he was obsessed with the story of Malta, its history, its trials, its heroism. After lunch we looked at the palace. It was built in 1586, and named for Cardinal G. M. Verdala, an illustrious Grand Master of the Knights of Malta. The stone walls are I-don't-know-how-many feet thick; the roof was built "proof against ordnance." And the sturdiness with which it was built almost four hundred years ago comes in handy now. We dove down steep stone steps; we crawled into chalky white oubliettes where hooks for chains are still set in the walls; we mounted the broad, spiral marble staircase where the steps are only two inches high, so that priests could ride up on mules which wore sandals. There are several rooms, dungeons, which the servants believe to be haunted, and which even today they will not enter. In the dining room are two frescoes. "We will now," said Lord Gort, "see how clever Mr. Gunther is." And I was asked to identify the biblical scenes portrayed in the frescoes. The only thing I could think of to say was that one bearded gentleman looked like George Bernard Shaw. Then everybody laughed. Of all the multitudinous guests who have been in that room, no one has ever been able to tell what the frescoes do represent. Later we inspected a magnificent broad room with a ceiling thirty feet high. This will be where Eisenhower sleeps. "Do you think the general will be comfortable here?" Gort asked anxiously.

This afternoon Gilling and I wandered into the headquarters tunnel opposite P. Mansions in search of Captain Sir Rupert Clark, General Alexander's personal assistant. In the gloom I saw a figure in a glittering white uniform approach. We were deep down; surrounding us was slimy rock; I have seldom felt so entirely encased by walls. I recognized the approaching figure at about the same moment he recognized me. He exclaimed, "Well, you certainly are *inside* Malta!" It was Lord Louis Mountbatten.

At dinner in the Phoenicia someone asked, "How are the girls in Cairo?" Reply from a young PR officer: "Oh, all the fat colonels have them now."

We saw some mild ack-ack tonight. It looks like Roman candles. The successive shells burst so very slowly.

Malta, Friday, July 9.—Late to breakfast in the 947 mess today. Half a dozen British officers were loafing, and three were reading the one-volume edition of H. A. L. Fisher's *History of Europe*. This, I found on investigation, is the only good book still available in Malta bookstores, and all three officers had picked it up quite independently. Indeed the British are a remarkable people.

I found myself surveying this group of officers with great curiosity. Here I was, eating, working, living, with the flower of the united Anglo-American command at a moment of supreme climax. What did these officers talk about, think about? The British are more seasoned than we are, on the whole; what was a surpassing adventure to most of the Americans—who were quaking with excitement—was pretty much a matter of routine, even though it was a climax, to these First and Eighth Army veterans. Also they seemed more detached, more sophisticated, and more literate. Here they were, spending a free half hour reading H. A. L. Fisher. . . . I looked to see what the Americans were doing. Poring over the tantalizingly inadequate morning paper or pacing restlessly back and forth. The British and the Americans get along better than the British and the British. That is, all the British, without exception, go out of their way to be friendly to the Americans; sometimes the Americans are gauche in replying to these advances. But some British will not willingly talk to other British. They stratify themselves by voice. This morning I had tea with a Guards officer with as pronounced an Eton manner as anyone I ever heard. A young lieutenant who probably went to a Welsh grade school came up to join us at my invitation. The Guardsman quite deliberately finished his tea as quickly as possible and moved away, then sat alone two tables off.

Many of the British officers here are bored; many are lonely; they don't like to have to sleep without sheets; but I get a strong impression that many of them *like* war. It relieves them of personal responsibilities; it submits them to an arduous discipline, but maybe that is better than having to live in an uncharted world of free will; they are busy doing the job for which they have been trained all their lives; they are now in active performance of their profession at a moment for which their entire careers have been a preparation. There is no worry about frictions at home or the dull necessity of earning a living. Besides, many officers appear actively and positively to enjoy military life. It is like a perpetual camping trip, and if you're the kind of a man who likes camping, you enjoy it. I heard one officer say, in fact, "How nice all this would be if only you could eliminate the bloodshed, the killing." He had been having a spectacularly exciting time during the whole course of the war. But it was unusual to hear any-one talk of death even in an impersonal manner. Death was never present in P. Mansions. (But one officer with whom I had breakfast that sunny morning was killed in Sicily the next week.)

The one thing that everybody misses most is mail. When we arrived Gilling brought a cargo of letters. The men snatched at them virtually tearing him apart. It is an odd thing, and I don't understand it, and of course any foreign correspondent is in a wonderfully lucky spot be-cause, by and large, he can quit and go back home any time; but what I have enjoyed most so far is the aloneness. Before long this emotion will change, of course. Not a soul in the world knows where I am; it is inconceivable that I should get a letter; I have no impulse at all to write anybody. (Hour after hour, most of my colleagues and many officers write letters, letters, letters, endlessly.) But to be temporarily alone is a considerable luxury, I find. And I am busy every minute. Of course it is ridiculous for me to talk since I only left New York twelve days ago. I simply have to confess that for the moment I enjoy the isolation.

British officers are known by cabalistic letters and numerals indicating their jobs. For instance "Bill" (E. T.) Williams, Montgomery's intelligence man, is "G.S. (I) G.S.O. 1." This means simply that he is a lieutenant colonel in the intelligence section of the General Staff. The doors in our tunnel are placarded with as fantastic a set of initials as I have ever seen, and Lock is forever telling Trotter, "Run over to G Ops," which means the Oper-ations Room. It is quite possible for a conversation to run something like this, "Oh, he's N.L.O. Next door to

B.A.F.V. Look out for S.O.R.E. (I), though. He's near D.A.D. (Survey)." With my own ears I heard today, "The G.S.O. 2 is busy calling on the B.G.S. I" (viz., Brigadier, General Staff, Intelligence).

Ned Russell heard early today that Eisenhower and Butcher have arrived, and he called Butcher up, suggesting that the general see us all. Butcher agreed, and a press conference was arranged for eleven-thirty. Everybody having to do with the press was invited: Lock, Warrener, Duncan Clark, two British censors, the RAF and Royal Navy PR's, the Malta information officers, Gilling and myself as the two reporters assigned to headquarters, and Russell, Montague, and Gillard for the Eighth Army. We walked across the yard and entered 947's tunnel. By this time a severe security check had been installed, and sentries scrutinized our passes carefully. We reached Eisenhower's office—a cubbyhole where an oil stove was burning; Butcher let us in, and introduced us to the general.

This was the first glimpse I had of the commander-in-chief. Medium height with a nice solid build; a hard friendly handshake; sandy hair, widely set bright blue eyes under a fine broad forehead; a wide mobile grin; an impression of modesty, directness, guts, and common sense. His talk is very informal and homely, full of expressions like "darn it" and "you fellows." The conference lasted more than an hour. I marveled. I was bewildered. Here was the commander-in-chief of what was going to be one of the most stupendous and decisive operations in history, on its very eve; yet he spent sixty-five minutes in solid, earnest, friendly give-and-take with a bunch of newspapermen and press officers. We were, he said, to consider ourselves members of his staff; we would be treated as such, and held responsible as such. "The censorship is purely for security. We want to play it your way just as much as possible." He was engagingly frank; we could gang up and "bust him," he grinned; but also he could "bust" any one of us if we didn't behave. He added, "Now listen; I want to co-operate with you fellows and I want you to co-operate with me." He was extremely eager to have everything centralized under the control of one officer. "I'm responsible," he kept saying, "so I want everything to go through one man who will be responsible to me." No human being could have been more helpful, more eager to listen; but I detected too a note of essential toughness, even ruthlessness.

All our talk was on press matters. We brought up the whole vexed issue of direct communication from Malta; Eisenhower appeared amazed that this technique hadn't been thought of before and hadn't been worked out. Some details were extraordinarily abstruse, such as the relation of the non-pool navy men to the rest of us, and the differences between "policy" censorship at Algiers and "security" censorship here. Eisenhower caught most points like a flash. When he didn't understand, he always said so. He would turn to his chief of staff, General Whitley, and say candidly, "Sorry, Jock, I didn't get that." And once he said to the navy PR who was pressing him hard, "Maybe I'm dumb; repeat that, please." I continued to be amazed that an officer with, shall we say, several other things to think about should be giving so much detailed attention to such a comparatively minor matter as press communications. But this was vital to us; and he won us all. Duncan Clark, polite, stubborn, pointed out that one of the general's own suggestions wouldn't work. "I'm sorry, sir," Duncan kept saying, "but that would violate security, sir." The general took it. It was refreshing in the extreme to hear a youthful captain tell Eisenhower what he could and could not do.

Gilling and I had been informed by Lock that we might write "dope" stories when the campaign began but that we could not touch actual operations; this would be unfair to the men in the field. We put this up to the general and asked him what, in detail, we could send. We were, after all, assigned exclusively to his headquarters; if we couldn't write operations, what else was there to write about? "Darned if I know," Eisenhower wrinkled his broad forehead. We suggested several possibilities and the general appeared to be thinking these over. Then he assigned an aide, a general, to work on the whole press setup, draw up a report, and submit it by that evening. His last words were, "I know how it is, you want everything there is just now, in the way of news, but this is just the time, above all, when all of us are scared to death to say a word." And he cautioned us to be moderate in our reporting. "Don't even call it a *big* attack. Maybe it's going to fail, and then where would we be, if we had claimed it was something very big." He chuckled. "But I don't think it's going to fail."

Lunch. Then a quick swim. All of us were all set now. At four, General Alexander saw Gilling and me briefly. Eisenhower had arranged this since the morning. Ned Russell, who had done so much to fix up the meeting with Eisenhower, was sick with disappointment at not being included. But the C.-in-C. has apparently laid down a rigid rule: Gilling and I are the only correspondents to have access to direct headquarters material; this is a fair division of labor, since the others have operations to write, and we haven't. Hereafter in all the Malta talks and interviews, Gilling and I are to be the only two correspondents present.

We had a good talk with Alexander. I will describe this later. He looks a little like W. Somerset Maugham, with an uptilted chin, a beautifully poised head, neat brown mustache, and an aware upward look that might be called supercilious if it were not so serene. His voice: quiet and cultivated; his manner, tactful, wise, intelligent. He wanted to know first how much *we* knew. Then he "filled us up." What is going to happen soon—very soon—will be the greatest amphibian operation in military annals.

Back to P. Mansions. In the middle of the dusty yard we walked into Butcher. "I've been looking for you lads," he said. He took us into the tunnel, and then again led us in to Eisenhower. The commander-in-chief had a minute free. With a zeal and an eye for news that would have well become any city editor, he began to sketch the kind of stories Gilling and I might write. He had been thinking all afternoon, he said, about our function; we had been quite right, we *ought* to have something special out of headquarters every day. He would "lay it on," he promised. Then at once he began to describe with hard-boiled vividness a story he wanted written about Anglo-American co-operation. But he insisted on one inflexible rule: nothing whatever about himself personally. No word at all about Eisenhower, except when mention of the C.-in-C. was essential to the story, and then only in connection with the other high officers of the Allied command.

Dinner. We ate quietly. Then up to the roof of the Phoenicia. Only a couple of minutes to wait now.

That afternoon swimming we had seen whitecaps suddenly dance across the water, and Alexander had told us he was worried about the weather. "Usually the wind goes down at sundown," Alexander commented pointedly. But it hadn't gone down. Indeed it had increased steeply. A wind was howling sideways through the interstices on the bomb-shattered roof, and below, in the glimmering darkness, we could see trees bend and sway. This must be a forty-mile wind at least. Maybe more. Lock glanced out toward where the invisible sea was. We had to shelter ourselves from the wind now. Lock muttered angrily, "To think what bloody casualties this —— wind may cause!"

At nine-twenty-two we saw the first planes skim over. They were transports carrying parachutists and glider troops for the airborne landings. The invasion of Sicily had begun.

Chapter IV

D Day

Malta, Saturday, July 10.—This has been a fine and strenuous day. No wonder, since it is D Day at last. We saw the airborne stuff go over last night, but the actual amphibious landings did not take place till dawn this morning.

Breakfast full of rumors; no actual news until about 10 A.M. Montgomery's landings have apparently been successful, but there is no authentic word about Patton yet. A signal officer who had been in the Operations Room all night gave us a quick, blurred, excited account of having overheard pilots talk to one another, orders to the Navy to blow hell out of an objective known as P for Peter, and German aviators ducking for cover when they saw our Spitfires. So far as we know there is no sign of German counterattack.

"Just like Georgie Patton not to let us know a darned thing," one officer complained.

I wrote a brief story, very early, couched only in general terms but to the effect that the battle for Europe had begun, that American troops were assaulting the continent of Europe for the first time, and that a new front had at last been opened.* Three points seemed worth making:

* In Washington months later I discovered that this brief story was the first word that the Bureau of Public Relations of the War Department received as to the beginning of actual operations. Of course the chief of staff had received messages direct from Eisenhower but mine was the first press story to arrive. It never made any impression in print,

First that Sicily, a gigantic triangular rock at the foot of
Italy, is in enemy hands an obstacle to both horizontal and
vertical routes across the Mediterranean; therefore, we
must take it. Second, inasmuch as it is the master plan of
the Allied High Command to beat Germany first, an attack on Sicily follows Tunisia logically and is the first
stroke in a great upward campaign toward the heart of
the Axis. Third, an amphibious operation on this scale is
one of the most difficult feats known to military science.

At about ten Butcher gave us stuff for a second story,
a feature on how Eisenhower spent last night. The generalissimo went out to a point on the beach and waited in
the moonlight. He fingered some lucky coins he always
carries—one silver dollar, one five-guinea piece, and one
French franc—and murmured Godspeed as the planes
whipped over. Once they were overhead, nothing more
could be done. The stakes of this operation are so stupendous—the liberation of Europe and the winning of the
war—that one fairly shudders at the notion that something might go wrong. Eisenhower's emotion must have
been an amalgam of worry and confidence, of almost un-
endurable curiosity and intense yearning that all would
be well. The worst moments are those after you know your
troops have landed but before you get definite information
as to what has happened.

I wrote a third story out of some things the general
told us yesterday. He wants it to be made clear that this
campaign is not an American show, not a British show,
but something directed by a truly *allied* command—a
command so melted down and fused together that it has
become almost impossible to tell what share of activity
belongs to what nation. It's his dearest wish, he told us,
to be regarded not as leader and commander-in-chief of

---

however, because it arrived sometime between midnight and dawn, New
York time, and of course was quickly superseded by thousands upon
thousands of words of subsequent copy which poured in all that day.

various American, British, and other military, naval, and aerial establishments, but of a single *united* force. Eisenhower is in supreme command of five separate and distinct entities—the American army (which includes the American Air Force), the American navy, the British army, the Royal Navy, and the RAF. The immensity of the task of correlating and synchronizing these disparate forces into one smoothly oiled machine is something to stagger the imagination. The general's own tact, candor, freshness, and general efficiency have had a good deal to do with the excellent results so far. So have the good humor, the good manners, and the good sense of his British collaborators. When Eisenhower arrived here he was met and specially greeted at a secret rendezvous by his three chief lieutenants, Alexander, Cunningham, and Tedder. It touched him considerably that they paid him this tribute; what touches him more is that all three have such authentic regard for him. I think that what they like best is his indisputably genuine modesty. When he was named commander-in-chief last July Eisenhower was, of course, outranked by such men as Cunningham, who is an admiral of the Fleet. Even as a full general he was outranked. So the British devised the pleasant fiction that all American ranks are one degree higher than British ranks. When Eisenhower was a lieutenant general they considered him a full general. Now that he is a full general they regard him as the equivalent of a field marshal. Eisenhower realizes quite well that there are always possibilities of friction in an allied command. Lots of Americans and British have an atavistic dislike of one another. So what the generalissimo does is accept the fact, instead of blinding himself to it; likewise he demands that every officer shall frankly talk up about any irritations. Also, one of his rules is that every unit of his command, no matter how small, must include both American and British officers.

Even in these cubicles here there must be people of both nationalities in every room.

Another example of the way he tries to keep in the background as much as possible is that he continually, in all conversation, stresses his responsibility to Washington and London. He will not allow correspondents to dateline anything as from "General Eisenhower's Headquarters." He insists on the term "Allied Headquarters." One more item: I never saw him wear more than two decorations, though many of his men are bedecked like awnings.

I haven't written any spot news by cable in competition with agency men for years and years, and something happened after lunch which both pleased and disconcerted me. We are to handle the spot news too! That is, it has now been decided that for the next few days Gilling and I will not only do the special headquarters stories, but also the factual operational news hour by hour. We will be briefed every day by Lieutenant Colonel D. W. S. Hunt; no other correspondent will attend this briefing. My two spot stories today when cleared at 1:33 P.M. and 1:41 P.M. One is to the effect that we are exploiting our landings more quickly than anticipated, the other gives details about the Italian forces in the field.

I think I must try to explain this further, why now we are writing operations too. Lock takes down our briefing, and transmits it to Tunis and Algiers; Duncan Clark also makes note of it for "censorship guidance." The official communiqué is then written. In other words we have access to what the communiqué will say, and to hedge against breakdowns in transmission it now seems advisable that we should, independently, be permitted to cover the same material. What we are writing goes into the communiqué that is issued the *next* day; therefore, if our stuff gets through, we are twenty-four hours ahead on anything except eyewitness stories from the beaches. To guard against breaking security, our spot news copy is not sent direct to New York, but, after preliminary censorship by Duncan Clark, it goes by courier to both Algiers and Tunis. This means that we are writing stuff that, although censored, is still not for public issue until the communiqués appear. So it is marked MOST SECRET. It gives me quite a kick to see our stories handled in this way.

At four we crossed into the tunnel and had another talk with Eisenhower. He seemed very pleased. "By golly," he kept muttering, "I don't understand it! By golly, to think we've done it again!" Because by this time it is apparent that our landings have taken the enemy completely unawares; we have achieved not merely strategical but tactical surprise. The general rocked back on his wicker chair, his heels caught in the lower rung. He grinned from cheek to cheek, and told us something strictly off the record. His grin was more disarming than ever: "Every once in a while I like to tell you fellows something like this, because you might hear it from somebody else, and if *I* tell you, it shuts you up!"

I looked carefully at the room Eisenhower works in. It measures about 10 feet by 14; there is a single table covered by a gray blanket and a small white blotter. An oil heater is burning, and a rug is on the clay floor, but the room is cold and damp. The general tossed away one of his cigarettes today and asked, "You fellows got a dry cigarette?" But all cigarettes, dry or wet, are very scarce.

We went to the Monico and I bought a bottle of Scotch for £4. Russell and his group are still stuck here. They are annoyed because they say that unless you get way ahead with the armored cars, you'll be too late to pick up loot. Warrener showed us Montgomery's order of the day. It cannot be released yet but we read it eagerly. The concluding sentence is "Good hunting in the home country of Italy!" Someone smiled, "What a gorgeous ham!"

I keep hearing a great deal about Tedder, and I hope I

will be meeting him soon. He is a hunter, a "killer," people say. Both his wife and son have been killed in this war, and so he has good reason to hate the Germans. But this doesn't keep his passion against them from being cool, scientific and methodical.

Late this afternoon we saw some of the LCT and other landing craft chug back to harbor. An officer sighed, "Can you understand the relief we feel when those ships get *back*?"

Malta, Sunday, July 11.—Wrote four stories today, about twenty-five hundred words in all. Two were about operations, and one was a small political piece, to the effect that, so far as we know today, our Sicilian landings, against an enemy, Italy, have cost us fewer casualties than our landings last November in France. For some reason the political censor thought this comparison was invidious, and didn't want to let it through. But Duncan Clark argued himself black in the face with this other censor, and finally it passed. Aside from Duncan, we have, of course, three other censorships; Navy, RAF, and Maltese. Normally there is very little trouble. Trotter rushes duplicate copies down to Information headquarters, and the navy and RAF people only pay attention to particular details in their field.

When we got up this morning, very early, and saw the Malta paper, we were shocked. All of us here have made the most scrupulous effort not to give anything away, and, above all, not to exaggerate unduly the importance of the operation. But the local paper is full of the wildest stories —many of them sheer speculation—from various agencies out of Washington and London and cabled back here. One or two stories are inaccurate guesses at just what Eisenhower wants most to conceal. Also we are told that there has been one serious leak from the front; in some inexplicable manner a dispatch from a Canadian correspondent got through which names and locates various

Allied divisions, which could be very damaging to security. The wires burned up on this. Someone—nobody here—slipped in censorship.

We had a moment with Eisenhower and Butcher; and Butcher asked Gilling rather cryptically if we had heard anything from the Navy yet. Apparently a trip is in prospect. Eisenhower dictated a statement commending the Royal Navy, and then arranged for us to see Cunningham, who is very chary about receiving journalists. The general's main point: The Sicilian landings were—or are—beyond doubt one of the most stupendous *naval* operations ever known. Vessels of every kind and description assembled from ports many thousands of miles distant and reached their destination through divers narrow channels; they made rendezvous at a precisely designated moment and went through highly intricate maneuvers on the day before the operation. D Day—yesterday—they set out for their Sicilian objectives under the very nose of what was once the most powerful air force in the world; they found the appointed beaches with great accuracy and landed a prodigiously varied assembly of men and equipment without a slip and with very small casualties and while maintaining complete surprise. All this, too, under weather conditions that had suddenly become sharply adverse.

I heard a story today that horrified me; I wonder if it can be true. The Germans in Tunisia not only mined their dead; that we know; but they also mined the wounded. The report is that a Scots guardsman was mined; but as he lay dying he managed to whisper to a rescue party not to touch him, because the Germans had fastened a booby trap under his back.

The kind of current operations material we are handling is roughly this. Both the American Seventh Army and the British Eighth are advancing from their bridgeheads against gradually stiffening enemy resistance. We have taken about four thousand prisoners in thirty-six hours. Junkers 88's are strafing us in some quarters, but mostly we have complete command of the air. The greatest thing in our favor is the complete quality of surprise we achieved; the Germans and Italians had no warning and were completely caught off base. Our tanks are now moving ashore in modest numbers, and we are getting supplies in at two or three different points. The American beachhead now measures roughly 22 by 8 miles, but there are signs of a strong German force concentrating near Gela. The British have taken Syracuse, Avola, Cassabile, and Floridia, after fierce fighting at the latter place; they have made contact with the following Italian divisions: the Fourth Livorno, the Fifty-fourth Napoli, and Coastal 206 and 207. The civilian population is quite co-operative and friendly on the whole.

At four-thirty Captain Dorling, the navy public relations officer, took us in to see Admiral Sir Andrew Cunningham, Commander-in-Chief, Mediterranean, who is salty as the sea. His cheeks are red-veined, glazed; his eyes are like none I have ever seen, with the underlids lined with bright red, like a bulldog's. He was direct, sparse, keen, and good-humored. Dorling introduced us by saying that we represented the entire Anglo-American press. Cunningham replied, "How frightful!" Later he said he could not allow us to use anything of an operational nature in direct quotation, because, he snapped amiably, "Every time I see the press, I get scrubbed by the Admiralty." When we left he called to Dorling, "Now, Dorling! See that none of this is used against me!"

Cunningham has just returned from a quick visit by sea to the beachheads his tremendous organization has helped make secure. We asked how many ships had taken part in the invasion, in all. He replied, "Bless me, how should I know? We'll have to count 'em." The heavy swell made some of the landings difficult, and it was still interfering with the smooth unloading of heavy equipment, the admiral said. Lighters, barges, landing craft of every kind, were rocking and pitching and bouncing while trying to transfer their cargo to the shore. The American sector had the worst weather, and he was much struck by the quality of American seamanship, especially since many of our sailors have had little actual experience afloat. Cunningham signaled one American admiral, "I fear you've had the worst of the deal. Hope you'll have better weather tonight." The American replied, "Thank you. All proceeding satisfactorily."

Cunningham had eight vivid and crowded hours along the beaches. It was an astounding spectacle, he said; it all looked like the Spithead review or Brighton Beach on Sunday. The brilliant Sicilian sunshine poured down on creamy rollers, while a breaking sea dashed briskly up the beach. The shallow water was swarming with landing craft of every kind. Most enemy batteries were silent by midafternoon and those afloat could hardly believe that the landings were taking place in enemy territory; the villages looked deserted. And there was no sign at all so far, Cunningham said, of the Italian navy. "I hope," he added, "that these very pleasant conditions will continue to prevail."

I heard tonight that the first U.S. parachute plane to go in was called Mister Period; the second, Miss Carriage.

Chapter V

With Eisenhower in Sicily

IT GAVE me an odd feeling to be the third American to set foot on this part of Axis Europe. The first was General Eisenhower, the second his naval aide, Commander Harry Butcher, U.S.N. It happened that I was right behind them. I was the only American newspaperman in the party of eleven that made the trip. The place was a beach near the southeastern tip of Sicily off Cape Passaro; the time was 10:24 A.M. Monday, July 12. I was busy taking movies with Butcher's camera but close enough to hear the first moment's conversation. I had hoped Eisenhower would say something in the Stanley-Livingstone tradition, for instance, "My name is Eisenhower." What the commander-in-chief did say was good enough. There was no warning whatever that he was arriving. He walked up to the first British officer we saw, a colonel with a long dusty mustache and said, "Good morning, I'm General Eisenhower." The British colonel almost passed out with surprise.

Our trip began the night before. A lovely lopsided moon dappled the shining water. We assembled near a blacked-out quay. A car with quadruple dimmed headlights slipped around a dark corner and a brisk gray-haired officer in white uniform stepped out, Admiral Cunningham. A moment later came Eisenhower's car, also with quadruple headlights and bearing the United States flag. Normally this car carries British and French flags too, but the gadget which holds them had been broken when the car was shipped here from Africa. Eisenhower and Cunningham talked a moment, then shook hands. We stepped into the admiral's barge. Cunningham said, "Good luck, General." Eisenhower replied, "Thanks, sir." Eisenhower glanced at the barge; "I'd trade you a lot for this," he grinned. Cunningham replied, "Wait till your dinner starts to go up and down."

The destroyer lent us by the Royal Navy looked sleek and powerful as we drew close. We climbed up a joggling rope ladder and Eisenhower chuckled, "I never know what to do when they pipe me on."

Our party included two American generals, one British general, a British commodore representing the Navy, a young American parachute officer, Gilling and myself. Our generals, except Eisenhower, were in full regalia—steel helmets, knapsacks on their backs, canteens and torches in their belts. Butcher, Gilling and I had toothbrushes, but nothing much else. Again I inspected with admiration the neatness and efficiency of American equipment; all the harnesses fit so very perfectly. But our generals seemed embarrassed by the plenitude of their kit, especially the helmets, and one of them apologized, "Georgie Patton won't let anyone ashore without one."

Most of us went to sleep in the wardroom as the destroyer slipped out of the harbor. A young ensign lent me a bedroll, and I stretched out on the floor. This destroyer had picked up four German aviators the night before; they had been in a rubber life raft ninety hours. A British lieutenant, naked to the waist and with shaggy black beard said, "They were pretty pooped. We almost chucked one of them over. I said to him, 'I guess you've had it, old boy'." Later the Germans were brought up to the deck of the destroyer and shown the prodigious display of our warships steaming past. One German said, "I don't believe it. It can't be true." He had swallowed whole the Nazi propaganda that the British Mediterranean fleet had been sunk.

Next morning we were called at five. By the time I got to the bridge at five-thirty Eisenhower and Butcher were already there and Sicily was in sight. Its purple shore was outlined against a rosy dawn streaked with fast-moving light clouds. Aircraft were overhead and someone remarked jovially, "Hope you don't shoot down our own by mistake." Then we approached our first destination and transferred from the destroyer to a small squat boat. The swell was high and glossy and we landlubbers tumbled awkwardly down the rope, bouncing into the new craft. We slithered across rollers, reached General Patton's headquarters ship, and climbed aboard.

Then suddenly the urgency and dramatic quality of this mission became manifest. We were invading the continent of Europe. For the first time we were about to set foot on Axis territory, Europe itself. The first landings had taken place only forty-odd hours before; others were still going on. And it became sharply clear that War was very close. An American cruiser was about a mile offshore. It began to bark. First a flash, then a crack, then a whish of shell, and finally the echo plunging back from the drear Sicilian hills. We watched the floating cloud of smoke, first white and gray, then an ugly incandescent yellow. A naval officer said dryly, "When it makes yellow smoke it's called smokeless; I don't know why." The rate of firing suddenly increased and another officer, American, said, "They must be on target now."

We saw big fires quite near, and I asked the colonel when the Luftwaffe had been over this harbor. He replied with suggestive brevity, "Constantly." There were one hundred and eighty Nazi sorties yesterday and they did some damage. I walked up to a senior officer in khaki with three stars but I didn't notice that he wore a black tie, signifying Navy, not Army; I said "Good morning, General." He replied, "Hell, I'm an admiral." Indeed he was; he was Vice Admiral Henry K. Hewitt, Commander of the American Naval Forces in the Mediterranean. Another officer came up, leaned over to light a cigarette, fumbled and put his mouth over the match instead of the cigarette. He said, "I'm the captain of this ship. I haven't had any sleep and God, am I tired!" Finally he got the match to the cigarette and added, "Guess I can't see straight yet."

The harbor was jammed with shipping. Every kind of craft was busy rushing to shore unloading, returning, reloading. I counted more than a hundred ships. Our cruiser continued to bark angrily, but there was no sign of the Luftwaffe just now. The admiral said, "The devils sneak in from those hills. Their spotters squirt information to them by radio and they skip low through ravines before our boys can spot them, and then dash away before our craft can get down. The lads on the beach have been machine-gunned quite a lot and they have nervous trigger-fingers. Sometimes they let go at our own planes. It's hard to tell our ships from Messerschmitts at ten thousand feet." Another high officer said, "We felt kind of helpless last night. The Luftwaffe came, dropped flares, bombed us to hell and left undisturbed. We haven't any night fighters yet."

Meantime Eisenhower was having breakfast with Patton, whom I'm sorry to say I didn't meet. We took leave, and Patton stood at the edge of the rope ladder looking like a Roman emperor carved in brown stone. He waved good-by. We bounced back to our destroyer and started to coast along the beach—if coast is the proper word to describe a speed of almost forty miles an hour. Eisenhower talked with the captain on the bridge, Butcher sat in a wooden chair high above, and the rest of us clustered around. The crews of a British destroyer are a picturesque-looking lot of brigands because most of them grow beards. The captain wore a blue turtleneck sweater, and an old pair of white shorts. At eight-seventeen I heard signalmen chatter in quick code; two aircraft sighted. The captain, not moving, said quietly, "What do they look like?" They turned out to be our own Spits, but for a few minutes the scene was remarkably like Noel Coward's movie "In Which We Serve." The crew leapt to the alert; they swung gun barrels upward sharply and trained sights while blinkers clicked with signals. And I reflected how strange it was that when you see something real you are likely to compare it to something fictional in order to gauge its true reality.

At about nine we approached an American squadron and Eisenhower ordered a message sent to all ships, "Best wishes and good luck." By this time the spectacular success of our landings all along the shore was being confirmed; most of the villages, as far as we could see with glasses, seemed empty. We passed a lighthouse roughly at the point marking the American right flank, and Eisenhower walked smoothly to and fro around the deck. At nine-forty-five I was standing with the general when a sharp call came suddenly, "Action stations!" The crews jumped up and manned our big gun aft. They stood in line, like pirates with rough towels or rags on their heads, and began to feed the long sharp shells forward. We heard the snort of gunfire, and saw splashes; we were being fired on by a German battery hidden in the groves behind the beach. This was something! The commander-in-chief himself under fire! I kept thinking that, to put it mildly, it would be a good story if we got hit. A senior officer, British, asked Eisenhower to take cover. But someone else said, "Oh no, let's stay out here and watch." Eisenhower, polite and unobtrusive as always, said, "I'm afraid I may be in the way," to which came the rejoinder, "Sir, the commander-in-chief is never in the way." Our guns were now ready to fire. The ship's officers seemed nervous at the responsibility of having Eisenhower aboard. They passed around cotton for our ears, and someone rushed forward with a couple of steel helmets, and asked the general to put one on. He tried to do so but the strap only came under his nose. He laughed, "If I use this I'll need two men to hold it on." Eventually we walked forward and took shelter. Eisenhower bantered, "It seems I'm the bird in the gilded cage." Then he added, "The last time I was shelled near Pantelleria the shots fell three hundred yards away but now they're missing by four hundred. I guess we're doing better."

Eisenhower wanted to visit Sicily for several reasons: to confer with Hewitt, Patton, and his other officers, to see for himself how things were going, and particularly to salute the Canadians who were associated with the British and Americans in a big-scale operation for the first time. He stood on the deck and watched the shore flow along beside us and constantly stressed—again—the *allied* nature of this tremendous operation, and his appreciation of the "exquisite" co-ordination achieved by all. He talked about how Cunningham, Alexander, and Tedder, each working perfectly in his own sphere, had assembled the whole machine into action with consummate efficiency while he was only "chairman of the board." Of course he is much more than this. But Eisenhower's modesty is, as I've said before, incontrovertibly genuine. He's the least stuffed-shirted general I ever met, and all his colleagues admire extremely his suppleness and tact. He never had concrete battle experience before Tunisia, and yet he found himself a superior to veterans like Alexander and Montgomery—he who had only been a lieutenant colonel a couple of years before. In Tunisia he quickly proved himself; it was he who worked out the final strategy. Another thing: his informality, his use of homely language, is disarming; but he never loses a nice healthy dignity; and don't think he lacks force. You get a sense that he's very sure of himself, very shrewd, very tough, and conscious of his own worth.

We rounded a bend in the Sicilian shore; Eisenhower

watched with aware attention, grabbing his glasses now
and then; yet he was free enough in mind and relaxed
enough to reminisce about his career and his ideas. He
said any military man, any general, had to believe above all
in his own luck in the game of war, otherwise the awful
strain would get him down. He added, grinning, "Of
course anybody can draw a bad card sometimes." When he
is tired and he wants to slump after a hard day he knows
his friend Butcher will cheer him up. Eisenhower went to
the Philippines with MacArthur in February, 1935. He
returned to the United States in January, 1940. He was
certain that war was coming but he thought it would strike
us from Europe first. He was strenuous in his warnings,
and friends kidded him, calling him "Alarmist Ike." He
went to work with the Third Army at San Antonio, and
he told me he has never been so busy in his life as during
that period. On the morning of Pearl Harbor Day, worn
out, he took a nap and left word that no one should disturb
him under any circumstances. Then an aide got news of
the Japanese attack, and consulted another aide who said,
"He'll murder us if we don't wake him." They did so, and
Eisenhower said simply, "Well, boys, it's come." A few
days later General W. B. Smith, then secretary to the chief
of staff, telephoned him to say, "Ike, the chief says hop a
plane and come to Washington." Smith is now Eisenhower's own chief of staff.

Eisenhower has enormous respect and admiration for
General Marshall. On the night before D Day—he is a
plainsman and a Westerner and he knows weather—he
realized that the sudden wind had reached forty miles an
hour or more, which might be ruinous to some phases of
the operation. When he returned to headquarters in Malta
he found a message from Marshall in Washington. It
read: "Is it (meaning the operation) on or off and what
do you think?" Marshall asked for an answer within four
hours. Eisenhower had fifteen minutes wherein to reply.

He answered, "It's on. There's a high wind but I think we're going to have good news for you tomorrow."

Eisenhower is as sound as can be on the essential strategy of war; he speaks from experience of the comparative dangerousness of the Germans and the Japanese. And he knows we must beat Germany first for the most substantial and elemental reasons.

Just after ten we approached the beach near Correnti. Again the bustle of shipping in the crowded harbor, again the pulsating beat of our aircraft overhead. We slid down the ladder and this time boarded a duck—the remarkable amphibious water wagon that looks like a truck, has a propeller, and navigates on land as well as water. I did not realize that a duck was a duck, and to my utter astonishment suddenly we found ourselves well up on the beach, dry shod. Eisenhower stepped out and then came the colloquy with the officer I described at the beginning of this chapter. The general carried no flag or other identification. He said directly, "I want to talk to the senior Canadian officer of this beachhead."

"This is a Canadian beachhead, sir, but headquarters is some distance inland," was the reply.

Eisenhower went on, "I don't care if it's a second lieutenant, I want to talk to some Canadian officer."

All around us troops were busy; some swimming in the creamy surf, some unloading ducks and barges, some laying down roads, cooking, erecting green pup tents, building signal boxes. It was hot. There was no shade. The nearest cultivation was a ragged tomato patch. I looked around. So this was Sicily. A young British officer came up to me. He thought I was an officer and asked, "How are we progressing elsewhere, sir?" Another officer glanced at the men in all varieties of undress, as they stared, awed, at the generalissimo and as word spread of his arrival. The officer said, as if apologizing for their casual appearance, "They're a cheery lot of rascals, sir."

After a moment Eisenhower decided to go inland himself to find the Canadians. He repeated, "I want to welcome Canada to the Allied command." He borrowed a jeep and we followed in our duck; I tried to take pictures as we bounced forward. That duck may have had rough passages in some waters, but nothing it ever experienced could have been rougher than these narrow, twisting, dusty Sicilian lanes. We bumped along, trying to keep up with the general's jeep; we got stalled in other traffic, and lost it. We ground through tall reeds and prodded into thickets, and I reflected that this would be a fine place for the generalissimo to get lost. The enemy wasn't far away, and on the beach we had heard that snipers were still busy and that three of our sentries had been killed the night before. But the first Sicilian I actually laid eyes on was a kid of about fourteen riding a bicycle. He smiled, waved, and asked us to take his picture. We went back to the beach. Eisenhower and the jeep returned a bit later. He had found a junior Canadian officer, Captain J. E. Moore of Vancouver, and so his mission was accomplished.

Our return was, as they say, uneventful. Eisenhower pointed to the duck near a thicket and asked, with his aware grin, "Is the flagship ready?"

"Aye, aye, sir, if you are prepared."

"Set sail," another officer said, and we mounted the weird thing and were off.

Two minutes later we slipped from land into water, and rode smoothly to the headquarters ship of a British admiral. We sat down to have a drink when the captain exclaimed, "Oh, blast! I'm afraid I'm captain of this ship and that's the red signal. I'm afraid I'll have to leave you." A red signal means an air raid alert and before we finished our drinks we had two of them.

Then we discovered that Eisenhower had already left the headquarters ship for our destroyer; there was great commotion as Butcher and I thought—not very seriously

—that we might be left behind. The admiral—who is known as a "tiger," and who has run more convoys through the Mediterranean than any other officer—said in the most vigorous tone of command I have ever heard, "My barge! Superspeed!" So the barge drew up and after an interval we were back on our destroyer once again. Then we began the return trip to Malta. The American Generalissimo of the Allied Armies of Liberation had set foot on the soil of occupied Europe for the first time.

Chapter VI

How to Cover a War, When Lucky

Malta, Tuesday, July 13.—Two stories today. The operations piece described the capture of Canicatti by the Americans, and of Augusta by the British. One of our officers said, "The Italians fought with great dash and spirit. They really did. The bloody fools."

The other story was an interview with Air Vice Marshal Sir Keith Park, the Air Officer Commanding, Malta. We cannot, however, release it until later, since it is still the most hush-hush of all possible secrets that Malta is playing a dominant role in this operation. Park is tall, gray, gaunt, with a beautifully organized, neat mind. Like so many British officers his reticence, his good manners, make you feel for a moment that he lacks vitality; then you discover that this is far from being true. He took the initiative from us right away, and told us just what *he* wanted us to know, point by point, with a fine discriminating symmetry. Most of what he said was off the record. But he did let us disclose some details of the extraordinary activity of the RAF stationed here. For instance in the past four days aircraft based on Malta have shot down no fewer than 106 enemy planes.

Malta, he pointed out, is of supreme value because of its geographical position as a pivot. Planes here can transfer their attentions from one sphere of the Mediterranean to another with remarkable ease. Last summer the Maltese

squadrons went after the Axis supply lines to Tripoli and
fed on enemy shipping—particularly tankers—along the
Adriatic coast and the shores of Greece; also they re-
peatedly bombed Benghazi and Tobruk. Then after the
Allied landings in Africa in November they changed direction to attack Sicily, trying particularly to knock out enemy
torpedo bombers. During the Tunisian deadlock the Malta
planes switched toward Tripoli again to assist the advance
of the Eighth Army, and during the final phase in Tunisia
they turned northward once more to pin enemy fighters on
their home grounds. Malta fighters have, Park said, rendered extraordinary service these past few days to American bombers working out of Africa. The RAF meets
United States bombers over the sea somewhere, and takes
them in to their targets; if a bomber is damaged, or gets
off course, the fighters bring it in to Malta as a provisional
stop. Aside from this the Malta planes have helped the
Sicilian campaign in three ways. First, their task was
reconnaissance; they swept the sea and photographed the
beaches. Second, they protected Allied shipping, and still
protect it. Third, they gave indispensable fighter cover for
the landings themselves.

Park sought to impress on us the enormous change that
has come over Malta. When he arrived, not so long ago,
the only streets open were a few main arteries; all the rest
were impassably choked with stone debris. The schools
had to be closed, and the people were on virtual starvation
rations. Last August a British convoy tried to fight its
way through to relieve Malta; out of fourteen ships which
left Gibraltar, only five arrived. The siege then began in
earnest, until relief came in the shape of a more successful
convoy in November. But when this latter convoy finally
did get in, the length of time that the island could hold out
was being measured in days, not weeks.

I liked what Park said about Eisenhower: "By Jove,
what a fine man! A magnificent co-ordinator, don't-you-

know? And so *simpatico*. You know what that word means, don't you? *Simpatico*. He's a good mixer, but not too much so. And by Jove, what a person to rely on!"

Also today we worked on a navy story, and attended the briefing of a group of young officers on the motor torpedo boats which harass the Sicilian coasts. Then as I thought my work was finished for the day we heard that the first group of enemy prisoners to arrive here was being disembarked. We had half an hour with them until an indignant British sergeant rushed up and shouted, "But you are not allowed to talk to prisoners, sir!"

About sixty or seventy Italians were dumped off a boat, and seven or eight young Germans. What a difference between them! The Italians were inadequately uniformed, dirty, sloppy, unshaven; they wore a nondescript variety of headgear; several were so tired that they fell flat-faced in the dirt. The Germans segregated themselves from their Italian allies as if the Italians were infected. The Germans were youthful, alert, bronzed, excellently uniformed and equipped, gay, and confident; they looked like the lads I used to ski with in the Salzkammergut or Semmering. They carried themselves not like prisoners, but like tourists off on a jaunt; they said cockily that they did not consider the "war situation" at all hopeless, and one kept making a gesture as if he were strumming a guitar. "I feel sure we'll have a good time in America," he announced. Normally stories about prisoners are heavily censored or not passed at all. But this one made everybody so angry that they let it through. "So he wants a good time in America," Duncan snapped. "Son of a bitch!"

Tea with Warrener, an able citizen. He has got "body-space" for Gilling and me to go to Sicily with the Eighth. I had never heard this phrase "body-space" before. Another expression both Warrener and Lock use all the time is new to me, the word "marry" to denote military union. Lock said the other day, "See, chum, we push the background communiqué to Algiers and it marries the Tunis stuff there." Warrener remarked this afternoon, "I came by a hell of a slow convoy from Alexandria, but we married a fast escort two hundred miles out."

Walking with Duncan Clark near P. Mansions we heard a radio near the entrance to a tunnel. Duncan, indefatigable, rushes out somewhere and monitors the BBC four or five times a day, so that we will know what is going on. (We have no radio in our office, strangely.) But this sound was different. A noncom welcomed us in with a strange accent, "Cawm in, sir." We listened then to a perfect Oxford voice giving the most unimaginably distorted view of the campaign. In a second it dawned on me; this was Berlin! After a time one of the sergeants said "Crap!" simply and turned the machine off.

Looking through my notes this evening I found something I had taken down on the destroyer yesterday. It was in the ship's scrapbook. Half a dozen officers asked their wives or sweethearts or friends to list "The Ten Things I Love Best." This is the answer I thought the most distinctive:

Salzburg in deep snow
The moment just before I fall in love
My children asleep
Etoile d'Holland roses in a white bowl
The slow movement of Beethoven's last quartet, Op. 135
Donne's love poems
The curtain rising on the first act of "Rosenkavalier"
A Viennese waltz with the perfect partner
Singing old songs by candlelight
Chelsea Embankment late afternoon in autumn

I wondered why I should have wanted to write this down; then it occurred to me that from a limited point of view it was about as good a summary of what we are fighting for as anything I know.

We are just about out of cigarettes today, and I scrounge

for them shamelessly. I stole a pillowcase this afternoon, stuffed my overcoat in it, and slept with as deep satisfaction as if I were in the Ritz.

Malta, Wednesday, July 14.—Our briefing goes somewhat like this: Lieutenant Colonel Hunt is, like Williams, a youngish Oxford don. I don't know what he taught, but he is amazingly learned in several fields; the other day he showed extraordinary knowledge of antiquities in Sicily; then I heard him say a word or two in perfect German; also he has had wide experience in the modern Balkans. Normally he breezes in to 947 a little before lunch. He has himself just been briefed by the intelligence staff. Then he passes on to us—and to Lock and Duncan—what he thinks we ought to know. He talks so quickly and in such a slurred monotone that it is hard to follow him; yet we have to take notes with great accuracy. Samples of his conversation:

"Ah, a monstrous show."

"It was all rather melancholy." (In ironic description of what had happened to a German detachment.)

"Oh bugger, wish I had known that. Damn."

"There's a bit of a stop (censorship restriction) on that."

"Now listen, old—."

"Absolutely. We were the cat's whiskers there."

"But for Christ's sake, don't print that."

"Oh, my aunt!"

"I don't know. That's your baby. Best of luck."

Our big talk today was with General Alexander, and I was even more impressed with him this time than last. He took us right into that supremely secret sanctum, the War Room, and patiently explained what was going on, tracing every detail on the huge maps that cover each wall. I cannot, for security reasons, describe these maps; but nothing I have ever seen has fascinated me more—their technical proficiency, their infinitude of detail, their extreme up-to-dateness, and the wonderful draftsmanship and lithography they represent. Have the Germans as good maps as these really super-maps, I wonder? . . . Alexander talked most about an engagement now taking place at a bridge above Lentini. British parachutists took this bridge. Then it was retaken by footborne German parachutists; this must be the first battle in history between rival paratroops fighting on the ground. Now the British have retaken it again; but Alexander was grave pointing out that the British unit is still half-encircled, and that a small group such as this cannot hang on indefinitely, without supplies. It certainly is something to have a battle explained in such detail by the commander directing it! Then Alexander, who has great respect for German military prowess, predicted that the Germans will fight long and stubbornly in Sicily and Italy. Also he pointed out what a difficult problem they have—that of defending an exposed coast line with a great deal of *long* beach. Alexander was as completely unruffled, as calm and serene as a lecturer in a college. When we left the tunnel I heard someone say, "Wonderful bloke, Alex!" I notice that when people mention his name, their faces light up.

An officer just back from one of the beaches gave me a line which I used in a second story, that in some Sicilian villages the signs *Evviva Mussolini* have been crossed out and replaced by *Evviva George VI*. I hear varying reports about what the attitude of the population is, though everybody agrees that the Germans are hated. Some eyewitnesses describe the Italian townsfolk as entirely inert; they see us march through their streets and pay no attention; others say that our troops are actively welcomed, with enthusiasm.

At tea today the talk was all on what we will do with Italy when the conquest has gone forward more. A major who is a well-known artist—assigned to the Eighth Army to make a pictorial record—asked about this and I said that I thought Mussolini would get kicked out in due course or shot, or maybe would escape; that then some *putschists*, à la Darlan, would offer to trade us the Italian fleet for better terms; and that Badoglio would probably form a government. Most of the group seemed perplexed and worried. Questions: Will we have to feed the whole peninsula? Can we make a government with the grandson of the king as regent? Surely we will keep Tripoli after the war? Would Italians temperamentally be able to live under a republic? Why not give Libya and Cyrenaica to South Africa, thus bringing South Africa to North?

We can now reveal what 947 is, the headquarters of what is known as the Fifteenth Army Group. This number was arrived at by the simple expedient of adding the 7 of the American Seventh Army to the British Eighth. So our date line is henceforth, "Fifteenth Army Group" instead of the euphemism we have been using; we cannot, however, disclose that Malta is headquarters. Duncan Clark again showed what a nice guy he is. First he went to bat with the other censors for me on a political piece, as he did once before; then he noticed that Gilling had forgotten to insert the word "censored" in his story about Alexander. This could mean that it might be held up for hours in London so Duncan went to an infinitude of trouble, telephoning for half an hour, to inform the cable head and get the missing word inserted before the story went off.

We had a bottle of beer at the mess tonight; the beer ration is one pint a week. And we got fifty inexpressibly foul Indian cigarettes, known as V's. Even men starved to the point of insanity for tobacco cannot easily smoke them. I saw five men light cigarettes from one match. Nobody is superstitious any more. As Gilling put it, "Matches are too bloody scarce, owld boy."

A signal came from Joe Phillips, "Gunther Gilling movements unrestricted." We have been waiting for this for several days, and it means that we can go forward to Sicily when this headquarters closes up.

A British officer suddenly got hysterical tonight; he screamed, "I can't stand the filth, the bloody dirt; I can't stand it!" I am crawling with fleas myself, and today there was no water even to shave in.

One of our American friends is sick. "It's just the drizzles," he apologized.

Malta, Thursday, July 15.—Today we had a good talk with Lieutenant General Andrew McNaughton, Commander-in-Chief of the Canadian army. Alexander introduced us to him yesterday. He has just arrived in this theater and is naturally proud of the way his Canadians are behaving. McNaughton is fluent, energetic, practical. "I'm a factual sort of bird," he said. "I don't suppose I'll tell you any state secrets, but if I do, the censor can cut 'em out." He waved at Duncan Clark, who was in the room (we were in Eisenhower's office).

McNaughton said the most interesting thing about the Sicilian landings is the evidence they provide that the Allies can now strike with tremendous efficiency and force on any front, not merely the European front. Japan, he implied, was watching the progress of this operation just as carefully as was Germany. And Japanese morale, as well as German morale, must be jolted at the success of what is probably the most perfect example of combined operations ever known. The Japanese must be aware now that we can concentrate overwhelming pressure on any point on the world's surface—pressure brought from the four corners of the earth—at almost any time.

McNaughton has been training and nurturing his Canadians for several years, and this is their first big show. "Just as there is an undefended and unfortified boundary for three thousand miles between the United States and Canada, so in Sicily today there is a common front between Americans and Canadians fighting the same enemy." McNaughton added that his troops—who have never served in the Mediterranean before—had assembled in Britain on plans worked out elsewhere; very few of his officers had any personal knowledge as to what was going to happen. "The plans were transmitted to us in England and we went to work." The landings had to be scheduled, various craft waterproofed, and everything loaded so that the right material would be on top. The Canadians arrived at the correct rendezvous on the minute, they carried out complex maneuvers exactly as planned, and they landed "on the button."

I wrote the McNaughton story—for release later when it is officially confirmed that the Canadians are here—and then a second piece on operations. For a third story today I'm indebted to Colonel Hunt. Expert British and American observers are, it seems, becoming more amazed day by day at the pitiful inadequacy of Italian equipment. Airplanes that can't fly; artillery that is ludicrous; guns that don't shoot; antediluvian tanks that burst into flame at a single hit—this is the price the Italian people are now paying for twenty years of "efficient" leadership under Fascism. Italian ration boxes have been found with only a thin layer of provisions on top and a pile of gravel underneath; fire extinguishers actually make fires burn brighter; tins of meat are rotten; the soup is dishwater. For years some Right Wing folk in both Britain and America have had secret—or not so secret—sympathies with Fascism; most explained or excused this sympathy on the ground that Mussolini "cleaned Italy up"; he chased beggars off the streets and made trains run on time; the Fascist regime was, if nothing else, workmanlike and "efficient." But as things turned out the Fascist regime was *not* efficient. Corruption and *in*efficiency have so deeply bitten their way into the core of the state that the Italian army is not even capable of feeding and equipping its own troops. Hunt's explanation for this is ingenious. He thinks, first, that Italy under Fascism was governed not merely by one bureaucracy but by two; this made for fantastic duplication of effort, maladministration, and corruption. Second, in the Fascist setup every man is a complete boss to those below him, a complete slave to those above. As a result everyone played his own game; there was no national co-operation or integration. The soul of a people was destroyed because no one in civil life would do anything except with an eye to feathering his own nest, particularly in the realm of political favoritism.

Apparently the public relations folk in Tunis and Algiers do not understand just how we are operating here, and they have sent an officer to check up. Lock couldn't understand why this should be necessary. "Am I dense," he kept muttering, "or mad?" Then everything was smoothed over, and he got a pleasant letter of congratulation from Joe Phillips.

Warrener has gone forward to Sicily. We found to our consternation that the body-space he booked for us has been canceled, since our permission to leave here was late arriving. Now we cannot get a signal through to Warrener; he is on the move, and it may take as long as three days to communicate with him. Moreover, we cannot proceed until he reconfirms our authority, inasmuch as Montgomery has just issued an exceptionally sharp order that anyone going to Sicily without permission—no matter who —will be "arrested." Our mess is full of disconsolate observer-officers (one arrived all the way from Cairo) who are not being allowed to proceed. Even McNaughton has been held up.

We had a swim today, and with glorious satisfaction (a) got fairly clean; (b) watched the Fleet go out.

Malta, Friday, July 16.—I cannot understand why we are not bombed. No one else can understand it either. Malta is, as is notorious, the most bombed spot on earth. And at this particular time, with the entire Allied command assembled here, and hundreds upon hundreds of ships of all shapes and varieties in the harbor, it is a better target than ever before. Yet we have been here a week, and there has not been so much as a peep out of the Luftwaffe. Every night I go to bed feeling sure that there will be a raid; I wake up puzzled, and, in a curious way, let down. Last night we had plenty of noise—our own depth charges apparently—but nothing from the enemy. The Germans send reconnaissance planes over every day, and so they must see all our concentration in the harbor; probably they do not, however, know the superior quality of the human game they might be stalking. Even so it seems almost inconceivable that in this week of all weeks, everything should have been so quiet. (Two weeks later I learned that the Luftwaffe did indeed come over Malta—the night I left. Two hours after I had gone our hotel got a direct hit, and an American officer who slept two rooms down from me was killed.)

We dismantled our P. Mansions headquarters today, and moved back into the Phoenicia mess. Our office will henceforth be a garret in the Information Building. We will not have so much privacy, or such an intimate sense of rapport between four men. Lock, Duncan, Gilling and I felt a rather acute emotion as we bundled up our papers, swatted a final fly, had the last cup of tea 947 provided, piled into a 1500-weight, and waved good-by.

People who lived here through the great siege tell with grim ex post facto humor what they endured. Apparently what everybody missed most intensely were the little things: no toilet paper, no soap, no razor blades, no shoe-laces, no books, no toothpaste, above all no matches. I too am finding out how these little things count. Yet with what astonishing speed one becomes acclimatized to shortages! I get along without much inconvenience and certainly with no sense of actual hardship. The chief nuisance is that there are no drawers and no hooks in our room, so that everything we own has to be piled into a bag three or four times a day and dragged out again. I went shopping today. One hundred sheets of typewriter paper cost 6s. 6d. I bought a thin inadequate towel for ten shillings, and two flints for my lighter (which is failing) for three bob. This morning neither Gilling nor I had a match left.

Wrote two brief stories, one on operations—a quarter of Sicily is now in our hands—the other about a trip Alexander just made to Sicily. He met and conferred with Montgomery there, and Duncan Clark suggested the "angle" for the story, that it must be the first meeting of these two redoubtable chieftains on *European* soil. This was Alexander's second trip over; on the first, with characteristic tact, he did not see the British but instead called on Patton and the Americans.

Looking out of the Monico window late this afternoon I saw a brown pile of stuff on the second floor of a building opposite. (Very few buildings in Malta have intact walls, and so it is easy to see in.) Someone said, "This really is Mediterranean civilization. It wouldn't be so notable to see manure on the ground floor, but to have it on the second floor, that is something!"

I have been bursting with ideas for stories these crowded days. I go to bed happy, and wake up feeling wonderful. Yet I feel that I have so much still to learn, and that every year there are fewer years left to learn in.

Malta, Saturday, July 17.—No story today. I started to write an article about Eisenhower. We had a lazy afternoon, and then wandered around the town.

Dana Schmidt, the United Press man with the British fleet, left yesterday. So I was astonished to run into him this morning. The big ship that he was on "caught a kipper"; it managed however to limp back to port. A German torpedo plane got it by skimming over at ten-foot altitude; no one saw the plane except, of all people, the parson who happened to be on deck; and it got away right through the destroyer screen—before anybody could fire a shot.

Tonight an officer staggered into the Phoenicia so drunk that he could only stand by bracing himself along the corridor. He sang, shouted, stumbled, and got very sick. I don't think I've seen anybody so drunk in twenty years. My chief emotion was wondering where on earth he had been able to buy or otherwise procure so much to drink.

Sample of dialogue from a British tank expert: "The Italians fought very well in Ethiopia, didn't they? Why should they collapse, now, while defending their own soil? Are they just *wet fish*, or what?"

We were almost shaken out of bed tonight by the reverberation of Montgomery's bombardment eighty miles away. The Eighth Army is getting ready—in its familiar way—for a really big attack.

Malta, Sunday, July 18.—Our permission and travel orders to proceed to Sicily came through this morning. The wiry Lock has been working on it steadily. For a time we could get no action because the only officer who was authorized to confirm Warrener's approval of our trip was absent in Sicily himself, but moving so fast that nobody could locate him or get word through.

At lunch an RAF officer told us that one of his comrades, working out of Malta in a Beaufighter last night, bagged five Nazi planes in one sortie, perhaps a world's record. How nice these British are! The officer's comment was, "You know, we're so strong now, and they're so weak in the air, it isn't quite fair!"

At about six Gilling and I said good-by to Lock and Duncan, and climbed aboard an LCI (Landing Craft Infantry). It looks like a tug with a forward ramp, and it was built in Perth Amboy, New Jersey, a couple of months ago. The skipper and crew are, however, British. We had brought along rations, and with two British brigadiers we made a kind of picnic supper on the upper deck. No smoking was permitted after sundown. We saw lights on another ship, and one of our officers said harshly, "The captain of that vessel ought to be shot."

We steamed slowly out into the harbor, and a destroyer nudged us into line with other LCI's. There was a lovely orange moon, and a Mosquito—surely the most beautiful of all airplanes—hovered gently overhead.

Chapter VII

Montgomery and Alexander

B OTH these eminent generals are lean, steel-hard,
spare, blue-eyed; both are in their fifties, and both,
like so many top officers in the British army, are North
Irishmen.* Everybody calls Montgomery simply "Monty."
The nickname is universal. Almost everybody calls Alexander "*General* Alex." The name is foreshortened, as a
token of affection, but it is rarely used without the title,
which shows the great respect in which Alexander is held.
"General Alex" is younger in years, but he is Montgomery's superior officer. Monty, the showman, takes the
bows; Alexander, the director, hovers in the wings. They
say that only Alexander can "handle" Monty, or call him
"Monty" to his face. Even though he is his junior, Alexander has toward him the attitude of a teacher proud of
a brilliant student.

Half the fun of covering the Sicilian campaign was
hearing stories about Montgomery. Maybe some are
apocryphal; it is always so with men packed with bounce
and color. Their personalities are so strong that they
create a kind of folklore, and the tinges of distortion add
a queer legendary touch to the essential truth, which
makes it truer.

Montgomery looks something like a hawk, something—
I don't mean this disparagingly—like a fox. He has the
most piercing and luminous blue eyes I have ever seen.

---

* Field Marshal Sir Alan Brooke, chief of the Imperial General Staff,
and Field Marshal Sir John Dill, British representative on the Combined Chiefs of Staff in Washington, come from North Ireland too.

He is very alert and clipped in conversation, and his most striking verbal mannerism is the way he repeats himself. When he talks, he puts the second finger of his right hand on the little finger of the left, and ticks off his points with mathematical precision, "One . . . two . . ." He recapitulates phrase after phrase, like this: "The point is," he will say, "Now, the point is . . ." Or, "You will remember. You will remember." Or, "The tanks will go through. Will go through. The tanks will proceed to their destination. Will proceed . . ."

Montgomery has a tremendous healthy ego, and is sometimes difficult to get along with. This is not merely a matter of conceit or vanity; it is based on complete self-confidence and an utter confidence in his men. He never refers to the Eighth Army as such, but always to "*my* army"; never to troops in such-and-such a unit, but to "*my* troops."

The King of England visited Tunisia last spring, inspecting the battle fronts. One afternoon the somewhat inarticulate monarch saw a patch of sunlight on a strip of sand; deeply taken by the color, a rich burnished tan, he said that he would like it for the ribbon of a new decoration to commemorate the African campaign. When the king received General Montgomery the next day he mentioned this. Montgomery looked up.

"Would Your Majesty kindly describe that color again?" the general asked.

The king did so.

"Why!" exclaimed Montgomery. "That's *my* color, that's Eighth Army yellow!"

Monty turned to his military assistant. "It's the exact color of my car. Paint up a sample for His Majesty. Or better, tear a strip off the car!"

But no story about Montgomery can be half so effective in print as in life. One must see and hear the general himself: the quick upward intonation of the sentences, the touch of style and dash he gives to every word, every gesture.

When I met him and presented my letter of introduction from Wendell Willkie, he looked it over calmly. "Ah, ah!" he exclaimed. "Willkie, Willkie . . . of course I know Willkie. He was my guest at Alamein. Ha, Willkie! Why, I showed him a battle once!"

Later he gave me a longhand letter to carry back to Mr. Willkie. He made the good score of misspelling *both* Willkie's names on the scrawled envelope.

The general's talk that day was a wonderful mixture of curiosity, incomprehension of any world not his own ("Have you ever heard of an American publication called *Life*, yes, that's it, a publication called *Life*, I believe that was the name, *Life*."), solid wisdom about military affairs, zest in the battle to come, respect and affection for the army he has created, and a courteous interest in such non-military occupations as the writing of books.

He told me that he has kept a diary for years, that he posted it every day, that he kept it under lock and key ("No one in the world knows where it is except myself"), and that it would "blow off everybody's head between Alamein and London." I summoned what little courage I have and told him that I thought he was making a great mistake not to give someone else access to it, because no future historian could write a true history of the African war without knowing what it contained.

"Tell me, would I get any money for my diary?" he asked smiling.

I replied, very deadpan: "About a hundred thousand dollars, General."

He turned to Lieutenant Colonel "Bill" Williams. "A hundred thousand dollars? What's that?"

"That's twenty-five thousand pounds, sir," answered Colonel Williams, solemnly.

"Well," Montgomery grinned. "Guess won't die in poorhouse after all." (His speech is so clipped that you can only give an impression of it by leaving the pronouns and articles out.)

Like any good actor, he likes to make his effects in his own manner, and many of his more outrageous statements are not to be taken literally. There is a certain waggishness about Montgomery. Once a group of correspondents approached him before Mount Etna, and asked him how the battle was going. "Ha!" he replied. "I have never fought under the eye of a volcano before!"

Some of his troops in Sicily suffered from "gyppy tummy," because they were eating fresh vegetables to which they were not accustomed. Monty turned to one of his aides. "We have advanced from Alamein to El Agheila to Tripoli to Tunis. Nothing stopped us. Now we are stopped. Why? Because the men are eating tomatoes!" Then with a complete change of voice: "Let them cease eating tomatoes!"

Montgomery's self-confidence and ego are one of the great sources of his power. When his own back was to the wall, just before Alamein in August, 1942, with the enemy only forty miles from Alexandria, he had the cool effrontery to tell Mr. Willkie, "It is now mathematically certain that *I* will eventually destroy Rommel." His orders of the day are full of this spirit; he simply will not allow any man in his command to conceive the possibility of defeat. For instance, he addressed his men just before the Battle of Tunisia, with these words: "The Eighth Army will destroy the enemy now facing us in the Mareth position, will burst through the Gabès Gap, and will then drive northward on Sfax, Sousse, and finally Tunis." His orders are always direct, concrete, personal. He likes to use homely phrases. He tells his officers, "Tomorrow we will give the enemy a bloody nose."

But for all his self-confidence let no one think that Montgomery is one of those men who never listen, who cannot bear to be countermanded. He loathes Yes-men. The officers of his staff have tea with him every day, and they talk almost as equals, with complete liberty to discuss, to criticize, to argue. One of his aides—a youngster in his thirties—told me that his own particular job was to tell the general, in no uncertain terms, exactly what he could *not* do. "I'm the No-man," said the aide.

Nor, despite the waggishness, should anyone think that Montgomery is anything but austere. In fact, next to self-confidence, the dominating note in his complex character is, as everybody knows, a rigid and compelling asceticism. He is given to odd quirks and idiosyncrasies; for instance he carries a big cage of chickens with him, everywhere he goes, so that he will always have fresh eggs. But at bottom his character is as stern as that of Cromwell, with whom he has often been compared. His father was a bishop, and he himself reads the lesson to his troops every Sunday morning. When time permits, he leads his own officers in exhausting five-mile runs, before breakfast. He eats sparingly, he doesn't drink, and he doesn't smoke. Nor will he tolerate anybody smoking near him. I told him that this was a characteristic he shared with Adolf Hitler —which considerably astonished him. Officers approaching toss their cigarettes away quickly and hide their pipes; I watched this happen in Sicily several times, when he was in the open field.

Montgomery has several rules for keeping himself on the razor edge of fitness. For one thing, he told me, he refuses absolutely to do any work after dinner. He goes to bed at about nine-thirty in the evening, without fail, and then spends an hour reading or, in his own words, just "thinking." He said that two other basic rules govern his behavior. First, never worry. Second, never bother with details. Details should be left to the staff, he told me. And also worries. "That's what a staff is for."

The general was born of an Ulster family in 1887. He

is a widower, with one child. He went to Sandhurst, the great British officers' school, and entered the Army in 1908. He served in France in the First World War, and was wounded and decorated; he had some years in Palestine, Transjordan, and India; when World War II broke out, he was in England commanding a division. It was Alexander who brought him to the command of the Eighth Army, in the black summer of 1942. But his appointment was based partly on accident; in fact his later career is a first-rate example of the importance of accidents in history. The officer originally chosen for his command, General W. H. E. ("Strafer") Gott, was killed in an airplane accident, and Montgomery took over as second choice.

He was heartily disliked when he first arrived in Cairo. He was cavalier about his predecessors, which was considered bad form in the extreme, and many officers thought him insolent. Monty paid no attention. He went up forward and wandered around for a day or two, inspecting every position, talking to every man he met, making intimate personal contact with the troops. What he had to pray for was time. "Give me a fortnight," he said, "and I can resist the German attack. Give me three weeks, and I can defeat the Boche. Give me a month, and I can chase him out of Africa." Meantime, he *took hold*. Within forty-eight hours the difference in spirit at the Alamein front was prodigious. The previous commander had scarcely ever visited or even talked to his own men. But within forty-eight hours of Monty's arrival, every man in Egypt knew that a fresh new wind was blowing, that their new commander was something quite different, something unique. He instilled into them, magically, his own magnificent superconfidence.

The plans for the Alamein battle, which opened on October 23, 1942, were made originally by General Wavell when the Italians were attacking in 1940; Wavell selected

Alamein as a good position for a last stand, if a last stand should become necessary. Oddly enough, the original Wavell plans were unaccountably lost; when the Germans threatened Egypt two years later, they were unearthed just in time. The actual conception of the 1942 battle was Alexander's. Montgomery was simply the executant. But he executed the job supremely well.

On his arrival in Egypt Monty knew very little about desert warfare. But he was flexible; he was quick to learn. On one of his first tours to the front, he saw men sleeping. They had been doing night patrols, and were worn out. Nevertheless he muttered, "Remarkable . . . Remarkable. *My* men . . . asleep by day. Get them up! Let them train!" But he soon found out that even *his* men could not work by night and train by day and still maintain efficiency. So he softened. He made several mistakes in the early phases of the Alamein battle, the nature of which are still military secrets. But, elastic, he reconsidered his original orders, rescinded his first directives, and started over again on a new track. He is a big enough man always to be *learning*.

Among others of Montgomery's qualities is, first, that he has made a profoundly serious study of the art of war —in theory as well as practice; second, that he is one of the comparatively few modern generals willing to take heavy casualties. Also, he has that characteristic of all great military leaders: foresight. He himself wrote recently: "The battle for the Mareth Line was the most interesting of all the interesting battles of the North African campaign, and I began to consider the problem of attack *three months* before I came to it."

This is his own account of part of the ensuing battle, which he made in a speech recently, as reported by the Sunday *Express*:

The last point of interest is the problem of the Gabès Gap. That was a strong natural position, and the point was what we were going to do about it, for we were now in the dark period, and all our operations had hitherto been carried out in the moonlight period. I had to decide whether I would take a chance in the dark period, or whether I would wait for the moon and give the enemy a fortnight to strengthen his position.

I decided to do two things I had never done before. The first was to attack in the dark, and the second was to attack in the center, in the middle of the Gap. The enemy was so surprised by those two things that the Eighth Army broke through the Gabès Gap in one day. Later on I asked General Messe, the Italian commander, after his capture, if he expected the attack, and his reply was: "We thought you would wait for the moon. We did not reckon on an attack for a fortnight."

Montgomery's greatest contribution—quite aside from the purely physical feat of chasing Rommel thirteen hundred miles in thirteen weeks—is in the realm of morale. He re-created, revitalized, reanimated the British armies in Africa. He did this mostly by personal contact, so that every human being in all his forces felt himself an essential constituent of the whole. He himself directs the "briefing" of his principal officers every day, and before action, he always addresses large bodies of troops himself, without fail. Again—another of his secrets—he takes good care of his men. He is utterly ruthless with inefficient officers. He summarily fired two generals who were slow getting the tanks through at Mareth, and once he sacked a major who failed to provide tea for a detachment of advanced troops. "The little fellow," one of his aides told me, "is certainly a stickler."

In Malta I asked the general what his rules for leadership were, and he replied that he had three. First, no failure can be tolerated. Since failure is inadmissible, the scope of operations must be limited to what is practicable. Second, the general in command must not be prodded into anything too grandiose for the means at his disposal. Third, the general must refuse to be rushed. He must be allowed to pick his own time. No matter what the pressure may be—and sometimes pressure is enormous—he must set himself against anything premature.

Then Montgomery added something like this: "It's a life work to make an army. A life work. An army is a tool, a weapon. You have to forge it, temper it, sharpen it, before you wield it. The first imperative is morale. Morale depends on confidence. On confidence. Also morale depends on victory. Men like an army that is winning." He smiled. "So do the politicians."

Montgomery has the most profound respect for Rommel, his greatest adversary, and one story is that for a long time he kept a photograph of him above his mirror. He would dearly love to meet Rommel when the war is over, and talk about the campaign, trace over the maps again and see why he and Rommel had done thus and so at such and such a time. He thinks that the Germans may have collapsed in North Africa because Rommel, ill at the time, was not "fit." "A man must be fit."

The general is not always respectful of certain eminent colleagues in his own army. He heard not long ago that a fellow officer had become a full general. "That man!" he hissed. "That man a full general! Bastardization of the rank!"

"General Alex" is a man of totally different character. When you mention Monty to people, they may curse or grin. Every time I asked anybody about Alexander, I got a reaction of pleasure, genuine warmth, and admiration.

General Sir Harold Rupert Leofric George Alexander, D.S.O., M.C., etc., was born in North Ireland in 1891. He was the son of an earl, and his mother was the daughter of an earl; he married an earl's daughter, by whom he has three children. Both his grandfather and father were in the Army, as is one of his three brothers. He went to Harrow and Sandhurst. For many years he served with the Irish Guards. You note the Irish in him right away—

his sense of wry humor, his subtle charm. Also you note the aristocracy. Take one look at him—the serene poised head, the carefully immaculate manner—and you instantly say to yourself the word: "aristocrat." Nor do I mean this in the snobbish sense of the term. I mean aristocracy in the sense of personal, not social, superiority—superiority in brains, courage, taste, and style.

Alexander has served thirty-three years in the British army. They sit lightly. He is youthful-looking and extraordinarily handsome. He was a famous athlete in his day; a champion miler in 1914, he would have represented Great Britain at the next Olympic Games had they not been called off. He listens well, and thinks carefully before he talks. He does not like to be quoted directly. This is not so much for reasons of prudence as shyness. "Shyness" in many Englishmen is simply a device whereby somebody with nothing to say has an excuse for not saying it. It is a shield for inertia, for lack of imagination, sometimes for stupidity. But Alexander's shyness is quite different. It is a kind of serenity, a deliberateness founded on tact and good manners.

Later I met a newspaper friend who went through the disastrous retreat in Burma with Alexander early in 1942. "I've seen more 'flap' (panic, disorder) in peacetime maneuvers," said my friend succinctly. Nothing ever ruffles Alexander. He was the last man off the beach at Dunkirk; he coasted about in a motorboat, seeing that everybody else was off. But he did it in his usual quiet way. He is as unspectacular as Montgomery is spectacular.

This general does not wear his heart on his sleeve, but no one should think he is dry-as-dust. Quite the contrary. As a young man he was an exceptionally dashing officer; he always carried an Irish flag hidden in his pocket, which he wanted to be the first to plant in Berlin. For a time he was in command of the Lettish Landwehr, in Riga, against the Bolsheviks. But even though vividly fighting them in the field he was delighted to acquire some Russian characteristics. He learned to ride straight-legged; he grew an enormous bushy mustache and wore his helmet deep over his nose.

As with so many British officers of high rank, the variety of his interests is astonishing. Once he learned tap dancing. He speaks four or five languages, including Russian and Hindustani. His hobby is water-color painting, and like Mr. Churchill he is good at it. He likes to fly his own airplane; he owns a little puddle jumper. The variety of his friendships, too, is considerable. In Riga many years ago he met Walter Duranty, who later became the Moscow correspondent of the New York *Times*. He liked and admired Duranty extremely, and gave him many of his early scoops. Duranty was the only newspaperman he would talk to, and I imagine they must have had terrific times together. During the middle of the Tunisian campaign, more than two decades later, he telegraphed Duranty asking why he wasn't there. When I mentioned Duranty to Alexander, the general exclaimed, "Duranty! Well!" in terms of deep curiosity and affection.

The outline of General Alexander's career is exceptional, in that he got his present command after being in charge of two defeats, Dunkirk and Burma. This was no small handicap to overcome. In France, during World War I, his record for pure personal bravery, courage, was—without exaggeration—extraordinary. He was wounded three times, and he won both the M.C. and D.S.C. Also, when he was a lieutenant, a platoon commander, he received the French Legion of Honor, which only rarely comes to a junior officer. During the years after 1919, Alexander served variously in Constantinople, Waziristan, and the northwest frontier of India. In 1938, at forty-five, he became the youngest major general in the British army, and was given command of the First Division at Aldershot, a prize assignment. In France, early in 1940, he was promoted to lieutenant general, in command of the First Army Corps. After Dunkirk, Alexander returned to England and took the Southern command, that is, the command that would have to bear the brunt of the Nazi invasion of England, if it came. It didn't come. But lots of other things did. In February, 1942, "Alex" went out to Burma, taking over there at the worst possible moment, when Rangoon was surrounded. He had to fly in, over the enemy's lines, in order to reach his headquarters. Forty-eight hours later the Japs took Rangoon. And he had to fight his way out. Then in August, 1942, he was promoted to Cairo and the command of the Middle East; he promptly summoned Montgomery from England, as we have seen. On February 20, 1943, after the miracle of Alamein and after Monty had chased Rommel across Africa, he was given command of Allied land forces in the Mediterranean, under Eisenhower. He created the Eighteenth Army Group, which finished off Tunisia, and then the Fifteenth Army Group, which made the invasion of Sicily and Italy.

I talked to several British officers about Alexander. One said, "He has the best judgment of human beings I have ever known. And in seventeen years, I've never heard a man say a word against him." Another went on, "The main thing about Alex is that he cares nothing for himself. He takes everything at face value; he never says anything he doesn't mean. His simplicity is almost childlike. When he finishes work he simply goes to bed."

Another officer commented, "He's the most unselfish man I ever met. He always gives praise to the other chap. He'll give anything away. My God, I remember how things were in Burma. We were in a really tight spot. There were a million refugees all around. How Alex bucked everybody up! If a woman would stop and ask for water, he'd halt and give it to her. He gave away things

that were really important, you know. I took quite a dim
view of it! I didn't approve at all."

The general's tastes and habits are, as one may guess,
simple. In Sicily, he lived under a roof for the first time
since Burma; even so, he liked to slip out and make his
bed outside. From Cairo to Tunisia, he lived (like Monty)
in a "caravan"; Alexander's is a three-ton, specially built
four-wheel drive Chevrolet. It looks like a ship's cabin,
with a bunk at one end, a big desk at the other. He likes
open cars, and occasionally he would leave the caravan to
drive alone in a jeep. Like every British officer I met, he
is crazy about our jeep, and he hopes to get one for hunting after the war, but he is afraid that it may be too
expensive to maintain. "They use a great deal of petrol,
you know." He told me once that driving a jeep fast on
the desert was like skiing.

The first time I met Alexander, he talked—off the
record so far as direct quotes are concerned—mainly
about two things. He was tremendously interested in what
seemed to be the decline of the Luftwaffe. One reason, he
thought, must have been simply that the RAF and the
American air force were just too good. Also the Germans
were working their pilots far too hard. They treated
them like land troops, they ran them from pillar to post,
they shoved them into battle without proper rest. If you
treat pilots this way, they go to pieces, since airmen are
notoriously sensitive and emotional. The British, on the
contrary, always pull a pilot out of action and give him a
long recuperation at other work, at the first sign of
nervousness.

General Alexander is convinced that the secret of success in modern warfare is correlation of "the three elements we live in," land, air, water. It is the greatest lesson
of the war, he thinks, that nobody can win unless these
three elements are united, co-ordinated, synchronized in
the fullest possible way, and mastered. Army, Air Force,

and Navy must become a brotherhood. It's quite obvious that linesmen alone cannot win a football match. Nor can any single element of a modern army win without the others. The Army can't get stuff ashore unless the Navy leads the way, and the Navy can't lead the way unless the Air Force helps, and the Air Force can't work unless it gets landing fields, which makes the circle complete.

Alexander and Montgomery, who are very close friends, are something more than a team. They have been a kind of entity; the great point about their careers is the way they interlock and complement each other. They worked together for years; Alex commanded a brigade when Monty commanded one of his regiments; Alex commanded a division when Monty had a brigade; Alex had a corps when Monty had a division; then Alex got a whole army group, with Monty as his army commander. Neither has ever done so well separately as together. One of their best officers put it nicely: "Alexander is the cannon, and Montgomery is his shell."

Chapter VIII

Battle Pictures

M Y EXPERIENCE was very limited in Sicily. I
did not stay long: because I wanted badly during
the course of this summer to see something of the eastern
Mediterranean too. I saw nothing of the American army
in the field, only the British. I never met General Patton
or General Clark or General Bradley. I saw no major
battle, and I had no "adventures" in the storybook sense of
that overworked term. I was a short-term visitor to the
Eighth Army at war, and though I worked hard that is
about all.

It is not easy to describe a war, or a battle, and I will
confine myself to what I myself heard or observed. The
temptation to exaggeration is considerable. You want it
to be the way you thought it would be. But often it is very
different.

An army encamped at the front is an enormous
mechanism. No matter with what advantages, you very
seldom see more than one small fragment at a time. The
Eighth Army, during the brief time I lived with it, was
scattered over an immense arc—covering at least sixty
or eighty miles—around the slopes of Mount Etna. The
various sections of this army were almost perpetually in
movement, as headquarters changed or units moved forward or sometimes back. What happens is that a tremendously complex organization superimposes itself on
the countryside, finding cover where it can, adjusting
itself to the nature of the terrain, and existing as self-

sufficiently as possible. Every tree, every brook, every building, has its use, and every man his function. It is as if a stupendous array of visitors suddenly arrived as house guests in a stupendous house already occupied.

The nucleus is of course headquarters. This is known simply as "army." People do not ask, "Where is army headquarters?" or "Where is 'the' Army?" They say, "Where is *army*?" It is important that people shall be able to find their way about, and so everything is named and numbered. But this is mostly in a kind of simple code for obvious security reasons. For miles, the trees, telephone posts, gates, buildings, are placarded with hurriedly prepared signs; at each camp, smaller signs with complex devices indicate what is what. In the British army the symbol "35" denotes army. "75" means corps (we have two different corps on our front), and "40" or "50" mean division. There are many other numbers which may not be revealed. Normally formations of an army, or a corps, or a division, are subdivided into "Advanced" and "Rear" units, but the Eighth Army—which always does things in its own peculiar way—uses the terms "Tac" and "Main" to denote this distinction. So "Tac 50" on a signpost, let us say, means the advance headquarters of such-and-such a division. "Main 35" (which is where we worked out from) means the main headquarters of army.

Every operation as a whole also carries a code name, and so do most of its constituent parts. The invasion of North Africa in November has been termed by various writers "Storm" and "Flame," to keep secret its real name, which is somewhat similar; a celebrated British operation was called "Knight." Officers discuss operations in code, even verbally; the code becomes a kind of argot. Someone will say, "You remember when we came down on Flame. . . ." or "On D Plus 1 of Knight, we hit Taffrail right on the nose"; Taffrail of course being the code name of a place. The multitudinous papers that comprise the orders for a big operation fill a volume. On our destroyer the other day I noticed something as large as a dictionary: this was the collection of papers the captain needed just for his share of the landings. Thousands upon thousands of such volumes have to be issued; yet the secrecy maintained is remarkable. This present operation, the invasion of Sicily, is called ———. Everywhere you see hefty books with ——— on the cover.

Just now Main 35 is located in a series of olive groves, behind low stone walls, covering several acres four and a half miles south of the town of Lentini. Tac 35 is of course several miles on the other side of Lentini, nearer the enemy. The various "75," "50," and "40" headquarters, both Tac and Main, are scattered in between and beyond, as are the armored units which are usually called "99." Between all there is an incessant surge of traffic. The two things that most distinguish the area immediately behind the front are the seething dust and the traffic. The M.P.'s stand at the intersections with handkerchiefs stuffed in their mouths, pointing blindly up and down roads choked with cars. The roads—who ever said Italians built good roads?—are ground to pulverization in a day or two; near Main 35 traffic has to be held to five miles per hour, in a vain attempt to keep the adhesive dust down. Tanks, armored cars, five-ton lorries, 1500-weights, command cars, bull-dozers, troop carriers, self-propelled artillery, motorcycles, jeeps—they lunge forward packed inch to inch, in a screaming, groaning, pulsating, never-ending and always forward-pushing noisy stream.

Perhaps you would like to hear how the group of correspondents attached to the Eighth Army does its work. This book is much more about the way a newspaperman sees the war than about the war itself, and I hope I don't have to apologize for one more section about how we did our jobs. I cannot speak for the American army, but in the British army, where after long experience press arrangements are very well worked out, things go more or less like this.

First of all, there are twenty-one of us, six conducting officers and fifteen correspondents, and we live in a camp quite near Main 35. We are an entity quite by ourselves, a close and exclusive group with our own vehicles, our own mess. Our "boss" is of course Bill Warrener, the Deputy Assistant Director, Public Relations, Eighth Army. He, however, does not live with us. He has his own caravan—a trailer located a couple of miles nearer Montgomery's headquarters. As soon as his driver halts, and pitches camp, Warrener can plug in electric light and a telephone; we have neither. The electricity net has of course been laid in the open fields by engineers and signalmen the night before. A couple of orchards beyond Warrener is the tent of Lieutenant Colonel Williams, the G.S.O. 1, or intelligence officer. And somewhere near by, but in a separate field, is Captain Patrick Synge, our censor.

The conducting officers are quite different. They live with us. They are a phenomenon new, I believe, to warfare. They are young men either majors or captains who are professional officers, not newspapermen. None have had journalistic experience, as a rule. This was because (during the war in the desert) they necessarily had to be men who could shoot, who could read a map and a compass, who could take active direction of a military operation in an emergency. It is the job and function of the conducting officers to take care of the newspapermen assigned to them; they are hosts, nurses, handy men, chauffeurs, guides. There were no British servants in our camp, no batmen, and the conducting officers drove the cars themselves and even did the cooking. The conducting officers are, of course, armed; the newspapermen are not. So they are in a sense bodyguards too. The way things work out is that one conducting officer makes a team with two or three correspondents; these three or four men either learn to get along together or a new group is formed. Each group has, in theory, its own transport—a command car or jeep. The main thing the conducting officer does is, of course, escort the correspondent to the front, explain what is going on, get him in touch with other officers, and in general show him the war. It is not expressly forbidden for a correspondent to go out alone, but it is rather rare for him to do so, largely on account of the shortage of transport. The conducting officer is, however, specifically at the service of the correspondent, not vice versa; it is for the correspondent to say what he wants to do and where he wants to go, and the duty of the officer—without incurring undue risks—to get him there.

Our conducting officers were a mixed lot, and one of our veteran correspondents said frankly one day, "Two are first class, one is worthless, one is crazy but a good fellow, and as far as I am concerned the rest are still on trial." What I noted first was that all had such nicely typical English first names: we had a Nigel, a David, a Geoffrey, a Gerald, a Michael. I liked them all. I got on beautifully with them all. The senior was Major Nigel Dugdale. He had a wonderfully subtle sense of humor. Once he saw me wandering around in the open field, after lunch, in pajamas, and he said simply, "Where's your necktie?" He had had a splendid career in Africa; for one feat he should have got the M.C. He was severely wounded (a shell blew his pants off); with great heroism he saved the life of his wounded chauffeur, and his lone tank got three Mark-4's, and damaged a fourth. I never met anyone who worked harder than Dugdale, and he was certainly one of the best tempered and most cheerful officers ever seen anywhere. Once, by some miracle, we found a few old grubby London newspapers. Nigel laid them out neatly, one just overlapping the other, on the rough ground. He called out delightedly, "Now we have a club!"

Another conducting officer whom I admired intensely was Captain David Heneker. He was quiet, almost dreamy, with gentle manners; his father was a full general. David always wanted to be a musician. He quit the Army seven years ago to devote himself to music; when the war came he resumed military service, of course. His whole soul was in music. This did not keep him from being the best man in the camp, after Dugdale. Then there was Captain Geoffrey Poole, dark-haired, brawny, and full of guts, and Captain Charles Kessler, who had perfect manners and was in charge of our mess. Mostly I went out with a vital black-haired Irishman, Captain Michael Davis, one of the most remarkable drivers of a vehicle I ever met. The most picturesque of them all was a naturalized Russian, Captain Soboleff, who had won the St. Andrew Cross fighting in the Russian army in the First World War. Soboleff was a huge creature with stiff mustachios; cocksure, an adventurer, gluttonous with vitality, and naughty. Some of our officers were supercautious; Soboleff always had original and advanced ideas. He was always scrounging chickens from farmyards no one else could get into, or inventing fabulous plans for buying cattle for a barbecue. The first time I met him he pounced on me and roared, "Tell me the complete story of your life in five minutes."

A correspondent has, in general, three main problems on a job like this: first, transport; second, communications; third, censorship.

It didn't take me more than half an hour, after arriving in Sicily, to understand why Eisenhower was so loath to accept new correspondents, and why Montgomery has ruthlessly clamped down on anyone coming here. A correspondent has to live on wheels, otherwise he is useless. For instance our camp is about two and a half miles from Warrener's caravan, and we have to go there at least twice a day. Also we must get to the front whenever we can;

and without transport, we can't budge. During one ex-cruciating interval our group of twenty-one had exactly three cars. We squeezed into them like ants clinging. One was a jeep (into which nine of us would crowd); one was a battered Humber station wagon which was continually falling apart after the fearful pounding of these unbe-lievable roads; the third was a Fiat about the size of a bathtub which Dugdale contrived to find somewhere. I will never forget one ride in that Humber, with Michael Davis driving. There was a bump, and he looked down suddenly. Both the front wheels had fallen off.

As to communications, we have to file in triplicate. This is a nuisance when working in a field without a chair or table, when the wind is blowing fiercely, and the carbons get lost, and nobody, for love or money, has a pin or paper clip. One copy goes to Malta or Algiers; I'm not sure what happens to the others. No communications are pos-sible by telephone or telegraph; everything has to be sent in scarlet PR bags by plane. These red bags are marked conspicuously so that attendants at airports will handle them quickly; Lock, in Malta, has a man on the watch for them at every field. But sometimes airplanes don't fly. Sometimes airplanes get shot down. And a considerable amount of copy, for these and other reasons, gets mislaid, hopelessly delayed, or lost.

The censorship is not serious here, and Captain Synge —a botanist by profession—is amiable. He gives the stuff a quick reading for security, and then ships it on to Phillips' staff in Tunis or Duncan Clark. Synge once led expeditions to collect orchids. It is certainly an orchida-ceous group he has collected here.

Normally we get up at about six, and after breakfast which Heneker or Kessler has prepared we pile into our cars and report to Major Warrener. He then takes us to Bill Williams, who does the briefing. This ceremony is rather formal. No one approaches Williams until Warrener leads the way; everybody stands during the whole session; everybody must wear a hat. And we take notes in the sparse shade of an almond tree. The surroundings are peculiar, because a couple of individual officers' latrines are only a few yards away. Just behind us there will be officers sitting down, concealed only by a waist-high strip of canvas; we can just see their heads and shoulders. A hundred yards to the left is another sight on some mornings: General Montgomery usually holds his briefing here, and he stands in the dappled sunlight surrounded by his staff, talking earnestly, gesticulating, listening, and pointing to the big map on the ground with rocks holding the edges down. Sometimes he passes us on the road, wearing his piratical-looking beret and in the car that has three compasses salvaged from fallen Messerschmitts.

We crowd into our cars again, and drive two or three miles to Synge's censorship headquarters. Here, having brought our typewriters, we sit down on the stony grass and write our dispatches. Synge censors them before a noon deadline, and Dugdale or Heneker or Poole take the scarlet bags to the Lentini airdrome. If a plane is flying, all is well. Then the rest of the day is free for work, which means visiting the front or looking about in town.

Now let me revert to my diary and get up to date.

Syracuse, Sicily, Monday, July 19.—Here it is D Plus 9, and I am back in Sicily. We arrived—Ted Gilling and I—early this morning. I watched the shore line from the deck of our LCI in the creamy haze of dawn; the coast looked serene and empty, with no trace of war except a few languid Spits circling in the sky. One of our brigadiers made tea expertly, on deck, and I stole into the captain's cabin and had my first shave with hot water since leaving Algiers. I watched with fascinated attention how the high-ranking British wash, while on safari so to speak. They carry white enamel washbowls, quite large, covered with a taut oilskin so that the bowls look like some kind of exotic tropical drum. Also they have an unwieldly contraption in the form of a canvas bucket, which is set up on a tripod of four wooden poles; also a canvas pail to carry water in. I have seen many British officers reeking with sweat and dirt, but never one that needed a shave.

The LCI warped to the dock, and we jumped off. An M.P. yelled crossly at me, "No smoking!" Petrol dumps are here, and there have been several large fires. An officer gave us a lift into town in a crowded 1500-weight. The first thing I saw was an Italian traffic cop, a *carabiniere*, very smart in a black uniform and shiny black boots, and armed. It seemed odd that anybody so recently the enemy, and still carrying a massive-looking gun, should direct us to our destination.

The problem was to find Bill Warrener. It took about three hours. The experience was much like that of our arrival in Malta, in that no one knew where we should go. We drove out into the fields in a small open truck without a windshield; the glass might sparkle in the sun and make a target. Motorcycles whipped past in the white dust, and M.P.'s wrinkled their brows trying to guide us. Some of the camps are named; one was Ladbroke Grove, and another Elephant & Castle. At one headquarters things were set up as neatly—in a rough, sloping olive grove—as if it were a bank on Piccadilly; one wooden sign said VISITORS and another ENQUIRIES.

I suppose what I kept thinking most was how fiercely hot it was. It was really hot. That is to say, it was almost as hot as New York. Then we heard the distant thud of guns. This might be Montgomery's attack on Catania which was due any moment. Our driver stopped his car suddenly, and pointed up. A dogfight. The cannons in the Spits sound like the very quick beat of horses' hoofs on hard dry turf; the burrowing sound of a German plane diving tore the sky apart. We could see little, on account

of the blinding sun. The driver said, "They certainly
have a lot of stuff around here. Last night we copped the
—— all right."

Warrener's press room is like none other I ever saw, a
deserted stone house set against a hedge back in an
orchard. We scraped through the trees getting there. There
are no windows, most of the stone is charred and broken,
and the single room is smashed to bits and littered with
jagged chunks of rock. Inside are two rickety tables,
smaller than an American card table; and two stools. A
couple of bedrolls lay against a fragment of shattered
wall. Here Warrener, Synge, and two sergeants temporarily live, work, sleep, eat. Warrener's handsome
caravan has not arrived yet, and he is praying for it
every day.

We reported; and heard that the pool is over, someone
"thinks." So from now on I can file in the normal way
to N.A.N.A. or the Blue Network. Warrener sent us back
to town. And we picked up with Gillard, Montague, and
Ned Russell, who have been here a day or two, after
having been stuck somewhere on the southern coast. They
were grim. As we bounced out of a jeep at a hotel known
as the Poletti, we met Poole and two Australian correspondents. They had managed to hook a boat ride and get
into Sicily without permission, and Montgomery's intelligence officer—furious—has peremptorily ordered them
to leave the island by tonight. They have their own jeep;
where they got it, God knows. (Later, through Warrener's intervention, the expulsion order was rescinded,
and Poole and his Australians became part of our group.)

The hotel seemed vastly comfortable, compared to the
Phoenicia. The first thing I saw was a sign over the
entrance desk, *La Libertà E in Marcia*, under the American and British flags; the first person I talked to was the
hall porter who had spent twenty-six years in Portland,
Maine. Gilling and I got a room four flights up. It actually

had beds. We had lunch, and I thought with pleasure that I was in a Latin country where cooking was understood. That is, lunch consisted of only one dish but it was a wonderful thick soup, crammed and packed with rich sauce, spaghetti, chunks of meat, vegetables, herbs, and garlic. The British, however, seemed to prefer their tinned rations, unspeakably cold, and dismal as they are. Gilling and I had brought a couple of loaves of bread from Malta. A tableful of officers went through that bread like ravenous wolves. "My God," uttered Poole, "I haven't seen bread since D Minus 1!" They ate the bread and ate it and ate it. (Of course when an army is moving fast, there is no time to set up bakeries, and for ten days nobody had had anything but hard tinned biscuits.)

In the room that Russell and Montague share, I saw and was considerably impressed by the posters General Alexander has just issued. Maybe we learned something in North Africa after all:

Whereas it is the purpose of the Allied Powers to deliver the people from the Fascist regime and to restore Italy as a free nation;
Whereas it is the policy of the Allied forces not to make war on civilian inhabitants of the occupied territory but to protect them in the peaceful exercise of their legitimate pursuits insofar as the exigencies of the war and their own behavior will permit—
Exercise of the powers of the Crown of Italy shall be suspended during the period of military occupation.
The Fascist party will be dissolved and all discriminatory decrees and laws will be annulled.

The correspondents are grousing a bit. One conducting officer cannot drive, and is hence useless. Copy has been murderously delayed, and even now some stuff is getting back to Algiers, describing the very onset of operations, eight or nine days late. And the manner of their life is wearing everybody down. Montague murmured today,

"Oh, to be in a place where there's water, where there's light at night!"

Joe Phillips is now enforcing a rule which pleases everybody, the "No Magic Carpet" rule. Correspondents may no longer date line any dispatch except from the place where they actually write it. Of course no reputable or conscientious correspondent would do this anyway, and the rule should have been put in force long ago. During the Tunisian campaign there was at least one American who wrote vivid and stertorous "descriptions" of "eye-witness" scenes of street fighting in such town as Enfida-ville, while he was sitting four hundred miles away in the Algiers press room; and already in this operation a couple of men in Algiers have tried to get away with date lines like "On the Sicilian Beaches" although they have never stirred from North Africa.

There has been one new censorship leak; no one can figure out how it happened, or whose fault it was. When the British took Augusta a few days ago they captured an enemy submarine, intact. This was of course of price-less value, because it meant that enemy codes, ciphers and so on on board were seized. But it is a very grave error to have disclosed publicly that the submarine was taken, because obviously if the enemy knows this, the codes will be changed.

Catania is not ours yet. The fiercest fighting is at the Primo Solo bridge on the Simeto River, and Russell drove up there today. This is the bridge General Alexander told us about the other day. The Americans are somewhere above Santa Caterina and are moving hard toward Palermo. The opinion here is that although the capture of Palermo will be a first-class moral victory it will not mean much strategically. Palermo has no contact with the eastern part of the island; the only lateral railway to Messina goes through Enna, and this railway has already been cut by both Americans and Canadians. So Palermo is isolated from the possibility of relief by the Germans, the only people who could defend it.

Everybody talked about the raids that come every night here in Syracuse. I said I hoped not to miss one; I even asked Montague to wake me up, which provoked considerable laughter. Our hotel is smack on the water front, which is the Luftwaffe's chief target; and a battery of our Bofors antiaircraft guns, with their long slim barrels, is in the garden just below my window. "They put up a very good show at tracer," was the way Montague expressed it. The others were less understated. "By Christ, it'll blow you out of bed," exclaimed one conducting officer. It was like Guy Fawkes' Day last night, so he said; you could read a newspaper in it, but you scarcely heard the sound of the bombs, because our own ack-ack is so very close, and hence much noisier. Some of the men sleep out in the fields, because of the choking smoke.

At dinner I met a crowd of AMG officials;* one was Captain (now Major) John Boettiger, the President's son-in-law. The lights were out, and we talked in complete darkness. This was eerie; to have animated discussion with people whom you have never met, and cannot see. AMG is working hard and well in this area, people say. The overriding idea is to effect the transference from military to civilian authority just as quickly as possible, in twenty-four hours if all goes well. We heard incidentally that Rome was bombed today.

We climbed upstairs. An American colonel clicked on his flashlight for a second. "The security officer will shoot your ankles for doing that, sir," his aide said respectfully.

Lentini, Tuesday, July 20.—We moved up here this morning. At first there was great difficulty getting transport, but Nigel Dugdale commandeered a three-ton truck, and about twenty of us piled in.

---

* AMG—Allied Military Government—was called "Amgot" at this time, but later the name was changed.

The road wound through a hot, dusty, stony landscape. Two or three bridges were out, and we had to make long detours down dry-slippery slopes of ocher sand. The trees are so yellowish with dust that they look painted. We passed very few civilians, but occasionally there would be a boy on a burro, or a gesticulating woman in a bright blouse and black skirt, and it was hard to believe that we were not somewhere near Málaga, say, or on the Riviera above Antibes.

Then half an hour out of Syracuse, as we were continually stalled in long traffic blocks, the taste and smell of war became very acute. This is the road to the front. And going up to the front—the actual front—quickens your apperceptions; it presents the same emotion in space that the rising of a theater curtain presents in time. We saw a number of lonely graves with helmets on the crosses; dumps of used petrol tins; then a lot of tanks near camouflaged haystacks—the tanks looked for all the world like a herd of gray elephants grazing there; then shattered pillboxes and a few German road markers still; and we began to smell corpses.

We arrived in Lentini, searched for an hour, and finally found our headquarters, which Soboleff had spotted and seized yesterday. An eleven-year-old Italian kid guided us there when the M.P.'s couldn't find it. We are to live in the Conzorzio Provinciale Antituberculare Dispensario, on a notched crest above the town. This is a remarkable place. A group of neat white rooms surround what was the doctor's office, and there are two bathrooms, one on each wing. But the building has been stripped; there are no chairs, tables, or other furniture, and the water works only at certain occasional hours. Downstairs is a laundry and a kitchen, and we set up a mess hall in the stone pantry. Captain Poole rushed up apologetically and said that, through some slip-up, there was no place for me. But I planted myself in a room nevertheless and dumped me

my gear on the stone floor. With me, in a space about 10
feet by 12, are Major Lewis Hastings and Frank Gillard.
Hastings is an interesting character who seems to be at
once a professional hunter from Rhodesia, an officer, and
an expert on Africa for the BBC.

Outside our villa, or clinic, is one of the most extraordinary views I have ever seen. We are above the rest
of the town, and we look down on lines of sharp gray
terraces, steep cuts through the rock, and a conglomerate
mass of tile roofs packed together like a crazy quilt, but
without much color, because the fierce sun blots out the
natural tones. Then come sloping grayish-green fields and
the skyline inevitable to an Italian town—a white church
here, a pine grove there, and rows of slanting vineyards.
Beyond is the plain leading to Catania, which the Germans
hold; the plain is mostly a dull khaki color, but spotted
with occasional pools of cultivation. About six or seven
miles away is a heavy ridge of darker green; here a series
of sharply bending rivers, the Gornalungo, the Dittaino,
the Simeto, converge to the sea like lines in the palm of a
hand. Here, also, is where the Germans are. Above the
rivers, as the plain gradually slopes up, is a second dark
green ridge, on the flanks of Mount Etna. The volcano
itself rises in calm, cold, insolent majesty; and it smokes
when it feels like it. Catania, our objective, is in direct
and open view. It nestles on the slopes of Etna like a
white bouquet pinned on a giant's brown shoulder. It is
quite rare, I am told, for an army to see where the enemy
is so plainly.

A broad court surrounds our clinic. On one side a film
unit—and these tough photographers who have come all
the way from Alamein are a band of real pirates—has
pitched camp. The film men despise us and our mess; they
cook, eat, and sleep outside. One end of the court is fairly
shady. The other has the savage sun all day. You get out
from the shade and it is like being struck on the head.

The battle for Catania, we found, is in deadlock just now. We have crossed the Simeto at four points, but the bridgehead is not yet secure. Suddenly we heard artillery. A big turnip-shaped cloud sprang up near Etna, at first gray, then greenish at the edges, then yellow. The bombardment goes on off and on all day.

It is very exceptional for correspondents to be in camp as close to the front as this. We are only two and a half miles from the advance headquarters of the Fifth Division, or "Five Div," as the British say. The correspondents who have followed the Eighth Army and this particular corps —Thirteenth Corps—have never known a press encampment to be so close. In the fluid warfare of the desert there was no front to see, and in Tunisia the press headquarters were usually fifty miles or more behind the lines. It happens now that we are right on top of everything.

Captain Kessler went into town and returned with a Sicilian boy and a cook. None of us knows any Italian to speak of. And these toughly seasoned veterans are somewhat shy—almost embarrassed—trying to get along with a civilian population in a foreign language. They fiddle with a dictionary, they look stern and apologetic at the same time, and they fumble with gestures—gestures not being a mode of expression normal to an Englishman. We got lunch somehow. I slept for awhile in the afternoon and then sat down on the stone floor with my typewriter on my knees and wrote a story.

Of the correspondents two are Australians and the rest British. Ned Russell—who was once a tennis champion— and I are the only Americans. The Australians are competent, hard-boiled, sure of themselves, not very talkative. John Redfern of the *Daily Express*, who is ill with gyppy tummy, joined us at Syracuse. MacDowell of Allied Newspapers has a fine Scottish accent; I love to hear him call "thirty" "theyrty." Alan Humphreys of Reuter's is an old hand at this kind of game, and so is the veteran

Christopher Buckley of the *Daily Telegraph*. When Buckley, a tall man with one pane of his eyeglasses missing,
is not indefatigably seeking action he is quoting Shake-
speare.

This evening a crowd of Canadians roared in. They
were led by an old friend from Montreal, Lionel Shapiro,
and after dinner they took me to see the Catania battlefield close up. We drove in a jeep, without lights of course,
which was uncomfortable and dangerous. The road is
gutted, narrow, and twisting; we drove against a thun-
dering stream of blacked-out trucks, lorries, troop carriers,
command cars, lurching and churning around blind turns,
grinding uphill in the middle of the road without lights.
We got out about a mile below the Simeto. No one wanted
to cross that bridge in the dark. The Canadians were high-
strung and overconfident; one said we might get into
Catania before morning, if we stayed put. This is nonsense
of course; it may be a week before we take Catania. We
cautiously walked a few feet into the fields, and listened
to the heavy vibration of the traffic. Then on the slopes
of Etna we saw a group of fires. One looked as if a field
of grain were fiercely burning; it stretched out like a taper
dipped into flame and held laterally. Other fires seemed
to come from burning villages, or possibly massed groups
of transport; we couldn't tell. These fires made us suddenly very sober. They were not very far away, and we
did not know if they were made by us, or the enemy. Up
flashed some Very lights, first green, then amber. But the
no man's land is so narrow here, and we are so close,
that we can't tell who is firing them. Then from the left
came a slow series of great fanning explosions; what
seemed like tents of light shot up into the sky, as if they
were summer sheet lightning; this was certainly our artillery, but the sound was almost inaudible, it was a faint
pulsating sensation rather than a sound, on account of the
peculiar acoustics of this valley. Finally we had an ack-

ack show, as we stood out there in the naked plain; yellow
pin points flickered and then red tracers; then after a long
wait the sky went dark again.

Back to the clinic. We almost got hit twice. I went to
bed, but at 3 A.M. the noise of a fairly big bombardment
woke me up.

Lentini, Wednesday, July 21.—Up at six, and then to
our first briefing with Bill Williams, the officer who took
me to see Montgomery two weeks ago. It is hard to take
notes while standing or squatting and with the maps held
open in our hands. Williams has a fine ironic touch. He
said today, "The Catania Plain is what the tank experts
would call a natural tank battlefield, which means that it
is full of obstacles which tanks cannot get through." This
is a very hard battle, he informed us. Both sides are tired,
and whereas we are exposed in the plain, the Germans
are high up, with good cover. Our object is to encircle
Mount Etna and take Catania, the stiffest job the Eighth
Army has had since Alamein. "The enemy is tough. A real
lot of sods."

We asked about the fires last night. They were made
by the enemy. The Germans ambushed and destroyed
some of our advance transport. "Not a pretty sight,"
Gillard said.

Journey to the front at ten-fifteen. Our party: Montague, who inherits some of his famous father's disen-
chantment, the astute and wary Gilling, Michael Davis
as conducting officer, and myself. "Oy say," Ted started
us going, "We have got to see that bridge, you know."
The drive was over much the same ground we traversed
last night. After an hour we reached the Simeto, then
turned sharply west. I suddenly felt very far removed
from Radio City and Fifth Avenue at dusk and my flat
on 61st Street. We got to a point about six miles above
Lentini, and about three thousand yards from the German
lines. A tanned, sweating, heavy-kneed major took us

along a row of British guns and then let us go forward
until we were about a quarter-mile beyond them. So we
were in what was authentically no man's land, between
our artillery and the enemy's. The major said blandly,
"Every day we fail to advance, more good Sicilian wine
goes down those unworthy German throats."

The barrage began. I jumped. The British guns let go
right behind us and we watched the short sharp flashes
from 25-pounders half-hidden in the field. The sound is
much like that any housewife can make by wrapping a
dishpan in a wet cloth and banging it hard with a wooden
masher. Then instantly comes the noise of the shells
whishing directly overhead; they go "Yee-yee-ow-ow-ow-
youuuuuuuuuu." We can see these same shells explode on
their targets forward; it is quite a different type of noise
then, that of huge firecrackers angrily snapping. And a
thick pall of smoke rises, like the spume of a gray waterfall going upside down. It is remarkable to be able to
sit directly in the middle of a battle this way and see
both sides. Without moving, we can see the British fire,
hear the shells go over, and watch them explode.

The major's headquarters were half a lorry. Knots of
men lay in foxholes, sucking lemons. The earth is khaki-
colored here, and they melt into it. One of the astonishing
things about a battle is that you see so very few men.

"The whole area here is dry as bloody tinder," the
major said. "The whole blasted business bursts into flame
if you touch it. Yes, we give 'em a burst every half an
hour. We want to knock out their anti-tank guns in that
shallow grove. Sometimes they throw stuff back. Right
here. Oh, yes. We tried to break through last night but
those fellows have good ground. They're high up and
they're very strong."

Later, "Jerry is a good tough fighter, I must say. The
paratroops are the best. They are young Nazis and they
are picked more for their political fanaticism than be-

cause they jump well. When we kill them they have sneers on their faces. We got a most interesting prisoner last night. He said that he and his comrades had served in Russia but that the last couple of nights have been the most unpleasant of their entire lives. We really are giving it to them, you know. Bloody good thing, too."

He sipped some water, sweating.

"It's most uncomfortable here, I must say. We can't do much except at night. If we move an inch by day, it brings all their stuff down on our heads. My dear fellow, it isn't any fun at all."

We poked warily forward, and found a shelter near a dip in the road. We made a kind of lunch of bully beef and cognac and I found out something that no one in the British army had ever bothered to find out, that if you squeeze lemon juice on bully beef it tastes pretty good. Our car tore some wire, and signalmen came out of nowhere to repair it. We fell into a foxhole and found frayed shreds of an orange parachute. But we could not tell whether it was British or Germans who had used this foxhole, perhaps only a few hours before.

We went forward now and reached the Simeto Bridge. This is the key position of the entire campaign, the bridge that has changed hands several times in the past week, and which controls the main road to Catania. It is still under heavy German fire. I inspected it carefully. It is of metal, not heavily built; the span is single, and it is perhaps 140 feet long. And I reflected how extraordinary it was that in this elaborately mechanical age such a simple example of engineering could be the vital point at which a tremendous army might win a cardinal victory, or which could be an obstacle to success for weeks to come.

The guns were going off now with the sound of corrugated iron doors slamming and slamming hard. Then a bright splash of dirt; smoke up like a plume; the cloud then turns greenish, and under it flames begin to roll, as if an umbrella were on fire.

Around us were scenes of cruel and terrible devastation. Red Cross posts half shot up; the pillboxes at both ends of the bridge splintered, charred; tanks on their backs, prostrate; burning timber and scorched fields; twisted piles of metal that might have been any kind of vehicle; uprooted kilometer posts; the shambles that were sentry boxes; gutted patches of broken dirty rock; watchtowers caving in; fragments of machinery and burnt-out guns; to one side the gaunt skeleton of a British glider; close to it the crumpled wreck of a German plane with an incinerated jeep inside—like some monstrous mechanism destroyed at the moment it was about to give birth.

We waited cautiously for a few moments, and then crossed the Simeto Bridge. It seemed a long time before we reached the other side. Here were bodies everywhere. The shelling has been so intense, from both sides, that there has been no opportunity for burial parties. We saw charred lumps of men, bodies without faces, a heap of old clothes with a leg protruding upward like a signpost, and bloated corpses melting blackly into the earth. The smell was sharp and obscene.

Driving slowly we reached a point about seven hundred yards from the edge of trees marking the German position. Michael Davis thought this was close enough. We got out and a shell whammed over. Davis thought the car ought to be camouflaged so that it would not glint in the sun, and we tossed a net over the top. "Now we are going over there," Davis said. He told us to walk very slowly, about a hundred feet apart. He said not to run. If the Germans see a few men just walking they do not bother to shoot, but if they see you running they get annoyed and interested. Davis went first. I followed him and then Gilling and Montague.

The bomb crater we came to after the slow walk of

about two hundred yards across no man's land, in the bright sunlight, was the command post of an advance battalion. The six men living in it have not been able to leave for four days. The thing that amazed me most was how clean it was. The crater is about 14 feet by 20, crumbling at the edges; at the least shove, the brown wall caves in. The earth is stony; big lumps make the parapet. Subsidiary holes are dug inside the crater, one for the radioman—who was talking sharply in code all the time we were there—and another to hold rations. The dirt floor was uneven, full of rocks, and crowded; but as tidy as if it had been scrubbed. Every man was shaved; and I would not have been surprised to hear that they dressed for dinner. The officer in charge wore lavender socks— the distinguishing mark of his famous regiment—and a bandanna handkerchief on his head to give some protection from the fierce, biting sun. A private leapt forward to the lip of the crater and snapped a picture. The officer said calmly, "Get down, Jock. You'll get pipped." And indeed a minute later we heard the clatter of German machine-gun fire, though I am not sure it was directed against us.

The officer went on: "They're damn cunning, those Boche up there. They go to ground and stay to ground. We never see them. But they watch us every minute." He looked up. "The aircraft overhead are a great nuisance. We don't always know; they may be the enemy. We must hide anything that's white. They usually catch me when I'm shaving. I have to put away my towel and even wipe the lather off my face." He resumed: "In general the Jerrys don't start anything unless we do. Why should they? They're neat and comfortable up there. Some of them are quite good chaps, you know. They've had a fearful lot of shelling and they stand up very well. Once or twice we catch a bad one. A parachutist was captured the other day and he spat full in the face of our sergeant.

What happened? The sergeant took care of him, of course. My dear fellow, what else could he have done? The Boche spat in his face. We don't like that sort of thing."

The men in this crater can only be supplied at night. Rations are sneaked in under cover of darkness, including every drop of water. The men will be relieved in a day or two.

The heavy soaring bellow of the British guns behind us made the earth vibrate; then the shells screeched over whistling and exploded in the German grove. "We're doing a bit of murder on them now," our officer said. "That's the word for it, a bit of murder." He pointed. "They have an 88 up there. That's quite a gun. They get the bridge with it, and, by God, what a shambles it makes. We have that gun pin-pointed now. We're going to get it."

German equipment is superb, the officer told us soberly. The medical supplies are admirable, and German officers even have small mosquito nets just to cover the face. They take special "energy" tablets "to keep going," and the luxurious profusion of their rations makes the British jealous. The Germans have coffee in quantity, splendid cheese, and plenty of fresh butter.

"There's one funny thing about the Boche, though," our officer said. "He doesn't bury his dead well. Too shallow. Isn't the stink something frightful?"

There was a movement along the crumbling lip of the crater—one of us had displaced a cubic yard of earth by moving an inch—and another officer popped in, sliding down fast. He was a full colonel. He lived in the next crater forward. He had seen us come across and he wanted to visit. He was jovial. "My boys are having a wonderful time chasing chickens with bayonets," he said. "We had six for lunch." There are cattle just inside the German lines. "Wish we could drive off some of those beasts. They look like fine animals and they would make quite admirable beefsteaks. They only get killed staying around here, and it is so much of a nuisance to have to bury them." The colonel foraged for a bottle. "Have a drop of wine? I must say this is a poorish country for wine. After Tunis I find it deplorable."

After an hour we filed slowly back; and it seemed a quite long walk. The colonel's last word was, "The snipers are apt to become offensive. Really, we must do something about it."

We drove home, and reached our clinic at about five-thirty. Charles Kessler had a steaming tank of strong tea ready, and I do not quite know what we would have done without that tea.

I wrote two long stories, one for N.A.N.A. and the other for the Blue Network. I cannot broadcast from here; what I am hoping is that the Blue will simply read my dispatches on the air.

Chapter IX

Main 35

FOR a good many reasons the British Eighth Army, that unique organism, is unlike any other army in the world; it has an individual character, an *espirit*, quite its own. What is it that makes an army *élite*? For one thing consider its worship of its leader, General Montgomery, which is little short of idolatrous.* And Montgomery has imparted to his men something of his distinctive personality; Monty, his officers say, gave the Eighth "its soul." Another point is that, above all, the Eighth is an informed army. It carries its own printing press everywhere, and publishes a small but fairly substantial daily newspaper. Montgomery, as I mentioned in Chapter VII, briefs his own officers, and the officers in turn tell the men the essentials of every forthcoming operation. This is valuable in case an officer or man gets into difficulties. First, he knows without having to await orders how to put himself right again; second, if he is taken prisoner his knowledge of the operation as a whole makes for more rather than less security, since he knows just what he should keep his mouth shut about.

Another point about the Eighth is its self-sufficiency; it is one of the most self-contained of all modern armies. Discipline is strict, but the camaraderie between officers and men is remarkable; probably this is a result of long

* As everyone knows Montgomery left the command of the Eighth in December, 1943, to become leader of all British land armies under Eisenhower.

experience of hardships in the desert. A great institution was, and is, the "brew-up," the afternoon cup of tea which is invariable no matter where the men happen to be. In the desert, officers and men, working together in small armored car or tank units, always had tea together; there was little distinction in rank, and each unit maintained its solidarity not only out of necessity but as a matter of principle. Paradoxically, this served to make for a pronounced atmosphere of hospitality; in the desert, no visitor was ever refused anything. And the "brew-up" led to "vehicle feeding," whereby clusters of tanks would meet toward sundown and have tea together.

One peculiar instance of the superb morale of the Eighth is the fine contempt most of its units have for every other unit. Divisions get shuffled and reshuffled, but every division in the Eighth likes to think of itself as something special. But let any rash and unwary outsider say anything critical about a division and all will band together to hurl fury on the interloper. The Eighth as a whole has an utterly magnificent disdain for any other army. Its men call outsiders "palefaces," and they say sardonically, "Wait till their knees get brown." What they despise most in the world is any creature so witless as to be seen wearing a sun helmet. The Eighth itself fights in the fiercest of all possible suns, but any trooper would be seen dead rather than in such headgear. This is odd; because for many years the sun helmet was practically a trademark of the British in the East.

Of course the desert, next to the personality of Montgomery, has been the greatest single factor that has shaped and molded the Eighth. It is desert-bred and desert-trained. Its men are proud of the appellation "Desert Rats," and many are what the officers call "sand-happy"; this is a phrase almost equivalent to punch-drunk, except that it does not mean lack of fighting instinct. The Eighth has, of course, its own insignia: a white Crusader's shield on a black background, with yellow crossbars. And the atmosphere of the desert, its vast and starry emptiness, its windswept loneliness, has given many Eighth Army men something of a crusading spirit. The exigencies of desert warfare have also contributed to the way the Eighth looks. The men wear, it seems, any kind of old uniform; many are naked to the waist, with ragged shorts and every variety of headgear; they look like pirates, ragamuffins. But they're tremendously clean. The life of the desert enforces an extreme and drastic simplicity. There are no women; there is very little alcohol. The health rate of the Eighth is always astonishingly high, and it is characteristic that before any engagement the rate of illness goes sharply down; the men *want* to be fit to fight.

Consideration of the desert leads to another point: the Eighth Army doesn't like Sicily very much. Partly this is because no army enjoys terrain in which it is being stalled, held up, no matter how temporarily. And here in this convoluted and corrugated battlefield, it cannot easily use its favorite weapon, the tank. But above and beyond this there is something else. The desert did something to these warriors; they cannot get over it and they miss it; they are unhappy to have conquered and thus lost it. The desert was hot, yes; but not so hot as Sicily. The desert lacked water, yes; but water is very short here too. Above all the desert was clean, and the Eighth Army veterans despise Italy—full of bugs and choking dust—as "a filthy place."

When the Eighth was advancing in Tripoli the troops dreamed of grass, of fresh fruit; they prayed for the sight of green, for trees, for vineyards. And when they arrived in Tunisia they were delirious with excitement. Every man picked flowers; on every tank, every jeep, there was a bouquet. Now a certain amount of green does exist in Sicily. But even so this isn't quite the place they thought it would be. This is not the "sunny Italy" of picture post-

cards. In Africa the Eighth Army had a kind of good-
natured contempt for the "Wogs," Italians. But here even
the character of the Wogs seems changed. The troops
simply cannot understand the crowds of young men,
civilians, squatting along the streets. Of course the Eighth,
used so long to working in small detachments and alone,
does not like crowds in any case. Many of the men have
never been in a foreign city before. And they find the
complexities of a town like Syracuse or Augusta bewilder-
ing.

I asked one officer why the Eighth Army was originally
called the "Eighth" army. He replied, "Oh, that's easy. So
the enemy would think we really had seven others."

Lentini, Thursday, July 22.—We are going crazy with
frustration, anguish, and a kind of masochistic delight at
the complexities of our domestic situation. Our two four-
teen-year-old houseboys are Antonio and Vittorio. They
make V signs with their grubby fingers, and beg cigarettes; they say the word "Mussolini" with a grim chortle
and then make the gesture of cutting their throats, with
appropriate gleeful groans; whenever they see one of our
planes, they shout with congratulatory pleasure. Also they
are magnificently uninhibited and mischievous. They are
scamps. We caught one of them peeing on the open floor
of the kitchen today, next to the soup kettle. Our daintiest
conducting officer shrieked "Naughty! Naughty!"

The boys are filthy but then so is everything else. The
father of one calls at our terrace in the evening and tells
us how proud he is of them. The boys are quite normal
kids; nevertheless they drive us frantic. This is largely
because they do not, of course, understand a word of
English. We all eat at a square table, crowding around a
space not meant for more than six or eight. We have no
dishes, only mess kits. When we finish something, we
scream a word meant to sound like *Lavare*, and the boys—

in theory—take the mess kits, tripping wildly over whoever is in the way, and wash them out. But nothing gets very clean. Between the shouts and screams they try to bring in what comes next to eat. Then somebody loses his temper; and when the boys are yelled at, they get rattled. At lunch Antonio dipped his dripping fist in Montague's soup. Montague, one of the quietest and best-mannered of men, roared, "Get away from me, you little horror!"

The key to everything is the lack of water. It goes on for about an hour in the morning, and then for a few minutes—maybe—at night. We fill the bathtubs and all the pots and pans we have been able to scrounge, not many. The tubs are of course somewhat unclean, but to-day, in desperation, Gilling asked seriously if we could not make tea out of what bath water was still there, since otherwise there would be no tea. The water is dependent on a pump about a hundred yards across a rocky court-yard. We did not discover this till tonight. Then Poole, Ronnie Monson (one of our Australians) and I made a search party; Monson got the water turned on. Hosannas! Everyone dived for every receptacle he could find. We filled a washtub out in the yard. Then the pump stopped. We woke up the youngster who is caretaker, and demanded to know why, if water does in fact exist, we cannot have it all the time. The caretaker said that the doctor from whom we have taken over the sanitarium has hidden some vital key without which the pump cannot properly function. I thought Poole was going to strangle him. Then we all collapsed in helpless laughter.

But, really, it is no joke, though I hope I don't sound petulant. Put twenty-one men in a small villa, men who have been driving in jeeps or open cars in unimaginable dust and a temperature over ninety; and for the whole lot provide not more than a couple of gallons of water per day, for drinking, shaving, bathing, cooking, washing dishes, flushing toilets, and in general mopping up; the state of filth that arises will be bizarre.

I did not have so much as a sip of water from bedtime last night until after a late lunch today. Then we found a cache of cool drinking water; someone had it stowed away. I drank a cup. Almost instantly, sweat broke out in every pore of my face.

In spite of outlandish handicaps the cook whom Kessler has found does quite well. We have a kind of soup of tomatoes and fat bacon for breakfast as a rule; a thick stew for lunch, made out of Compo rations supplemented by whatever we can buy; and cold bully beef for supper. We have some tinned fruit, and today we bought oranges. Usually dessert comes out of a can, and, incredibly enough, it is almost always Christmas pudding, thick with cold lard and heavier than lead. This in a steaming cellar in Sicily in July! We have not managed to get any bread yet, and although the countryside is full of chickens, they are scarce at our table. Some of the shortages perplex me. For instance we have several hundred pounds of assorted rations, but until I asked for some today, no one had thought to provide any salt. Nor—to turn to a different field—have we been issued any Red Cross kit, or chlorine tablets to disinfect the water. We get seven cigarettes a day each, carefully doled out by Kessler, but no matches; every other day, we get a stick of chocolate. I searched the whole establishment today for some iodine. Soboleff cut his finger opening a can and in a day the wound was septic. Yet we are in a hospital! The most serious lack from the point of view of comfort is of course that we have no furniture. But I have learned by this time to type quite comfortably sitting cross-legged on the floor and holding the typewriter on its own case. Some of us, more accomplished, can even typewrite on their knees in a moving jeep. Finally, we have no radio. This seems to me a strange shortcoming. We are entirely cut off from any knowledge of what is going on, unless we scrounge transport and travel a couple of miles and listen in somewhere.

We were early up, and listened to the briefing. Not much news. This is a period of lull.

This afternoon we had a swim. Ned Russell, who is patient, amused, and a bit sardonic about everything, the silver-haired Montague, Michael Davis and I drove forty minutes through blinding dust. At times the road seemed to buck like something on Coney Island. We got lost twice, and for a time drove north along the beach, through thick reeds, until we thought we might be fairly close to German patrols. I was nervous. Those elegant folk who, in former days, were wont to loll on chic Mediterranean beaches should have seen us swimming today. It started with a bang—literally. Michael found a couple of unused hand grenades along the beach and he exploded them. There was a big grave near by, hung with parachute gear, and marked Unknown British Soldiers. These must have been lads who fell into the sea on the airborne operation and were washed up later. A flak ship stood just offshore, and as we were dozing in the fine hot sun we suddenly found—of all things—that we were watching an artillery battle. Catania is straight ahead, in as clear view as from our villa, but closer. British artillery opened up on it, and as we lay there naked and perfectly secure we watched the explosions in the town, the great onion-puffs of smoke and black-lined flame.

I wrote a story, for a Sunday broadcast, and then sat out in the shady part of the court, in one of the Desert Victory jeeps, and read in *War and Peace*, the only book I have with me.

Tonight we had a parachute scare. Paratroops have, so our officers say, been dropped behind us. I felt alarmed. I told Ned how distinctly I would hate to be taken prisoner by the Nazis. He said grimly, "You don't need to worry. Paratroops do not take prisoners."

We drank good red wine in the evening—though Montgomery has just declared the cafés and wineshops out of bounds—and talked till late, while a medium artillery bombardment was going on.

Lentini, Friday, July 23.—Briefing early. The enemy paratroops are Italians, it seems, so they cannot be serious. Three groups were dropped, in civilian clothes, and most but not all have been rounded up. One man had never jumped before; his story was that he was made to do it as punishment for some delinquency. Is this the way the enemy runs a war? We asked Bill Williams what would happen to the jumpers, since obviously if they were in civilian clothes they should be shot as spies; he replied wryly that in a couple of months someone would probably begin to wonder about them, and that they would then be let off, after a light slap on the wrist.

Montague said this morning: "I don't know what's been happening to our stories."

Russell: "I do; they fall into the sea."

Montague: "You cheerful beggar."

We asked Williams how he explained the comparative inactivity, the lull, at the front, and he had several theories. First, the heat. Even in the fiercest stretches of African desert, the Eighth Army has never faced anything quite so punishingly hot as this; the men have never felt a sunshine so murderously sharp. The Canadians, stanch as they are, suffer most particularly, because they did all their training in northern climates, and have never seen action in a hot country before. Second, whereas the American army advancing on Palermo is only facing Italians in the main, the British army here is up against first-rate German troops. Moreover, the Germans are still getting reinforcements in; their flak over the Straits of

Messina, under which they slip stuff through at night, is as terrific as anything in the war, we are told. Many of the Germans are what Williams calls "Old Sweats," veterans from Africa who have been resting in Sicily; some, however, are inexperienced. We do not know who the German commander is, though we have now identified most of his divisions. Third, the nature of the terrain. The enemy was rushed out of his early positions, but now he has excellent high ground, and he is concentrating his power just where it is hardest for us to strike, and where tanks are useless, in a well-wooded terrain interspersed with stone villages and split with sharp ravines. Fourth, the troops on both sides are extremely tired.

We wrote our stories, saw them censored, and went for a swim again. Near the beach a plane bounced off the ground ten feet away and not more than a dozen feet over our heads. We stared. An airport has been put in operation here (near Agnone) since yesterday. The plane is one of the little artillery spotters that can take off in twenty yards and land in three bumps.

Our luck on this beach is remarkable; again we saw an artillery battle, and this time British bombers went over Catania too; it is like something out of Tolstoi, this actual witnessing of a battle in full view. Two angry fires were burning in Catania, and into them the British kept firing air-bursts. Once when planes went overhead the anti-aircraft men on our flak ship, just offshore, took battle stations; but we were not bombed. There were new graves on the beach today, and I stepped on the body of a dead German in the water.

We have lost two jeeps, which is serious. We are help-less without transport. Buckley's went bang into a stone wall at the turn of a road, last night, and will be hos-pitalized for some days. The other was pinched by a conducting officer (not one whom I have named in this diary); without permission or indeed a word to anybody, he drove off toward Palermo and hasn't been heard of since. Everybody is angry in a helpless sort of way.

I had a splendid hour yesterday with Major Hastings, talking about Africa. Some day I want to write an "Inside" book on Africa, and Hastings' discerning conversation—full of vital love for Africa and eager zest to communicate his feeling—made me want to start on it at once. I took notes carefully on what he said: what "Johnny" Smuts was like, and how a great man named Huggins is Prime Minister of Rhodesia; what are the best hotels in Pretoria, Victoria Falls, and Johannesburg; what a Bantu is and the difference between Bushmen and Hottentots; how the history of the Indian ocean and Portuguese colonization has played a considerable role in African development; how it is important to steer a middle course between two "damnable heresies," the sentimental view of African natives and the old-fashioned superior "white man's" attitude; and finally how Africa is a microcosm of the world's great problems.

Late today, Michael Davis took me into town. We have been so busy that this is the first time I have had a look at Lentini itself. An astounding percentage of the population consists of young men, of obvious military age, who are not—and so far as external evidence would show—have never been in uniform. We went slowly from shop to shop, and were almost mobbed. People wanted cigarettes mostly. Yet, along the curbs, the young men watched us with a certain surliness. We bought oranges, and then I saw a magic word—*Ghiaccio*—ice! We rushed into the shop, bought a sizable chunk, and slipped it into our jeep. None of us have seen ice for weeks. Most of the shops were pathetically empty; they were stripped. We could not buy soap, or sugar, or paper clips, or a fountain pen, or razor blades, or paper, or a knife and fork; but it wasn't clear whether all these articles had been natural casualties of years of war, or whether the Germans have lately pared everything clean as they withdrew. The delicate old women in black lace shawls, the wonderful brown-eyed children, the heavily lined, squat, broad shouldered men who seem made of leather—I have always liked these people, and it was only too obvious that they have suffered terribly. It seemed inconceivable that any Italian town should not have a major café; and we set out to find it. It was just around the corner from the main square of course; it even contained a three-piece orchestra. People streamed in after us, but we could not buy drinks for them in public, since all cafés are forbidden to men in uniform. Now I am an old Chicagoan and therefore, if I may say so, I understand Sicilians. So we penetrated to a secret room behind the bar. The proprietor toasted us and we toasted him. The head barman had twin daughters aged eleven. They thought that Michael's feathered hat meant that he was some kind of British *Bersagliero*, but they roared telling us that, however, they knew he was different because Italian *Bersaglieri* always went backward and the British went forward. Within twenty minutes we had met most of the notables of the town. There was a fabulous hogshead of crude, powerful red wine, and we filled a large jar we had brought with us, letting it drip slowly from the leaky spigot.

Back to our villa. On the terrace we encountered a weird sight. Kessler had collected every canteen, every empty bottle; there were dozens of them of every variety and description, from old olive oil vials to gin bottles, beer bottles, whisky bottles; Charles was bundling them all into a jeep, to the accompaniment of wild shouts from the two houseboys, the cook, some women who were supposed to be doing our laundry, and a vast concourse of skeptical onlookers; the bottles bounced, slipped, and banged; the idea was to get down to the town pump somehow, and thus get some water.

Meantime Russell and Gillard had invented a parlor

game. They poured small puddles of vermouth on the floor of our room, hoping thus to attract the flies. In each room there are about a thousand flies. When a few dozen had settled on the sweet sticky vermouth, Ned would flop down on them and kill a few.

We had a fierce argument at dinner, twenty of us shouting in the small stone room with its reverberating boom of confused echoes. The cook became desperate and the houseboys rushed in and out, dropping mess kits with clangor and scattering soup and stew on our knees, scrambling over the jagged piles of empty cans and shouting. The core of the argument was how to get along with the Italians. My theory is to be polite always, say *Prego*, and above all, smile. Also I thought that Charles should issue us extra cigarettes for purposes of barter; we can bribe our way into anything with cigarettes. This was frowned upon, because it might "spoil the Italians." And my idea that you could win almost any Italian with a smile was shouted down. Sir Gerald Boles, one of our officers, kept insisting that if you smiled at them, the population would consider it a sign of weakness!

Outside, the continuous stream of trucks and tanks grind along our roads, without lights, pushing through the darkness relentlessly, noisily, never-endingly.

Six weeks ago in New York if I had walked from Fortieth Street to Sixtieth and got in a mild sweat I would have rushed home and had a shower and changed my clothes. Here we are soaking wet all day long, a shower is an unimaginable luxury, and we fall asleep instantly on a single layer of canvas on a stone floor. And of course I have never felt better in my life. I have not had a cough or a sneeze or a sniffle. Before I fall asleep I think how lucky I am. If I had been even a day later out of New York, I might have missed all this. And I love every second of it.

Just before I turned in I heard Buckley's fine conscientious sober voice: "I am not satisfied with my story today. I am not sure that I understand exactly how the battle went."

Lentini, Saturday, July 24.—At briefing today we learned that the Americans have taken Palermo. "Well done. Good chaps," MacDowell said in his rich Scotch voice. But I thought I detected a faint note of jealousy among the British, and a healthy resentment (not against the Americans but against the enemy) that Patton goes forward so nicely, while we are still stuck.

Dugdale, Poole, and I set out to find a camp. We are being expelled from our clinic, thank God; a group of nurses is going to be quartered there. We drove two or three miles behind Main 35—hitherto we've been forward of it—and came to a grove beyond Geoffrey Keating's photographic unit. This spot looks pretty good. There isn't much shade, but we have a spring; what's more the spring leads into a concrete-encased pool. Water! We licked our chops, and staked out a field. We have no tents, of course, but this won't matter.

Drinks with Bill Warrener at the Naval Liaison tent. We were having a fine amiable talk when the phone rang and I heard a code word, the name of an American city. Warrener and the naval officers jumped up, precipitate and embarrassed; Warrener said his orchard has an "exposed flank." A parachute scare. Men came running; officers dashed up heavily armed. One of the naval lads said, "It's just like playing at soldiers, isn't it?" Yes. The German lines are not more than seven miles away, yet somehow the quality of make-believe overcomes that of reality.

We couldn't move till the alarm was over; then we went into town again. The people are coming out more and more; they look as if they had been hibernating for years. But they behave as if very little had changed; almost the most remarkable thing about this whole story is that, after twenty years, Fascism has apparently rolled off these people like water from a duck's back. The Germans today cannot even rely on the Italians to fight for or in their own homeland. "Nothing ever changes in this country," Buckley murmured. "The eternal things are still the olive and the vine."

Mount Etna had a small eruption today. Nothing like a volcano to give a live touch to a battlefield! One of the photographers said, "It wasn't erupting; it just gave a little f—."

Lentini, Sunday, July 25.—Briefing. We have cut the road near Agira, and our bag of prisoners is sixty-five thousand so far; nevertheless the Germans are still reinforcing. It is hard to get accurate information here even on what is taking place in the next valley; never in the desert did officers feel so isolated. "It makes for general untidiness," Williams put it. We wanted to know when the identity of the various British divisions on this front would be revealed; that of the Canadians has now been made known, and all the British—to whom this is an important story—feel that this is unfair discrimination. Williams terminated the discussion with one ironic sentence. "Ah, you must remember that one of the defects of the Statute of Westminster is that it did not confer Dominion status on the British Isles."

A quick swim with Ned Russell and Michael Davis. And for the third time we saw a battle from our beach at Agnone. Really this is remarkable. And this time it was a naval battle. Directly before us, not more than half a mile offshore, a workmanlike-looking British cruiser appeared steaming calmly for Catania. It got closer and closer to the German defenses. We saw white waterspouts splash up near the ship, as the Germans went after it with artillery; we heard the sharp crashing bark of enemy guns. Imperturbably, the cruiser continued across the brilliant blue water; imperturbably, arrogantly, dis-

daining any note of apprehension, it kept pushing its nose
further in. Then, very close into the harbor, it opened up
with its own guns. We watched the shore and the ship
exchange salvos, and for a second I could not believe that
this scene could possibly be real. Warily, cockily, the
cruiser heeled about and began to withdraw. Almost at
the same instant, a big flight of our bombers flashed north
very high. This was all so exhilarating that it was a welcome anticlimax when someone said, "Bloody silly those
naval chaps! They'll knock the place apart! Won't be anything for us to see!"

On the way home we were sideswiped by a truck.
Michael jumped out of our Humber, gray with fury. I
have seldom seen a man so angry. He walked with teeth
clenched up to the truck, and then, to his considerable
consternation, discovered that its driver was a major, who
of course outranked him. Laughter. We got started again
and the Humber broke down. We had a long wait until
we thumbed a bumpy lift on a 1500-weight.

Domestic details today are: (a) I got eight oranges
for one cigarette; (b) our laundry has finally arrived. I
looked at some handkerchiefs and marveled. They had
been done with as exquisite precision as if they were
Valenciennes lace; they were folded into delicate frilled
fans like little napkins; and I felt again what nice people
Italians are.

Into town. Called at the AMG headquarters, and had
a long talk there. AMG's main job is of course to feed the
destitute and to restart production. This is not too easy in
this area, because of the enormous influx of refugees, of
which there are eight thousand here. First, AMG tries to
get agricultural workers back in the fields; then it does
everything possible to provide water, because without
water the mills and bakeries cannot operate. Also there is,
naturally, a great shortage of transport for getting produce into the towns. Almost everywhere, electric power

has been shut off, either as a consequence of bombardment or because of German sabotage; so another paramount problem is to get the power on again. These preoccupations seemed to be more pressing than political issues; so far as I can gather politics are not much of a problem, at least in this district. First, AMG establishes itself in the local Casa del Fascio, the headquarters of the Fascist party, and hangs up big American and British flags outside. Any outspoken or subversive Fascists are arrested, and security officers carefully go through the books and dossiers. Then an effort is made to get the mayor to co-operate; if he is friendly, all goes well; if not, he is replaced. Then the banks are sealed, the local police rearmed, curfew regulations established, and traffic officers put to work. Usually a radio with a loudspeaker is established in the main square, and this bellows out announcements; also, posters go up everywhere, and a town crier parades through the remote alleys and suburbs. Disorder is rare, though in some isolated villages the people have been surly. There has been practically no looting in this area. But Fascist headquarters have been burned in some towns; in Carlentini on the hilltop a few miles away, the angry citizenry displaced and ground into dust the marble plaque celebrating Mussolini's battle over sanctions; a rude sign, Long Live the Allies; Long Live Democracy and Liberty, went up instead. I asked one AMG officer what happened to the actual Fascists. He replied, "The only real Fascists are those who made money out of it."

The AMG folk offered to put me in touch with some non-Fascist Italians, and in an hour I was having a talk with a young man named Natale Verra, a lawyer who had recently been a political prisoner in Syracuse and who is one of the local leaders of the Free Italy movement. I had never heard before of this movement, at least under this name. Verra said that anti-Fascists all over Italy, not merely in Sicily, are linked by a kind of vague word-of-

144
D DAY

mouth organization; he insisted that though it is not fully knit together or ready to function as a party, it could be the basis of a Popular Front all over Italy, uniting socialists, communists, and liberals. Lentini, he said, is a strong socialist town; Catania is largely communist. He talked of Mussolini with the utmost contempt. "We will leave him to you to deal with," he said. But when I asked him if in his opinion Mussolini had left anything at all worth salvaging, he said yes, the corporations, provided they could be reorganized on a democratic basis. His opinion as to the House of Savoy was that "the king should be nicely pensioned off somewhere, and Italy will become a free republic."

Back to the villa, and wrote two long stories; then dinner in circumstances that are gradually becoming more decorous; and so to bed.

Someone said tartly: "I must really ask you not to use that flashlight. Kindly remember we are in range of direct artillery fire."

I slept so soundly last night that I didn't hear some bombing. "Was it ours?" I asked. "No," replied Ned briefly.

A Camp Near Main 35, Monday, July 26.—We moved this morning. Keating helped with transport; otherwise we would never have made it. Ned Russell and I picked a tree roughly in the middle of a long rocky slope, and slung our bedrolls in its thin spotty shade. This will be the first evening I have slept in the open in about a hundred years.

At briefing we learned that Mussolini had resigned. Apparently the news was out last night—one wonderful rumor is that an eleven-year-old houseboy at AMG heard it on a clandestine radio and was the first to tell our commanding general—but we, who represent the entire press of the Anglo-Saxon world, didn't catch on until this morning.

These are my notes as I scribbled them after briefing:

"Musso out. Does this mean It. peace offer. Yes, of course. But all we *know* now is that M. is out (where?) and Badoglio in. M. probably arrested, I think, though Ted suggests he may have had a stroke or been bumped off." I wrote a short political piece for New York, trying to emphasize the profound potentialities of this event; that the Duce should quit or get thrown out just sixteen days after Italy was invaded shows—what has already been fairly obvious anyway—that the entire political fabric here is deliquescing.

Planes are incessantly overhead today, out to blast a town called Regalbuto. Perhaps we notice them more because we're in an open field. There are big flights of Bostons and Mitchells every twenty minutes; we counted 132 by noon, and then got bored.

After lunch Nigel Dugdale drove us to the airport. The engineers began building it the day we got here, and it was ready on D Plus 8. There were some wounded sitting under the wings of Red Cross planes, and we got a story on how they are being evacuated by air, a new development. An Irish doctor explained his work; up to 50 per cent of all wounded on this front are now moved by air; what this saves in human suffering can only be understood by those who have been over these unimaginable roads, which shake the stretcher cases to a jelly. Also the doctor told us of some tremendous air battles going on here. One wing of 60 Spits got 25 German planes in one operation; 21 were Ju-52's carrying two and one-half tons of petrol each. One German bailed out and landed plunk in the middle of the raging fire set by his own crashed plane. "Poor chap," said the doctor.

We drove to AMG headquarters to hear how the Mussolini news would be communicated to the town. At our café we were told that people were weeping for joy; but I didn't see anybody actually weep. Crowds had been filtering toward the square all afternoon; they lined the

streets, with children wriggling in the gutters. There was
no hand clapping or cheering, though some youngsters
grinned; mostly people wore a look of grim but taciturn
satisfaction. One gets the sense that the whole population
feels that a crushing weight has been lifted, but that they
don't quite know yet whether they can dare breathe again.
I felt that these people were so fatigued by Fascism, so
worn out by privation and war, that the news of their
liberation was almost an anticlimax.

Yet it all made an exhilarating spectacle; we were
watching something unprecedented, the celebration of the
fall of the first of the Axis dictators, as seen by those who
had been his own people. The setting could hardly have
been more perfect—a scribble of rooftops against a dark-
ening mauve sky, a great baroque church at the right, and
clusters of brilliant white houses on a hilltop. There was
one fine ironic touch; directly opposite the American and
British flags outside AMG is a building with the word
DUCE painted in black letters six feet high. And signifi-
cantly, the radio music which was blaring through the
loudspeaker was suddenly interrupted and obliterated
when an American bulldozer ground up a cobbled side
street, turned into the square, and with a rasping and
crashing racket plowed its way across the sidewalk. A
British general, Lord Rennell Rodd, slipped into the AMG
Building, and with two American assistants appeared un-
obtrusively on the balcony. Then a quiet English voice
began to read—in Italian—the ordinary news bulletins.
The efforts of the speaker to understate rather than exaggerate were positively heroic. The broadcast began with
a statement that the Germans were still tenaciously resist-
ing us on the Catania Plain, and the announcement that
Mussolini had fallen didn't even come first; it was tucked
in casually between other bits of news. There was no
effort to make the proclamation dramatic or colorful, and

I couldn't quite decide whether a great propaganda chance had been muffed or not.

After dinner we hitched a ride to a signals camp that had a radio, full of curiosity. *"Finito Benito,"* Frank Gillard said. But what was happening as a result? I don't believe I will ever forget that scene as we listened to the BBC. A profile of steel-helmeted heads against the dark sky; two soldiers cooking next to a bush; the lines of camouflaged vehicles; all of us crouched around the massive metal radio, and the signalmen adjusting it delicately; then the voice of London, so smooth, so resonant, so relaxed, so understated, so supremely confident. But we did not learn much. There is no news at all of actual political developments.

Back at camp late. I hadn't looked at my bed since morning, and it was full of rocks. A good deal of shelling took place over our field, and flares kept dropping.

A Camp Near Main 35, Tuesday, July 27.—All day at the front, visiting the sector held by Highland Div. Anybody who thinks Sicily is a green and verdant isle should have been with us today. We perched on a hilltop about a thousand yards from the enemy lines, from which we could survey a broad arc covering miles. As far as the eye can see, there is no single spot of green, no trace of water. The fields have been harvested, and a dry tawny stubble covers them; it all looks like Nebraska in a dusty heat wave. I asked a Scots officer quartered in a deserted barn where we were. "Man," he replied, "we aren't anywhere. This is a point on a map."

The Germans up here are full of fight. They are aggressive in their defense. They rake the valley with shellfire by day, and send out infiltration parties at night, crossing no man's land in small groups and seeking to get behind British units. Sometimes a German will call out in excellent English, "Halt! Who goes there!" thus trying to entrap a British patrol. But this stratagem doesn't work well in these parts, because, as I heard it said, "Jerry is up against the Argylls here, and they're too Scotch to speak English."

We met an officer who is called an "official observer"; this type of officer does not, I believe, exist in the American army. He is someone who was a journalist in civil life; his job is to pick up stories of individual exploits, with as many names as possible, and get them back to the provincial press in England, specially directed to the district where the men come from. Our official observer had a keen sense of politics. He talked bitterly about the Darlan deal; his opinion of the Mussolini downfall was that it was an "attempt to save the regime by sacking the boss." And, like every British officer I have met in Africa or Sicily, from Alexander down, he is intensely curious about the Russians.

"My men are tired," this officer said. "They're shag tired. That's the word for it, shag tired. The Germans are thickening up around here, mark ye. There was a bit of a shambles last night. One of our battalions was isolated up there for twenty-three hours; nobody could get any water or food to them, and they could not evacuate the wounded; the shelling was too heavy. It was a hellish business, mark ye. A man is useless after eight to ten days on this front. He needs a chance to recuperate, to replenish energy. My men get no sleep. The artillery and the infiltration parties keep them busy at night and, by God, there is no shade by day."

We had a slow trip back to camp, through Ramacca, Palagonia, and Scordia; the Humber collapsed just outside of division headquarters, and again we had to borrow a 1500-weight, after long delay. We saw fantastic big fires on the slopes of Etna; there were huge purple and orange explosions. No one could tell exactly what they might be, until Buckley suggested that the Germans might be burning their stores of magnesium flares, Very lights, and the like. Jerry never gives anything away.

To bed, and a group of enemy planes came over quite low as we were undressing, their motors desynchronized. They dropped no bombs; they were heading for Syracuse or Augusta, though they may have given us a parachutist or two en route. I had lost a slipper and was searching for it. Someone yelled at me to put my flashlight out. Then the ack-ack lit up the whole distant sky, in a series of rising yellow points, which became pyramid-shaped pulsating blasts of fanning light, far to the south and west.

Paid my mess bill tonight, one pound for all this so far.

A Camp Near Main 35, Wednesday, July 28.—We awake each morning, stretching and groaning, to the tune of a strange assemblage of sounds—the screams of birds, the grunt of cattle, and then the throbbing roar of aircraft overhead. First as a rule a peasant crosses our field, driving a pair of donkeys, or burros; they roam placidly between our beds, braying, and leaving traces close by which no one bothers to clean up. The cattle come next, lifting the early morning dust, and, unless I was dreaming one morning, we have had at least one incursion by peacocks. We can sleep through all this—even when the goats forage through the beds—but everybody wakes up when our bombers come. The sky shreds in their invisible path.

This camp is infinitely more attractive than the clinic. I like sleeping out. Dugdale and Heneker have, with great resource, managed to procure not merely cutlery and plates, but wooden beams out of which we have made tables, and a dozen dilapidated chairs. So we can now sit down to work. The mess is neatly placed alongside a stream, in a thicket of tall reeds; behind this is the pool, and in a cave back of a clump of brush we have cool drinking water. Our beds, so-called, are spread out two or three to a lemon tree. By day, the green mosquito nets covering them look like coffins. By night, every star in the world is out.

Briefing. There were 231 sorties over Regalbuto yesterday. Williams said it was a deliberate attempt at systematic destruction. "The expenditure of bomb power was considerable. We overinsured ourselves perhaps. But the object was, within a certain time and by making use of a certain effort, to learn just how long it will take to expunge totally a nodal point." Someone asked him rather stupidly what Regalbuto looked like today. Williams went swiftly into irony: "Like an English country village on Sunday at high noon." Then someone asked him if the bombing were not monotonous. "Perfection is always monotonous."

After a good deal of mind-searching I have decided to return to Malta for a week or so; I don't know yet whether I shall then come back here, or go on to Cairo. Bill Warrener has given me permission both to go and return. I want to get back to Malta for about four reasons: (1) It seems reasonably certain that we are going to be stalled here for at least another week, before the frontal assault on Catania takes place, which means that there will be very little to write about. (2) After all, I have taken this trip on commission from the Blue Network, and I can do no live broadcasting here. (3) I want to write a *Reader's Digest* story about Eisenhower, and I must see Butcher to have it cleared. (4) The political story is now more interesting than the military story, with Mussolini out; and there's no way to write it in a lemon grove near Lentini.

Hot this afternoon. And a storm began to brew up. Anything I write about Sicily needs censorship on the spot, and so I wrote four long stories to get all my Eighth Army stuff to date. What a luxury to be able to work sitting down at a table again! But the wind grew stronger and stronger; by 3 P.M. it was screaming half a gale. We

tried to hold things down. Hilarious. All our papers began
to blow down field. Then came a sudden stentorian gust;
the mess tables went over, the reeds were whipped from
their roots, mosquito nets got pulled out, the bedrolls
started flying down the field—so did all our orders, docu-
ments, and security papers. We dropped everything, and
chased bits of paper for a quarter mile, with the wind
still howling, great thunderheads massing on the horizon,
and large blobs of sticky rain about to fall. Hilarious,
indeed.

In the middle of all this we had visitors. Colonel
McCormack popped in from Algiers, and with him was
Hugh Baillie, of the United Press. Everyone had been
threatening friendly maledictions on McCormack, a fighting cock if I ever met one. But he brought pounds of mail;
no one has had any mail for weeks; and this mollified
everybody, more or less. We had a vivid dinner in the darkness. (Of course there are no lights at night in this camp.)
McCormack brought me three wires from the Blue Network and N.A.N.A. I wonder what the expression on
my face was when I read them. One was dated July 8
and asked me for a story the next day. One said somewhat
crossly, "Why no broadcast last night?" It had been filed
from New York exactly seventeen days ago.

A Camp Near Main 35, Thursday, July 29.—Up at
5:45; Charles was making the fire, and David Heneker got
tea ready. I packed, and David drove me into Syracuse
after breakfast. We had a good talk all the way in, about
children; music; and whether or not everything that happens is for the best. We passed long files of troops march-
ing; these are almost the only men on foot I have seen.
Again: how extraordinarily few men, whether afoot or
not, you see in any case. There must be upwards of fifty
thousand troops in this vicinity, but you never actually
run into groups of more than a dozen, which is one thing
that makes this war so peculiar.

I said good-by to David, and felt how deeply I would miss this group, in case I did not return. More and more I hated to go, now that I was going. The airport near Syracuse was choked with heavy bright-red dust. There was no weighing in, or even signing in; and no one knew whether a plane would take off for Malta today or not. The field had been strafed by Messerschmitts flying at treetop level about half an hour before I got there.

A public relations officer, Captain Salzer whom I had met in London years before, gave me tea and a cigarette next to his foxhole. And in a couple of moments I met by chance three other people whom I knew: an English boy who had been on an Oxford debating team; an American major whom I had last seen in Tunis ("For God's sake, you here!"); and a British economist who had been at a Geneva economic conference back in 1927. Another PR officer came up and introduced himself: "I'm called Scoop around this part of the island. My photographer is nick-named Flash. Scoop and Flash. Do you get it? Ha, ha!"

I strolled to the edge of the runway, boiling with the red dust, and there on a stone bench sat five men. I stared. Two were British lieutenant colonels, and one an extremely youthful American second lieutenant. Between them sat two other officers, smoking cigarettes, yawning, rubbing elbows with the men on either side, comfortably, casually. They wore khaki shorts much like ours. I looked at their insignia again and saw that both were Luftwaffe officers. They had been picked up out of the sea and taken prisoner last night. Now here they were amiably chatting. This is certainly an informal army. One of the Germans was from Vienna, a quick-spoken talkative lad; the other was a heavy-set Dortmunder. They were in the charge of the young American lieutenant, who had been assigned to this work because he was supposed to know languages; there had been some slip-up however, and the language he knew was Italian, not German. So he could not talk to his prisoners in their tongue; the Viennese, however, knew English well. We were not allowed to discuss politics, but we gossiped a bit about how Vienna used to be. Then the American lieutenant told us how he interrogated Italians "*All* Italians talk—sooner or later. The higher the rank, the quicker they spill."

We took off for Malta around noon. The only other passenger in the stripped DC-3 was an RAF group captain. This flight was really something. We flew at an altitude of about sixty feet, just skimming the roofs, turning between chimneys, and gliding over trees. The pilot didn't want to be caught in another strafing. His ship was unarmed, and his only safety was in keeping a few yards off the ground. It was hot and very bumpy; the plane made a deafening metallic noise; we tore bouncing and whishing across Sicily, swerving from side to side and fishtailing. I saw Malta presently, and felt very glad. From the Malta airport I called Lock, and he crooned into the phone, "Chum! Choom! I don't believe it!"

Then driving into town, trying to reflect on all that has happened in these past few weeks, I had two thoughts. First, how proud I was to be wearing for this brief interval the uniform of the Army of the United States. Second, that the worst thing about war is that so many men like it.

Chapter X

Malta—Stalingrad of the Mediterranean

FIELD MARSHAL LORD GORT, V.C., Governor and Commander-in-Chief of Malta, took me into a sunny garden outside Verdala Palace, and said with a good-humored grim irony, "You know, Napoleon once remarked he'd rather have the British in Montmartre than in Malta. Interesting statement, what? Ha, ha!"

The shrewd and courtly Gort has, indeed, every reason to speak with legitimate pride of Malta's struggle and the role he has played in it since he became governor in its grimmest days. Now the secret is out and the world knows how Malta revenged itself for its bitter months of embattled siege, how it became transformed from what seemed a hopelessly isolated island into an essential springboard for the invasion of Europe we have been witnessing.

A couple of nights ago from the balcony of Verdala Palace I watched Malta's 3,322nd raid. The overwhelming impression I got was that anything so terrible could also be very beautiful. The alarm came at about 11 P.M. We were several miles from the harbor; we could only hear the sirens faintly. Then the shafts of searchlights began to move slowly through the sky, until a dozen converged to the same point of focus; then solidly, smoothly—almost tenderly, if that doesn't seem too strange a word—they probed through the velvet darkness. The lights continued to finger their way sideways—so smoothly, so silently, so very slowly—until there came sharp pinpricks of yellow light, the bursts of ack-ack fire. The sound reached us in a steady succession of neat cracks. Then the real barrage went up. It was colored red, the color of rubies. Slowly, very slowly, with extreme slowness, so that you could see each individual light, the ruby-colored tracers expanded into successive rows and lines of jewels. Chains of these rubies spread evenly in the sky, so slowly, so confidently, and then met in sparkling criss-crosses—like bunches of ruby necklaces suddenly intertwined and torn apart. Then came pulsating flat flares, reflections of the Bofors guns firing. And finally every kind of noise barked out savagely, and one by one the rubies separated, faded, and disappeared.

Malta is a curious little place, with much to show. Its people are of mixed stock, who claim descent from the ancient Phoenicians; they are partly Arab, and they speak a language quite unique. Most Maltese are small shopkeepers, fishermen, and cultivators of olives and grain; above all, they are islanders. No Maltese has ever seen a railway, a streetcar, a river, or a wood—except in the movies, of course, or unless he has left the island.

The history of Malta, which ramifies back to the most remote antiquity, is remarkable. This island has successively been ruled by Romans, Carthaginians, Visigoths, Saracens, Normans, Spaniards, French, and British. For many centuries, as everybody knows, it was the home of the Knights of Malta and of St. John of Jerusalem, the grand master of which was its ruler. The last grand master —and the only grand master ever to be a German—was Ferdinand von Hompesch; he held power from 1797 to 1799, when he traitorously turned the island over to Napoleon. As Lord Gort put it, he was the first great Quisling in Mediterranean history. Malta has been besieged twice. The first siege, the Great Siege, came in 1565; it was made by the Turks, who were repulsed after four months of bitter struggle and blockade. Deriving a lesson from this, the Maltese knights set out to build the vast series of complex battlements which still engird parts of the island. The work took fourteen years. The knights, using slave labor from the Levant, erected walls ten to thirty feet thick; they set up formidable bastions and watchtowers; they tunneled deep into solid rock and made a city inside a city. And it is a striking example of the continuity of history that these identical battlements withstood another enemy in the second great siege in 1942, when German bombs blasted them in vain. Eisenhower, Cunningham, Alexander, and Montgomery, as we know, established their headquarters in the same caverns, tunnels, and underground passages which the knights built four centuries ago. The knights built well. No modern engineer could have constructed a more secret, a more ingenious or a safer shelter for the base of a great military operation.

Malta today looks like what it is—a community subjected to one of the most intensive and merciless attacks ever made anywhere. Down the narrow streets of the town are ruins—including what was once the opera house —where whole blocks have disappeared. A few broken pillars stand out of the white rubble, nothing more. Then you get near the harbor and gasp at the fury that once eviscerated it. Even now, months after the worst of the blitz, there is a harbor district known as Three Cities, once the bustling center of the maritime community, where exactly one street has finally been scraped clear. But to an amazing degree life goes on almost in a normal manner; in large part this is due to the work of Lord Gort and his officers, who took over when almost everything had disintegrated; they plunged stubbornly into the mess and made things tolerably shipshape again.

The story of the Malta siege is one of indomitable resistance against the most strenuous odds. The Germans opened up on the island on June 11, 1940, and have been at it ever since. There were 3,322 raids up to the date I left, and more than 16,000 tons of bombs were dropped. Some 6,000 tons descended in one month, April 1942— much more than were ever dropped on the whole of England in any single month. Yet the total area of Malta is only 98 square miles, its total population only a quarter of a million. On a per capita basis the Malta death toll—about 1,500—would thus represent almost 200,000 dead in Great Britain. Of course, hard boiled folk say—I have heard them say it—that no one on Malta had any business being killed at all. No spot in the world has a more perfect natural shelter system, and almost all buildings are of stone, so that there is little danger of fire.

One thing the Maltese are intensely proud of, I learned, is that the island caused more casualties to German airmen than it suffered itself. More than a thousand enemy craft have been shot down over Malta, which means at least 1,500 Nazis dead or prisoners. Most of the people will concede, though somewhat grudgingly, that the Germans did their best to avoid nonmilitary objectives. About 30,000 houses were destroyed and some famous historical monuments were damaged, but even though the island is cramped with everything close to everything else, the Nazis never hit the big hospital which dominates the entrance to Valetta. "Maybe they spared it deliberately in order to use it as a landmark," I heard it said. A queer item is that the only chapels destroyed in the great cathedral were the German and Italian chapels, and the only one damaged belonged to Vichy France.

The worst period of the blitz began in December, 1941, and lasted until the middle of May, 1942; the raids these months were incessant, day and night, and some of the longer ones lasted over thirteen hours without interruption —literally. If, at this time, the Germans had been able to locate and destroy the hidden bakeries that were feeding great masses of refugees in the villages, they might have

forced the island to capitulate. As it was—a curious detail
—underground grain stores built by the knights in 1565
helped save Malta in 1942. You can still see them, their
covers set in flagstones, before Floriana Church.

The turning point came explosively in May, 1942, when
some newly arrived Spitfires destroyed 102 German raid-
ers. One officer told me, "My God, what a day that was! I
was in the hospital, ill and shaken from the unbelievable
raiding all day and night. One afternoon I heard a dogfight and I looked out of the window and I saw ten Spits.
Then I saw twenty Spits. I couldn't believe my eyes. I saw
thirty Spits, then forty Spits. My God, it was wonderful.
Those Spits of ours were filling the whole bloody sky!"

I asked another soldier what the bombing was like,
whether the enemy came in high or divebombed. He replied, "Both, sir. Sometimes the Messerschmitts came in
much lower than the dive bombers and tossed grenades
at us out of their windows. That is something, sir, to have
grenades tossed at you out of an airplane window. Being
grenaded from an airplane is quite something, sir."

Then began the siege. It lasted from June, 1942, until
December, 1942, and tapered off in February, 1943. During all this time Malta submitted to what was nothing
more nor less than slow starvation. There was hardly a
ship in the harbor when Gort arrived, and for month after
month, none got through. Then came the November
convoy, which—British air superiority having become
more marked—reached Malta without too serious loss.
During the siege people were tried to their utmost; almost
everybody lost between fifteen and thirty pounds. There
was no fresh meat, no soap, and little bread. The total
ration for one person was one tin of bully beef, one small
tin of sardines and one and a half ounces of tea every
sixteen days. Petrol had to be guarded drop by drop, and
since power was so limited, there were no lights at night.
It wasn't a mere matter of a blackout for month after

month; no lighting existed at all. To save petrol, Gort and his men rode bicycles, and at the end the RAF was using petrol—on which survival of the island depended—"by the spoonful." Malta came within an inch of falling.

Probably it was the air factor which was decisive once the danger of starvation passed, but other elements contributed to victory. I asked Gort one morning what he thought were the main things responsible, and he answered three, first the Church, second Maltese nationalism, third Maltese loyalty to Britain. The people here are extremely religious, and the clergy was outspokenly anti-Axis. As to Maltese nationalism, the islanders like to say that they have never been "conquered" and that they are the only people who ever "volunteered" to join the British Empire. Any former leaning they may have had toward Italy was blasted away by the first Italian bomb and the knowledge that the Italian consul general, long a resident of Valetta, had probably told the Nazis where to aim. In the dark days of the Battle of Britain in 1940, the Maltese sent a message to England that no matter what happened they would continue to consider themselves "Britain's ally." The George Cross, as everybody knows, was awarded the island as a whole in April, 1942; but I found that many Maltese were somewhat indifferent to this honor. They said, "We have had enough crosses. Let us have more bread."

Why is Malta so important to Britain? Why did the Germans want so badly to knock it out? The answer is of course obvious; the island is the central crux of Mediterranean communications. If the Nazis could have reduced it they might have been able to maintain Rommel in Africa indefinitely. Had the enemy rubbed Malta out, the only Allied link between Gibraltar and Alexandria would have disappeared. Why then did the Germans not attack Malta even more fiercely, why didn't they attempt an actual invasion at the peak of the blitz or during the siege? The answer seems to be that Rommel, too confident, thought he could reach Cairo anyway. Marshal Kesselring, the German commander-in-chief in the Mediterranean, was not so confident. He wanted to assault Malta and try to finish it off. Rommel's point of view prevailed. This, I heard it said, was because Rommel could get the ear of Hitler himself, whereas Kesselring only had direct access to Goering.

A couple of months ago a Russian journalist visited Malta. He prodded through the smashed streets; he looked at the pulverized harbor and the terrible devastation in the town. He exclaimed, "This is war, all right. This is the real thing. This is Stalingrad."

Malta, Sunday, August 1.—This time I am staying, not at the Phoenicia, but at Verdala where Lord Gort has put me up. The contrast to the hotel is, to say the least, considerable. I'm in a room with screened windows, so that no nets are necessary; and the ceiling is higher than the room is broad. We get hot water to shave in, and a British servant brings early tea. Far cry from the lemon grove near Lentini!

The first thing I did here was check with Lock on how my stories got through. One filed in Sicily on the twentieth arrived on the twenty-third; one filed on the twenty-third arrived on the twenty-fourth; one filed on the twenty-seventh actually came in the same day. But five, filed between the twenty-sixth and the twenty-ninth, only arrived yesterday; all came together. Lock's headquarters have expanded beyond belief since I have been away. No longer is it a cozy and intimate kind of clubroom for two or three friends. The new setup is substantial, with several more PR officers and two new censors working with Duncan Clark. All of it is very professional, and no longer can we wander in and out informally and sit on anybody's desk. I had the feeling one might have returning to a small cottage, full of intimate personal associations, and

finding a strange skyscraper there. But Lock's zeal and
efficiency, even though almost everybody has been ill, are
as notable as ever.

Gradually I have come to find out that we were almost
completely in the dark about politics in Sicily. We were
right in the middle of it, and yet almost as isolated as if
on Mars. An army is as impervious and opaque as cement.
I did not know until breakfast the other day that Badoglio
had dissolved the Fascist party, nor that Eisenhower had
formally asked for Italy's capitulation in a message mentioning the House of Savoy. The papers and ticker services are boiling with diplomatic agitation, rumors of peace
feelers, and so on. Religiously all of us at Verdala listen
to the BBC at least three times a day; the first session
is right after breakfast, at 8:15 A.M. I have been thinking
how radio has made this war so strikingly different from
the last one. How did people in Malta, say, or some other
isolated outpost, learn what was going on in 1914? Of
course they had newspapers and wire services. But the
extraordinary factor of immediacy that radio provides,
its invisible and instantaneous spanning of oceans and
continents by means of an actual human voice, makes all
the difference.

Eisenhower and Butcher arrived here yesterday, and it
is wonderful luck for me that I am staying in the same
house. The more I see of Eisenhower, the more I am
impressed by two things: his considerable talent for that
most difficult and rewarding of all the arts, the art of
human relationships; and his modesty, his complete lack
of personal ambition. And he is quick, bright, realistic,
and packed solid with common sense. This morning he
decided to reveal at last the part that Malta is playing in
the campaign. I had been hoping strenuously that he would
do this, and at the very moment I was going to sound him
out, he suggested it himself. Feeling for words carefully,

he dictated the following memorandum. Butcher wrote it
down in longhand, and then I typed it:

The epic of Malta is symbolic of the experience of the
United Nations in this war. Malta has passed successively
through the stages of woeful unpreparedness, tenacious endurance, intensive preparation, and the initiation of a fierce
offensive. It is resolutely determined to maintain a rising
crescendo of attack until the whole task is complete. For this
inspiring example the United Nations will be forever indebted
to Field Marshal Lord Gort, the fighting services under his
command, and to every citizen of this heroic island.

The general, with his aggressive grin and cheerful
abrupt voice, said first I could have this story all to myself ("Let's give John a break"), but it didn't quite work
out that way, for various reasons. Eisenhower continues
to be as interested as an editor in what happens to news.
He had bothered—even before coming here—to ask one
of his generals how the stories Gilling and I wrote two
weeks ago had been played in the United States and England, and he even remembered what stories had been most
widely printed. Yet, always, his interest is strictly impersonal as regards himself. "I'm just a simple soldier," he
keeps saying.

He talked briskly at dinner and again at breakfast, on a
wide range of things; how divisional generals can "get
away from it" sometimes, but that for the commander-in-
chief there can never be any single moment of respite from
strain; how he was perfectly sure—this followed some
talk about the Japanese—that American soldiers too would
be willing to die to the last man in an engagement; how
this war differed from other wars in American history,
like the Civil War, in such matters as casualties and the
immense number of men that must now be kept in reserve
to support an operation; how he was perfectly sure that
the Italians wanted to quit the war, but that the problem
was how to get them out while their "pals," the Germans,

were on their territory. He talked about Mussolini and Badoglio and the unconditional surrender formula, but strictly off the record. And he exclaimed once, "I hate to get into forensics. Let's talk common sense. Take first things first."

I wrote a magazine story about Eisenhower's first landing in Sicily, and Butcher worked over the manuscript carefully, word by word, adding a few items and cutting it a little. After two hours we came downstairs. The general said, "What you fellows been up to?"

When Eisenhower left, his whole mind was fixed on Malta again, and his last words at the airport were an instruction to see that the Malta story was handled properly. One thing he said at the end was, "You know, I'm not one of those people who find it hard to hate my enemies."

It has been interesting these few days to meet a good many British officers, many of them of the Navy, and listen to their talk. One thing that struck me was their staggering ignorance of the United States, despite an intense friendly interest. For instance one full colonel asked me, quite seriously, if our Secretary of War was the same as the Secretary of State; one naval captain wanted to know if American states had governors, and if so, were they appointed by the President. Another thing is that almost every Englishman I meet confesses quite freely that he thought in May, 1940, that Britain had "lost the war." They talk of Dunkirk as a "miracle" which, rationally, they cannot "understand" or explain. I heard one young major say, with suppressed passion, "Ribbentrop was right. We *were* decadent. We were soft, we were spoiled. We scoffed at the splendid trait of loyalty; we despised tradition; we lost belief in belief. The rich were rapacious, and the poor were greedy; the banks were full, and the churches empty. All that had *made*

England seemed lost. . . . But even so, the Boche didn't beat us. And now, he never will."

One evening, presiding at his Spartan but excellent table, Gort talked a good deal about the last war, particularly its generals. He said that generals were like surgeons, that a general should not only be a specialist but a specialist within his specialty. A general should be chosen for a particular type of job on much the same basis that a brain surgeon operates on the head, a heart surgeon on the heart. Gort told fascinating stories about Haig, Foch, and Weygand. Once Foch was really happy. Both Pétain and Haig complained to him on the same day that he was favoring the other.

Tonight I had a long talk with an elderly staff officer; he described the Sicilian campaign as a whole.

"I was in on the planning, you know."

"You did pretty well, didn't you?"

"Next time we'll do a damned sight better."

Alexander came to lunch today. I got a considerable kick out of this. And when he left I had the strong and durable feeling once more that this is one of the finest men I have ever met. He reminisced a little; he talked again of Duranty. When he discussed what is going on in Sicily now he threw more light on the whole strategic situation, in fewer words, than I have had from anyone; he explained just why, in terms of future air power, Italy was so important, how its seizure would establish the practicability of all-year, all-weather, all-front bombing of the Reich. One thing that impresses him is the apparent failure of German intelligence in the Sicilian operation. The Germans, it seems, simply do not anticipate what we are doing, probably because of faulty information; and as a result they always reinforce too late. They began to throw everything they had into Tunisia *after* Tunisia was lost, and they are still throwing a good deal of stuff into Sicily even though Sicily will obviously be lost. Alexander said that if Hitler had reinforced Rommel *in time*, Rommel would have taken Cairo.

I gather—though not directly from either Eisenhower or Alexander—that our generals in the field are somewhat perturbed about the admixture of political considerations into the Italian battle. For the time being anyway, it seems that we are committed to a kind of ambivalent policy, that of hitting the Italians hard but not too hard. And perhaps it isn't wise to pull punches on a battlefield. The idea is of course to steer between two alternatives: to continue to attack in enough strength so that Badoglio knows we mean business, but not so violently as to drive him to desperation and into the hands of Germany.

All told two thoughts are in my mind, that the Badoglio regime will sue for peace quite soon, but that the war against the Germans in Italy will take a long, long time. Already people are talking about when the next D Day is to be.

Chapter XI

Across the Underbelly

Malta-Cairo, Tuesday, August 3.—Off to Cairo very early. The rising sun looked like a tomato. We waited around the airport, and saw twenty-four Baltimores assemble neatly on the runway, and take off one by one, a few seconds apart, for a raid somewhere in Sicily. Then our own DC-3, manned by Australians, lumbered up. As it wheeled on the apron one wing sliced the top off a lamp-post; our wing tip was damaged, but the pilot said it didn't matter, and we took off.

The pilot announced, "No smoking is permitted in this aircraft. If any of you gentlemen tries to sneak into the can and smoke, he will regret it. . . . Anybody who doesn't know how to use a Mae West? There are also a couple of dinghies aft. Thank you, gentlemen."

We passed a small island, Filfio, and a British colonel said that it grew smaller every time he saw it; the Navy uses it for target practice, and bits and pieces get continually knocked away. Aircraft on the coastal fields looked like leaden toys, and so did a great battleship in the harbor. My last glimpse of Malta itself was spectacularly beautiful: we were high enough to see almost the whole island, and yet each line of sharp cliffs was clearly visible, as if cut sideways out of plywood by a jigsaw; the island lay on the water like a solid relief map in gold and amber.

After four hours we landed at an airport in Tripolitania, near Benghazi. Clouds of red dust. No lunch. There were swarms of Liberators around, and American pilots, looking hot, tired, and exhilarated, talked in small groups. (I did not learn till later that they had just returned from the great raid on the Rumanian oil fields at Ploesti.)

We flew on toward Egypt, across the long battlefield which Graziani, Wavell, Auchinleck, Rommel, Montgomery, had so often traversed back and forth. The ground, except where it is reddish desert, looks as a rock might look—one of those rocks my son collects, full of bright speckles—if it were skinned and spread out on the ground. We passed Tobruk, and I thought of that grim day when Mr. Churchill heard it had been lost. We passed El Sollum, Hellfire Pass, Bir Hairam, and El Alamein, and late in the afternoon I saw the pyramids. A jet black road, very narrow and absolutely straight, looked like a seam in a tawny carpet.

It took a long time to drive into Cairo. I shoehorned my way into Shepheard's, and had a hot bath for the first time since June 27.

Cairo, Wednesday, August 4.—Lunch with the American minister, Alexander Kirk, and met Major General Lewis H. Brereton, Commander-in-Chief of Usafime— United States Army Forces, Middle East—and also of the Ninth American Air Force which has made a spectacular record in this region. They had pictures of the Ploesti raid —the most heartrendingly dramatic aviation pictures I ever saw—and Brereton said our casualties had been heavy. Much impressed by Brereton, as I am by all our air officers. He is direct, hard-minded, and extremely candid; he has pride, confidence, and a fine faith in what his men are doing; and there is no bunk about him. Most of the talk was, of course, about the campaign in Italy; almost everybody thought that we were being too slow, and that "we should bomb the bejeezus out of the Italians" whether they were going to make peace or not.

Dinner at the Mohammed Ali club with Colonel Philip Astley, the British public relations chief for this area, also

for the Eighth Army, and his assistant, Major Oakshot.
It never fails. These British PR officers are the salt of the
salt. Astley is adroit, friendly, civilized, and superior in
the authentic best sense of that term. He is Warrener's
boss, and it was he who created the PR system as I saw it
work in Sicily. Lord Killearn, the British Ambassador,
better known by his former name Sir Miles Lampson,
joined us: an enormous beaming man whom I had known
here six or seven years ago, bursting with shrewd confidence and humor. Astley and Oakshot were eager to hear
gossip about Sicily, and they told me stories of Montgomery and Alexander. Killearn was candid about the
political situation here.

Egypt seems very strange. Plenty of lights at night,
though in theory a dimout is in force. We dined on the
roof, hung with colored light bulbs, and later watched
fastidiously dressed women dance. Heaven knows I have
not been away from New York long, but all the normality
here, all the rather febrile gaiety, seems very odd.

I heard today that the Eighth has finally launched its
attack on Catania, and maybe it was because of this, and
my regret at having missed it, that I slept less well on a
bed with sheets than in that Sicilian lemon grove.

Cairo, Thursday, August 5.—I am beginning to realize
now that I am in an utterly new world. This theater is as
different from Sicily as Sicily was from Algiers. The hotels
are packed with rich people, and they are quite comfortable, except that the phones seldom work; the atmosphere
is lush and not what you would call martial. I have never
liked Cairo much. I'm sure I don't like it better now.
I have heard that there are forty new Egyptian millionaires
since last year, and the cost of living has gone up enormously; import of consumers' goods has been cut to 4 per
cent of normal. But there don't seem to be many serious
shortages, though three days a week are meatless, and the
hotel runs out of Scotch every evening at about 6 P.M. But

plenty of bourbon is available; I had a mint julep tonight served in a glass as big as a flower pot, and with something that looked like a tree growing out. The rank and file of the people, dressed in their shabby white nightgowns, trailing dirt at the hems, are of course as miserably poor, as diseased, as insect-bitten, as rapacious, as downtrodden, and as helplessly corrupt, as ever.

Also I have the impression that Cairo has now become a backwater. The crisis has passed and history has moved on. No one will concede this in so many words; but it is true. I had no very strong hunch about walking into military operations here—my main object is to get to Turkey—and I am sure after only a day that I am right, though there may be a small "step in" in the Dodecanese. But any really big show is obviously out of the question, because everything substantial has been drawn out of here to feed the campaign in Italy. And we do not yet have the capacity to support two major operations at the same time.

Yet Cairo remains important. It cannot be dismissed as a vacuum. This is because of the immutable factor of geography; Cairo and the Suez area are and always will be an indispensable pivot of Allied communications, especially now that the Mediterranean is cleared. For the Allied cause everywhere, Cairo is a root and a ganglion. It is a base, an entrepôt, a kind of enormous depot between two giant fronts, between—one might say—two giant wars. Because the Middle East will, in time, be just as important as a supply base and a shipping point for the Japanese war as for the present war in Europe.

What is a base? It is something much more than a mere depot in which supplies are stored; it is a reservoir not merely of munitions but of brains and labor; it deals not merely in provisions but in skills and maintenance. There are establishments and installations near here that can service anything from a tank to a micrometer. Some took more than three years to build; in one, more than thirty thousand people are employed. Also Cairo has the vital advantage of concrete and practical experience in the business of maintaining a great army in the field; it was from here, of course, that Montgomery got everything he needed for the long chase across Africa; and at the end of the campaign, Cairo was as important a supply base as Algiers, even for operations as far away as Tunis. Montgomery had to have 120 tons of water per day—which worked out to one gallon per man—during his advance. How Cairo got it to him every day almost without fail— even when he was isolated in the desert four or six hundred miles away—is one of the great and little-known achievements of the war. The details, alas, cannot be written now.

Everybody talks with huge good humor of the difference between Cairo a year ago and Cairo today. Last year Rommel stood at Alamein, forty miles from Alexandria. You could visit the front in a taxicab; lots of people did. On one day last July, I was told, Rommel could have taken Alexandria and Cairo with a dozen tanks. He could have driven straight through. This was the time of the great "flap," or panic. Rommel had reserved a suite at Shepheard's; and a lot of folk began to evacuate. The wind was really up; and people tell me that the Americans here did not particularly distinguish themselves for staunchness. Everybody I meet has a "flap" story or two. One day is now known as "Ash Wednesday," when various headquarters and embassies burnt their papers, to keep them from falling into German hands. You could see the smoke for miles.

At ten-thirty this morning I called on Lieutenant Colonel Robert Parham, Brereton's public relations officer; he is a former United Press man, and he does his job smoothly and well. He is helping me here as much as did Joe Phillips in Algiers. The Cairo setup is intricate and interlaced. On top of everything is what is known simply as "Middle

East"; this is British army headquarters for an area stretching all the way to Aden in the south, Tripolitania to the west, and regions to the north which are not precisely described. The RAF fits into this picture in a complex way, and so does the Royal Navy, under the commander-in-chief, Levant, who is stationed in Alexandria. Yet this is not a united *allied* command like Eisenhower's; for instance it would take a Byzantine theologian to figure out just how Brereton's command links up with Tedder, or the local RAF. Brereton is in charge of American ground troops in this region too. Also there are Free French, Greeks, Czechs, and Jugoslavs; and the Poles a bit further away.

Philip Astley arranged for me to meet General Sir Henry Maitland Wilson, the British commander-in-chief, Middle East, at noon. It took some time to penetrate the heavily guarded area, surrounded by barbed wire, of his headquarters. Wilson is known everywhere as "Jumbo" Wilson. This is partly because of his elephantine size; he is a very large man indeed; also he collects elephant curios as a hobby. He is sixty-three, a veteran of the Boer War; he was commander-in-chief in Greece and then in Palestine during the Syrian campaign against the French; he "created" the British Ninth and Tenth armies. He looks like Old King Cole, and shakes like jelly when he laughs. He was not very talkative. Mostly he discussed the ravages that the war—and the Nazis—have brought to Greece, and the necessity to get some sort of relief to the starving Balkans soon.*

I had a talk with Brereton today; in a quarter of an hour, compactly and decisively, he told me practically everything worth knowing about the essential strategy of this whole area.. All strictly off the record. What he said about Turkey was eye-opening. Then—through Astley's

* General Wilson was promoted to commander-in-chief, Mediterranean, late in 1943, when Eisenhower was assigned to London.

courtesy—I met Major General A. C. Arnold, the British military attaché to Turkey, who is here on a brief visit. This officer, I've been told everywhere, knows more about Turkey than any man alive; he probably counts in Ankara more than any other Allied official. He mentioned some things to watch for when I get to Istanbul.

Lunch with Kirk, and dinner with him also. Lunch at his town house, which he keeps only for entertaining at noon; dinner out near the pyramids in the house, beautifully decorated in the modern manner, where he lives. At lunch the guests were Killearn and Lord Moyne, who is deputy minister of state; that is, he represents the British War Cabinet in Cairo. Much talk about the Russians and the Poles. At dinner we met the King of Greece. The other guests were a fabulous miscellany: Egyptologists, generals who specialized in typhus control, sumptuous women from New York, Arab experts, officers whose work is in fields so secret nobody even dares to ask them about the weather. We saw an American movie. Not much talk of politics, alas.

I told Kirk that I had a letter to King Farouk from Wendell Willkie, and he replied in his dry way, "Burn it at once." I didn't know that Willkie's book, *One World*, had been suppressed here, and I still don't know whether it is the British or the Egyptians who wanted it banned. Apparently Mr. Willkie committed the indiscretion of saying that Lord Killearn was the real ruler of Egypt. This is of course perfectly true; but it annoyed British and Egyptians both. Also, with considerable shortsightedness, most Egyptians I meet—they are violently sensitive nationalists—say that Mr. Willkie wrote about them "unfairly," that he stressed too much the control of the rich pashas, and the lack of education. But the more I see, the more convinced I am that Mr. Willkie was a good reporter. Anyway the Egyptians should appreciate it that he is so much on their side.

This has been a busy day; I had a lot of minor things to tend to. I went to a bank and cashed my letter of credit for the first time since leaving New York; it seems odd to be in a place where money is a commodity. I had some inoculations, and wrote a pile of service messages and thank-you letters; Lock in Malta wanted a pair of desert boots, and I tried to get them off to him. In our PX I came across a nice example of the Americanization of the English language. An American sergeant said that something cost "a pound and a half."

There are pictures in almost every window of Churchill, Roosevelt, Stalin, and Chiang Kai-shek. To see pictures of Stalin in Egypt, of all places, is breath-taking to say the least.

Cairo, Friday, August 6.—I skipped lunch to write a story, and then called on Major General F. G. Beaumont-Nesbitt, formerly the British military attaché in Washington, and now head of Allied Liaison here. I have thought ever since I met him a good many years ago—and particularly since he predicted flatly early in 1942 that the Russians would never give up Voronezh and that the Germans would never take Stalingrad—that this officer is the single best informed and soundest military man I ever met. Today we talked for a crowded hour, mostly about Russia and the Balkans. What Russia wants more than anything else, he is convinced—and he is a profound student of Russian history—is not revolution, but security.

Dinner with Frank Gervasi of *Collier's*, who reminds me of Colonel Frank Capra, the movie director; he is similarly direct, likable, and friendly. We left Shepheard's after ten—which is curfew for all drinks in Cairo—and drove out to the Club de Chasse in the open air near the pyramids, where there is no restriction on alcohol, or almost anything else, at any time. It looked like the Stork Club outdoors, and it was hard to believe that a war was going on—just as it is often hard to believe this in New

York. King Farouk sat with a party a few tables away, and I observed the healthy informality of this powerfully built young man. Gervasi, who knows him well, introduced me, and the king sent over a couple of bottles of champagne for us to enjoy, almost as if he had been Sherman Billingsley. I did not tell His Majesty that I had in my pocket a letter to him from Mr. Willkie.

It's a curious fact that Egyptian neutrality has on the whole been a convenience rather than otherwise to the British. According to the terms of the Anglo-Egyptian treaty Egypt should certainly have gone to war against Germany, and the British were annoyed at first when it did not do so. The Egyptians sought to be both allies and neutrals at the same time; now they are called "nonbelligerent allies." But the fact that they have not actually declared war has helped Britain in several ways. For instance the Red Sea in the early days of the war was considered a neutral zone, and thus the United States was enabled to ship vast quantities of material here by this route, and to build a base at a site which must not be named. Also, the Germans never had a pretext for bombing Cairo —though Alexandria and Heliopolis have, I believe, been bombed—and as a result the British were able to use Cairo as a headquarters in almost perfect safety. The situation is strikingly like that which obtained in Shanghai in the early days of the Japanese war on China, when the International Settlement provided a wonderful vantage point for secure activity.

Almost all Egyptians I meet, even those most fiercely antagonistic to the British, seek to emphasize that they have been "loyal" allies and have rendered substantial service to the Allied cause, though "nonbelligerent." During the flap, when a Fifth Column might have been dangerous, Egyptian morale stood up very well. If two small bridges had been blown, the British at Alamein would have been cut off from Cairo; they were never blown; moreover, they were guarded by Egyptians. Also Egyptian man power has been very useful in policing roads, helping defend the canal, and so on.

There was a good deal of talk tonight about the curiously entangled political setup here, especially the enormous role that cotton plays in Egyptian affairs; but when I got home I was too tired to write it down.

Someone—an Englishman—said the other day that one lesson of the war is that the British do not do well if forced to fight on territory they have "exploited," e.g., Burma and Malaya. But it's unlikely in the extreme, now, that any fighting will ever take place on Egyptian soil.

Cairo, Saturday, August 7.—Another lunch today *chez* Kirk, in honor of Nuri Pasha, the Prime Minister of Iraq, whom I met in Bagdad years ago. He asked me if I remembered a barman named Jesus in the Hotel Zia there. Nuri is supposed to be in Cairo to sound out Egypt on an Arab federation.

Drinks late in the afternoon with Gervasi, Fred Sondern of *Reader's Digest*, Chester Morrison of the Chicago *Sun*, and the other correspondents who meet every day at Shepheard's. Grant Parr, of NBC., is helping arrange my broadcasts.

Cairo, Sunday, August 8.—I called at the Egyptian Foreign Office, trying to line up a talk with the prime minister, and, if possible, the king. It all reminded me of similar experiences in various Balkan capitals in the thirties. The building is handsome and venerable; the attachés are polite, sensitive, and inclined to think themselves superior to their jobs; they apologize for their English, which they speak perfectly. They ask you to submit questions; they deluge you with books and brochures; their talk is highly nationalistic and at the same time curiously defensive. But the two or three young Egyptians I met were bright and helpful. One—a department head of some rank —was busy reading Joseph E. Davies' *Mission to Moscow*.

And all of them talked with curiosity of the future role, not only of the Soviet Union, but of the United States, in the postwar world. As to Egypt, what seemed to bother everybody most was that it "has always been owned by someone else," ever since the days of the Pharaohs.

Lunch with Major Oakshot and Frank Gervasi, mostly in discussion of what may happen in the Balkans; then at five I had another good hour with General Beaumont-Nesbitt. He sent me on to a brigadier in charge of Military Intelligence, and then I saw an American colonel—a Yale professor not so long ago—who is also an intelligence officer. Everybody, including me, wants to know what is going to happen next in Italy. Of course some kind of negotiations with Badoglio, or, rather, negotiations to get in touch with Badoglio, are almost certainly going on. Everybody in Italy wants peace; but the Germans are reinforcing all the time. There is no clear indication yet of what is happening to Italian divisions in the Balkans, but it is a general theory that Badoglio cannot quit until he has time to get his Balkan troops out. Still: Is not Italy itself worth more than the couple of hundred thousand troops who, in the event of peace, might get stranded outside Italy?

Benjamin Welles, Sumner's son, took Gervasi and me to dinner in the country, and we met Kareem Tabit Bey, an astute Egyptian journalist, one of the editors of the great newspaper *Al Mokattam*. He was almost defiant defending Egypt's position in the war, and he said that Farouk was the first really "Egyptian" king in the country's history.

Cairo, Monday, August 9.—Ninety-six in the shade today, and one of the busiest days I ever had. I wrote two broadcasts, and saw them through censorship; there are five different censorships to pass here—U.S. Army, British military, RAF, Royal Navy, and Anglo-Egyptian political—but I had no trouble. Then young Parr helped me record both shows, for transmission later to New York.

Lots of nuisances. I got passport photographs and I had to buy, in a hurry, a complete set of civilian clothes, since we are not allowed to enter Turkey in uniform. And although I have my Usafime pass, which does away with most passport trouble, someone told me today I needed an Egyptian exit visa. It took most of the afternoon to get this, since I was not checked in when I arrived (I came on a military aircraft), and therefore the authorities said I wasn't here, and hence couldn't leave.

Then more trouble over tickets and priority. It isn't easy to get on the British plane which only flies to Adana, Turkey, once a week; and the problem of wiring ahead for *wagon-lit* transportation from there to Istanbul seemed to appal every travel agency. I sent about ten telegrams to friends along the line. Then came the big event of the day, a talk with Lieutenant General Sir Wilfred G. Lindsell.

This remarkable officer is known as the "greatest quartermaster general of the war." He, as well as Alexander and Montgomery, "won" the Battle of Africa, because he was the cool-minded genius who organized and maintained the whole route of supply, from Cairo to Tunis, during the entire campaign. Someone said of him once, "Oh, Lindsell's all right—if you give him his own way." He chuckled telling me this. He sketched the problem of communications and supplies in Africa in all their details, and talked about the new railway his men have pushed up to Beirut, so that Egypt and Syria are now for the first time linked by rail. On his desk is a sign, THINK OF THE MILES AND COUNT ACCORDINGLY. I said that I supposed he was the greatest logistics expert in the world and he laughed and said that he had never even heard the word until quite recently. He talks with brilliant symbolism. Logistics depend on three factors: (1) the scope of an operation; (2) its distance from a major base; (3) the amount of reserves or hand. "Nothing comes out until the whole pipe is full." Cairo's "pipe" to the United States is now "three months" long.*

Dinner with Lord Moyne. This was very pleasant. We saw, through General Brereton's courtesy, the movie made by the American Air Force and the RAF which was used to brief the Ploesti fliers. This is, I believe, the first time a great air operation has been explained to its participants largely through motion pictures. And I marveled at the masterful skill with which the movie was put together, and the infinity of cogent detail it contained. The whole Ploesti area was re-created in a model, and this was then photographed at every possible angle from which a pilot could approach it, so that the pilot could see in slow motion exactly what his "run" would be. We continue to hear extraordinary stories of the heroism of the Ploesti fliers.

Someone said tonight that the British have a wonderful quality of being able to conserve a last ounce of surplus morale for use at the extreme end of an operation. They expand, as it were, under the pressure of the supreme, final moment. And this wins wars.

Cairo, Tuesday, August 10.—I got kicked out of my place on the Adana plane tomorrow, but valiant work by Oakshot, Moyne, and Beaumont-Nesbitt put me on again.

I left all my personal papers with Ray Hare at the Legation, since I don't particularly want to take any confidential stuff into Turkey. Lunch with Bob Parham, and then some shopping. On Shepheard's terrace I walked into Larry Adler and Jack Benny, of all people. Dinner with Beaumont-Nesbitt and a group of officers. I talked too much, and so learned little.

Cairo-Adana, Wednesday, August 11.—Up at five, and we hurtled to the airport in the British Airways truck. Of course we did not get off till hours later. The plane is an old Lockheed, with wooden benches. I sat next to an

---

* General Lindsell is now stationed with Lord Louis Mountbatten in the India theater.

American official, "Packey" MacFarland, who was formerly a Chicago banker; everybody else on the ship is a courier or king's messenger. We stopped for a moment at Lydda, in Palestine; and I tasted of two luxuries: the wonderful Palestinian orange juice, served in chilled bottles by a pretty Jewish girl; and the Palestine *Post*, which is edited by my friend Gershon Agronsky. What a relief to be reading a really good newspaper, composed and written on the strictest standards.

We reached Adana at about one-fifteen, and then waited till three the next morning for the Taurus Express to carry us further into Turkey.

Chapter XII

Talking Turkey

I LIKE and admire the Turks; I always have. And it was wonderfully interesting to visit Istanbul again, after almost ten years away. Perhaps I was a bit disconcerted when, the night I arrived, I asked a friend what the Turkish attitude toward the war was; he answered, "Every Turk prays for two things: that the war will last as long as possible, and that they can keep out."

Of course my friend was not quite serious as regards his first remark. What he meant was that the Turks, as neutrals, derive considerable material advantage from their neutrality; both Allies and Axis court them hotly, with zeal and zest. Both Allies and Axis want certain Turkish goods; also they want to keep certain other goods from the other side; they outbid each other and prices go higher than the Taurus mountains. The whole field of economic warfare, and how it artificially stimulates a country's economy, is something that cannot be written about yet; but the Turks will have a wonderful story to tell if they ever tell it. Consider what they have received through Lend Lease—free. "Every day is Christmas here," one of my Turkish friends exclaimed.

Nevertheless the strain of remaining neutral in the middle of an exploding battlefield is irksome, and sober Turks know quite well that the political and economic favors and blandishments with which they have been showered will not last forever. Moreover, the longer the war lasts, the more Turkey is exposed to the possibility of being drawn in. So I do not accept the first part of my friend's remark quite literally; the Turks will be as happy as the rest of us when the war is over. But I do accept with full agreement the rest of what he said. Certainly, above everything, no matter what happens, the Turks hope and pray that they will be able to stay outside the war. Perhaps by the time these lines are in print they will have become belligerent—on our side, of course—but they hope to avert this contingency as long as humanly possible. The dominating characteristic of the entire Turkish political scene is the intense, stubborn, and un-wavering desire of Turkey to remain neutral.

Of course at the very last moment—particularly if, or when, the Russians attack the Axis in the Balkans—the Turks may change their minds, or pressure upon them will be too relentless to resist. Such a possibility in the realm of *force majeure* is not to be excluded.

The Turks are, it should be pointed out, at great pains to tell all comers that despite their nonbelligerency they are not strictly "neutral." When I saw Prime Minister Saracoğlu he said that Turkey does not consider itself "neutral vis-à-vis Great Britain and the United States," and that it only uses the term "neutrality" on account of the complications provided by "other powers." The coun-try is, indeed, bound by an important formal alliance to Great Britain. But even so the Turks are not, like the Egyptians, "nonbelligerent allies"; they are "neutral allies" or just "allies." The object of Anglo-American policy is to make them a little more "unneutral" on our side.

The Turks say that, even as neutrals, they have rendered substantial service to the Allied cause; and this is true. They are making interesting contributions in several fields right now. And as to the past, if Turkey had not been neutral when Germany smashed through the Balkans, the Nazis might be in Cairo and Bagdad this minute; Ger-many did not dare violate Turkish neutrality (partly be-

cause of a fear at the time of complications with Russia),
and therefore the barrier provided by Turkey kept the
Axis out of the East. Mussolini, I heard it said on quite
high authority, tried to persuade Hitler to attack Egypt
and the Middle East through Turkey instead of via North
Africa; but Hitler, knowing what the quality of Turkish
resistance would be, hesitated. Of course this argument
by the Turks that they "saved" the Allies in the Middle
East by being neutral is somewhat negative. Hitler has
attacked many neutrals. He was never dissuaded from
assaulting a country because of its neutrality alone.

It is certainly true that the British, at least twice, have
formally requested the Turks to enter the war, and on
each occasion (up to the moment of writing) the Turks
have formally refused. It is probably true, though it would
be hard to prove, that during at least one black interval
for the Allies—after the Nazi invasion of Greece and the
fall of Crete—the Turks were seriously tempted to enter
the war on the Axis side.

This danger has completely passed; most Turks, even
officials, now assert in fact that it "never existed." The
possibility of Turkey's becoming an Axis ally has altogether disappeared; the danger has been categorically
liquidated. There are several reasons for this. For one
thing the pro-Ally Turks have risen in domestic influence
as against the pro-Germans. Many Turks were impressed
by German power, and even if Germans were not particularly liked—there is no statue to Liman von Sanders in
Istanbul—they were respected. Many high army officers
were pro-German. But now the winds blow the other way.
The Turks, who are nothing if not realists, know quite
well that the Axis has lost the war, and they have no
faintest desire to end up on the defeated side. The mission
of Franz von Papen, the German Ambassador, has been a
failure, and Papen's influence is not more than vestigial.
Papen tried to sell the Turks a bill of goods: that they

had more to fear from the U.S.S.R. than from Germany, and that therefore they should be pro-German. The Turks still fear the Russians, certainly, but the general international picture has drastically changed. German pressure at the moment has been reduced largely to the economic sphere, and German influence is mostly "cultural."

As to the Soviet Union there is no doubt that fear and suspicion of Russia is still the pivot of Turkish policy. I found evidence of this in every talk I had with any Turk; it can be seen in almost any issue of a Turkish newspaper. The Russians were advancing on Kharkov when I was in Istanbul; the Turks watched this advance with positive apprehension; every new Russian victory chilled the country. Why? Mainly, it seems, the Turks fear the Soviet Union not because of communism but on straight nationalist grounds. They have little fear of Russian revolutionary activity; what they fear is Russian territorial expansion, either in the Balkans or toward the Dardanelles. They are cynical about Anglo-American friendship with Russia, and their mistrust is so great that it would still be a factor even if Russia were a democratic state.

I asked many people why the Turks hold this tenacious and atavistic fear of Russia, but I never got a really satisfactory answer. Turkey, like Russia, had a great revolution after the first World War; in some respects the Turkish revolution made alterations in the structure of Turkish life as profound as did the Soviet revolution in Russian life; one might naturally have expected countries which had experienced analogous convulsions at about the same time to become friends. And as a matter of fact, Turkey and Russia *were* good friends for ten years or more; Turkey was the first country to stretch out a hand to the struggling bolsheviks; Kemal Atatürk based his foreign policy on co-operation with the Russians. When I asked various Turks how they explained the contrary situation prevailing today, they were apt to answer, "The Russians changed; we didn't." But is this really true? And I began to wonder if the disharmony between Turkey and Russia could not be resolved somehow, if its historical roots could not be dug up and reburied. The chief point at issue is of course the Dardanelles. But worry about the Dardanelles represents, it seems to me, a somewhat outmoded conception of history. This is an era when the geographical importance of a strategic body of water has been largely superseded. Why should the Soviet Union want the Dardanelles any more? In time of war the Straits could be useful only for emergence into a larger sea, and the British, by controlling Gibraltar and Suez, have that sea locked up anyway.

It should certainly be pointed out that in spite of Turkish apprehensions and suspicion, the formal relations between Ankara and Moscow are correct. The Russian Ambassador, Mr. Vinogradoff, is well liked. There are no outstanding issues between the two governments; Prime Minister Saracoğlu himself told me that if you asked either government if there was anything overt to which it objected, in the whole field of Turkish-Russian relations, the answer would be No. Maybe I'm being optimistic; but as the war proceeds and the Turks see progressively (1) how deeply the Allies are committed to a policy of co-operation with Russia, and (2) how deeply they are committed to the Allies for a place at the peace table, the Turkish attitude toward Russia may become less inimical.

The other great preoccupation of the Turks is the Balkans. While I was in Istanbul people thought that when the Italians surrendered the Germans would gradually withdraw from the Balkan area, leaving a "Vacuum." And politics, like nature, abhors a vacuum. The Turks hope ardently for an Allied invasion of the Balkans soon; I even heard it said that they would like to assist it, in the role of auxiliary "policemen"; and if the country ever does get into the war, this is the way it will happen. Of course the reason the Turks want the British and especially the Americans in the Balkans (the theory is that the Americans will be disinterested) is to keep the Russians out. The greatest crisis in the history of modern Turkey will come, so almost every Turk told me, if the Russians march into southern Rumania or particularly Bulgaria. On the other hand, I never met a Turk who would admit that they themselves had any territorial ambitions in the Balkan area. One Turkish editor said, "The best thing that ever happened to this country was losing the Ottoman Empire."

A shrewd observer gave me this sketch of other Turkish attitudes. Toward England: considerable suspicion; they don't like the British as much as they pretend. Toward Germany: respect mingled with fear. Toward Italy: contempt. Toward the Arab states of the Middle East: a big-brother feeling, now fading. Toward the United States: hope. Toward the rest of the world: indifference.

Another consideration is that from certain points of view Turkey's entrance into the war on our side could be an inconvenience. First, the Axis might destroy Constantinople from the air, and it is even conceivable that the Bulgars would reach the Straits, which would be a damaging defeat to Allied prestige. Second, although Turkish air bases would be useful, the difficulties of getting a land army across the country are almost insurmountable.

Finally, Turkey is, as I heard it said, "a very sovereign" country. The Turks will risk absolutely nothing, they will play it safe to the very end; and nobody is going to push these people around.

Everywhere I went in Turkey I asked a leading question, "Who runs this country, and why?" The answers distilled to "Inönü and the Army."

The president of the republic, General Ismet Inönü, is

about sixty; for years he was known as Ismet Pasha, and as such he was Kemal Atatürk's first assistant during the early history of the republic; it was he who represented Turkey at the Lausanne Conference, and who helped drive the Greeks into the sea. When Kemal enforced on all Turks a Latinization and secularization of their names, Ismet chose "Inōnü" in commemoration of his most notable battle.

Oddly enough the great Kemal did not pick Inōnü for the succession; quite the contrary. Kemal had wantonly affronted Inōnü on various occasions, and he had been out of office since September, 1937. When Kemal died (October 1938), the two leading choices for the succession were the Turkish Ambassador to London, and Fethi Bey, a former ambassador who has since died. Both were strong men; both were liberals. But Inōnü played a wary game behind the curtains, and partly because of his considerable prestige, partly because of support by the Army, he got the job.

Inōnü is a recluse. With something of the xenophobia that attaches to almost all old-time Turks, he dislikes foreigners, and with the exception of ambassadors he almost never receives one. In fact, he scarcely sees anybody outside his own immediate circle; he receives even less than Stalin. He owns the largest private yacht in the world—it cost $3,500,000 and was given Kemal by the Republican People's party, the only political party in the country—but he almost never uses it. Sometimes, however, Inōnü does show himself in public. I saw him once—with a party of deputies—at Taksim's, the most celebrated night club in Istanbul.

On the Sunday that Tobruk fell, President Inōnü happened to be at the Ankara races. He heard the news. He thereupon walked up alone to the British Ambassador, Sir Hughe M. Knatchbull-Hugessen, who had not yet been informed; conspicuously, in front of hundreds of people, he put his arm consolingly and almost affectionately around Hugessen's shoulder. The news of this gesture spread fast. Inönü does not often make gestures. And it indicated to people that even on this dark day, Turkey was resolute in its fidelity to the British treaty.

The sources of Inönü's power are, first, the heritage he automatically derives as successor to the formidable Atatürk; second, his close association with the military. Inönü is, even among Turks who are all fiercely nationalist, distinguished by the intensity of his nationalism; definitely, he is the most nationalist of the Turkish leaders. He remembers well the days when his country was a kind of half-deflated football being kicked around by the great powers (so they thought); he does not intend that such days shall ever come again. What he wants is a strong, compact Turkey, with a strong army that can say No or Yes to anybody in the world, any time it pleases. Personally, Inönü's greatest characteristic is, next to stubbornness, his meticulous sense of detail, his devotion to routine.

The prime minister, Sükrü Saracoğlu, is an altogether different type of man. He is a professional politician ("a career politician," one of his Turkish friends told me); he was one of Kemal's early ministers, and he has held almost every Cabinet post; in 1938 he became foreign minister under Inönü, and in 1942 he acceded to the prime ministership. Saracoğlu is an able citizen. He gives you a sense of both astuteness and power. A vigorous good mixer, something of a backslapper, he knows all the tricks; he likes people, and people like him. He is convivial and hearty. He was shrewd enough, even in the worst days the Allies had, to see that Turkey should avoid any too-deep commitments to the Germans; the chief source of his power is that he has consistently guessed right on the international situation, while always making the best possible use of his country's strategic position. Of all the

Turkish men of state, he is the most pro-Ally and pro-American.

The American Ambassador to Turkey, Laurence A. Steinhardt, who has done a tremendously effective job in lifting and entrenching United States prestige in Turkey, took me out to see Saracoğlu on August 18; the prime minister was vacationing at the seaside resort of Florya, an hour by boat from Istanbul. We left the magical harbor of Istanbul—watching what is certainly the second most remarkable skyline in the world—in the American Embassy motorboat, and skimmed across the crisp blue water. Saracoğlu, sun-browned and sipping coffee, received us in a modest bungalow perched above a blazing white beach; he was vigorously outspoken. In fact, this turned out to be one of the frankest talks I ever had with a European politician. He was wary at first; he only revealed what was really interesting him toward the end, when he asked questions instead of answering them. He told us a good deal of what was going on in the Balkans—he is expertly informed on this kind of thing—and he thought that Italy was at the moment looking for a formula to surrender. One thing he said struck me vividly —that when Turkish neutrality closed the door to the East to Germany, the German attack on Russia therefore became inevitable. So Turkey is responsible for the Russian war! What he wanted to know was mostly in two fields; first, would the United States abandon Europe after this war, as it had abandoned it in 1919; second, what were basic Russian intentions toward Europe? In regard to the first question, Steinhardt and I replied with somewhat different points of view; as to the second, I offered a tentative idea for what it might be worth. The Russians want two things: (1) Strategic frontiers in the West, as drawn by themselves. What is more, they will get them, since no one in Great Britain and the United States is going to take on the Red Army for the sake of, let us say, Lithuania. (2) Fifty years of peace. On the other hand, the Russians might be tempted to become mischievous if (a) we overtly support reactionary or anti-Russian regimes in Europe, or (b) if their hand is forced by any attempt to build a *cordon sanitaire* against them. We had good talk about all this. Later came some mention of the Dardanelles. One hypothesis advanced: the Russians will not seek to expand in this direction, since this would bring them into direct conflict with Great Britain and possibly the United States, whereas recovery of territory in Poland and the Baltics will probably not.

Saracoğlu is, like all Turks, an ardent nationalist. In his last big speech to the National Assembly, he reflected the mood of his country by saying, "We are Turks, and we shall become a little more Turk every day."

The foreign minister, Numan Menemencioğlu, is again a different type: retiring, a student, not in very good health, modest, a beautiful linguist, and a politician who has sought to steer a razor-fine middle course between Allies and Axis. Once Steinhardt called on him, having spent the night before reading in John Bassett Moore on international law; he thought that by so doing he could the better present a case in which he was interested. He found that Menemencioğlu had also spent the night reading the identical chapters in the same book.

It is an odd point that Inönü, Menemencioğlu, and the Permanent Undersecretary of the Turkish Foreign Office, are all very deaf.

The political structure of Turkey has changed little since Kemal's death, and the economic realities remain about the same. Only one party exists, the Republican People's party (though a handful of deputies are appointed from within as a kind of "opposition"), and although the National Assembly has great power on paper, in effect it is little more than a debating society. But to be a deputy is important; because deputies—who are nom-

inated by the party and only very indirectly "elected" by
the people—have special privileges. Sometimes—in committee meetings though not in general sessions—a deputy
will speak out, and risk criticizing the regime. I heard it
said that a clique of about a dozen men runs everything
in the Assembly; no one else really counts. Between the
very small number of first-rate, expertly trained men at
the top and the bulk of the people, the drop is terrific.
And the chief social problem of Turkey is to bridge this
gap, to communicate decisions from the top, through the
vast bureaucracy down to the popular mass. Village officials often cannot read and write; everybody is stiflingly
poor, so that corruption is not exceptional; orders have to
be given six or seven times before anything is done.
Nevertheless, the quality of Turkish administration, after
heroic efforts, continues to improve; things are infinitely
better than they were under the Sultan, and better than
in any other Middle Eastern country.

I asked everyone I met how well Atatürk's social re-
forms had stood up, which of them had best survived, and
whether the country had retrogressed much since his
death. Without exception, everyone I talked to, including
Americans friendly to Turkey who have lived here for
many years, agreed that there has been some retrogres-
sion, though they disagreed as to how much. An Englishman said, "Kemal brought the country forward fifty
years, and it has now slipped back twenty-five." But I
think this is probably a somewhat bilious estimate.

Turkey was declared eligible to Lend Lease on November 7, 1941. Obviously the motives were in part political;
it was, even then, of substantial value and importance that
Turkey should remain neutral, and if possible be weaned
to the Allied side. The defense of Turkey was considered
vital to the defense of the United States.

The dollar value of our shipments to Turkey since 1941

has never, I believe, been officially published, but it reaches a considerable sum. Lend Lease shipments to "Africa and the Middle East" totaled a value of about a billion dollars from March 11, 1941, to April 1, 1943; in the six months between March and August, 1943, they ran to a value of $525,000,000. So the outward flow sharply increased; we shipped approximately half as much in six months in 1943 as in all the two years preceding. How much went specifically to Turkey inside the general category "Africa and Middle East" is unknown; the figures are not broken down. Shipments to Turkey, apparently, ebb and flow depending on political circumstance; when the Turks are behaving well, or when we particularly want them to behave well, they are apt to increase; when we consider the value of Turkish good will to be less acute, we shave Lend Lease down. To keep Turkey neutral we will pay a good deal, and of course if the country should enter the war on our side, Lend Lease would be multiplied. Conversely, if a contingency should arise in which Turkey was being obdurate, we might threaten to cut Lend Lease off altogether.

What the Turks want, and have been getting, are airplanes (almost all from Great Britain); tanks, trucks, lorries, jeeps; medical supplies; boots; technical equipment of all kinds; gasoline, telephone wire and telephones; wheat early this year; and a certain amount of armament.

Lend Lease is administered in Ankara by the B.A.C.C., or British-American Coordinating Committee. This committee considers Turkish requests, assembles information, and makes its recommendations, in both civil and military fields. In Washington Turkey is represented on the munitions Assignment Board, the chairman of which is Harry Hopkins, by the British.

Following the Casablanca conference Mr. Churchill flew to Adana—with full American approval—and there met Inönü and members of the Turkish general staff. The

Turks were invited to prepare lists of what they wanted, and told that they would get what they reasonably asked for subject (a) to its bona fide importance to Turkish defense, and (b) the country's capacity to absorb. Presently the Turks produced what came to be known thereafter as the "Adana lists." They were somewhat staggering. Among other things the Turks put in a request for three marmalade factories. They asked for enough machine tools to set up a whole series of vocational training schools. They have not by any means received all they asked for.

The Turks are doing their best to mechanize their army—and its mechanization and motorization might be of incalculable value to us in the event of Turkish adhesion to the war—and their requests for petroleum were therefore subject to special scrutiny. The Turkish army asked for 852,735 tons of petroleum products; the Turkish air force asked for 188,320 tons—in one year. Very little high-octane gas was included in the lists, indicating that the Turks were not thinking so much in terms of tanks or aircraft as trucks and similar vehicles. Of the total amounts the Army wanted 720,000 tons in automobile gasoline alone. Our experts thereupon calculated that this amount of gas would suffice the country for at least twelve normal years. There are only 7,000 trucks and busses in the whole country, and the consumption of gas is roughly 6,000 kilograms per truck per year. Trucks in Turkey average 1.83 miles per kilo of gas; so 720,000 tons would send one truck 1,317,600,000 miles, or 52,704 times around the world. The life of a truck is calculated at five years; therefore 720,000 tons would run 24,000 trucks, or more than three times the number the country possesses, until they wear out. If the war should last one more year, 720,000 tons would be enough to run 120,000 trucks for this period. Finally, to deliver this amount of gas to Turkey would take a fleet of ninety 8,000-ton tankers; 3,000 tank cars would be necessary in Turkey, two new discharging berths at Iskanderun, triple the present tankage (23,000 tons), and 80 railway sidings for tank cars instead of the 13 that exist at present.

The "Adana lists" also included requests for 75,000 tons of lubricating oil, which would be enough for 500,-000 passenger cars for one year; 22,000 tons of gear oil, enough for 1,500,000 cars for one year; and 16,000 tons of grease, enough for 3,000,000 cars in one year. (In all Turkey, there are only 4,600 passenger cars.) But these figures should not prejudice the basic picture. If Turkey comes into the war, every bit of these petroleum products will be useful, and probably will be used by us.

Lend Lease has been an enormous windfall not merely to Turkey but all over the Middle East. Countries are getting a prodigious new plant—for nothing. All the way from Khartoum to Basra, from Ankara to the Caspian, there are new harbors, new airfields, new railway stations; docks, roads, weather-reporting installations, radio towers, telephone lines; factories, machine shops, printing presses; fields sewn with our seed and bakeries feeding children with our wheat. Nobody except the singularly shortsighted will object. Because to raise the standard of living anywhere in the world means raising it at home.

The first word I heard in Turkey was *Varlik*. And I heard more about *Varlik* than anything else in the country, much more than about neutrality or the war.

Literally *Varlik* means "wealth tax," or "tax on fortune"; it is the name given to a special levy authorized in November, 1942, for "taxing heavily the extraordinary profits and accumulations of wealth resulting from abnormal conditions since 1939." On paper, the tax was just that, a steep excess profits tax, nothing more. But in practice it turned out to be something else, a kind of capital levy used as a weapon of extortion against the minorities.

There are about 320,000 Greeks, Armenians, and Jews left in Turkey; most of these are concentrated in Istanbul. Kemal Atatürk followed, in the main, a wise and tolerant policy toward minorities, but since his death, the trend toward integration has been reversed; the Turks now stress the differentiation between themselves and the minorities, and seek to relegate the non-Turks to a definite and permanent secondary status.

As *Varlik* worked out, the minorities got taxed, and the Turks didn't; discrimination was overt and flagrant. The law, as written, included two clauses which laid the way open to grave abuses; assessments were put in the exclusive hands of the local tax boards, which were invariably composed of pure Turks; and the law contained no proviso for appeal. Moreover, assessments had to be paid on top of the regular tax within fifteen days (with appeal prohibited); and the minimum assessment was set at £T 500 $275), a sum staggeringly beyond the capacity of most people to pay.

So application of the law produced fantastic and cruel absurdities. Greek office boys or Jewish stenographers who had never had £T 100 in their lives would be assessed £T 5,000. On the main street of a village a Greek shop and a Turkish shop might be side by side; the Greek would be assessed £T 20,000, the Turk £T 1,000. The house servant of a friend of mine, an Armenian, gets a salary of £T 40 per month; his assessment was £T 500.

It was this factor of discrimination which, of course, caused most protests and scandal. In Istanbul there are twenty-one shipping firms, twenty Turkish and one Jewish. The twenty Turks paid £T 465,000 *Varlik* in all; the single Jew was assessed £T 1,000,000. One substantial American company in Turkey has 353 employees; of these, 187 are Moslem Turks, only 9 of whom were

Varliked. Of the Turkish employees, 98.2 per cent were not assessed; of the minority employees, 96.1 per cent were assessed. Figures for the whole Istanbul area show that the Armenian community was taxed on a basis of 289 per cent, Jews 239 per cent, Greeks 165 per cent, and Turks 4.9 per cent.

The apologists for *Varlik* say, on their side, that the minority communities, and also some of the foreign business houses, had consistently and successfully dodged tax payments for years. For instance one big industrial house, foreign-operated, which does a business worth at least one million pounds per year, paid only £T 404 in the last pre-*Varlik* year. (Its *Varlik* is a cool £T 700,000.) Naturally all the rich screamed bloody murder. Turkish officials, defending *Varlik*, say several things; that everybody did cheat for years, especially those who put their tangible fortunes into jewels and so on; that most of those punished for failure to pay *Varlik* could have paid something, somehow, but instead attempted to outbluff the law; and that, if the Turks now relaxed *Varlik*, no one would pay taxes at all hereafter.

Nothing, however, is an excuse for the manner in which the genuinely penniless victims of *Varlik* were punished. They were shipped, without trial, to labor camps in the remote interior of Anatolia, where living conditions were execrable, without proper food or clothing, and forced to work on roads and rock piles. Moreover, sentence to these camps was indefinite, until the *Varlik* was paid off. At the rate of a piaster or two a day, this would in most cases take a lifetime. At the beginning 86,000 people were sentenced to forced labor in these camps—and for many elderly Greeks and Jews it was the direct equivalent of a death sentence—but the number was eventually reduced to about 30,000.*

* In December, 1943, it was announced that all the *Varlik* internees had been released; this probably followed informal representations by the British and Americans when they saw Inönü at Cairo.

As administered—to the regret of many civilized and decent-minded Turks—*Varlik* was beyond doubt a deliberate attempt to impoverish selected individuals, and to tax the whole foreign community far beyond its capacity to pay.

Chapter XIII

Outside Europe Looking In

Adana, Turkey, Wednesday, August 11.—This has been a long and fascinating day. A British vice consul, Hardy Blair, met us at the airport, and took us to a rest house which the British have installed here as a convenience to their travelers. So typical of the British to do this kind of thing. The rest house is a series of rickety rooms in a ramshackle kind of loft; but there were showers, beds, and tea. Mrs. Blair, the vice consul's mother, runs it; and a system has been worked out whereby Turkish money is advanced to people; very important, because you can't cash foreign currency here except at fantastic rates. Blair took charge of everything as if he were a super-dragoman; he arranged our transportation up to Ankara, and helped squeeze us on the crowded Taurus Express— no small job—when it arrived at 3 A.M. six or seven hours late.

Meantime we had spent the day loafing and looking around. It was very hot. Wonderful lunch at a hotel called the Yeni. That is, I thought it was wonderful, because I love Turkish food—the cucumbers stuffed with peppery nuggets of meat, mutton grilled on a skewer, and pilaff. We went out into the kitchen, which is allowed by Turkish custom, and chose what we wanted cooked. The hotel radio was tuned to the BBC. The German radio tries to blanket Turkey, and transmission and reception from Berlin are excellent, but all the local Turks seem to prefer British stations.

The plane on which we arrived at Adana returns to Cairo the same day. The Turks won't let any foreign plane fly further into the country. It has made this run once a week for three years; each week, however, formal permission must be wired from Ankara before it can take off. The telegram was late today, and so the plane was held up for three hours. This, the pilot said, was the kind of Turkish bureaucracy he could do without.

Adana looks like any moderately colorful Eastern town. At night it was brightly lit up, the first fully lighted city I have seen in a long, long time. We went to a big open-air restaurant-cabaret near the river. On a stage, plump Turkish dancing girls yowled and screeched and belly-danced. In the cabaret there were half a dozen Hungarian housegirls in evening dress, and I saw a line of green-white latticed *séparés*, little rooms where they may drink intimately. This was a trivial thing on which to associate memories of Vienna and Budapest, but suddenly an emotion that had been tantalizing me all day became crystallized; I knew I was in Europe again. Adana is, of course, on the extreme Asiatic edge of Turkey; nevertheless I kept thinking to myself, this *is* Europe. And it was good to feel that after all these years I am "in" Europe once more.

We went back to the rest house, and Blair telephoned the station every half hour to see if the train had come. We drove there at about 2 A.M., and there was another longish wait. I haven't seen anything like it since a railway station at Baku in the neolithic 1920's. Hundreds of soldiers lay sleeping in tangled piles on the hot pavements; they crammed the station platforms in sweating clusters; other trains kept puffing in, with troops crowded in boxcars like animals, and dangling out of windows. Somebody made a bad joke: "Turkish soldiers are forbidden to bathe more than once a week, so you can tell them from officers."

I hear that since Tunis and Sicily the Turkish attitude to the Allies has stiffened a bit; they feel that there is no danger from Germany any more, but that the war is getting closer.

Ankara, Friday, August 13.—We got in just before midnight last night, many hours late. The arrival of the Taurus is always a great event in Ankara, and dozens of people make parties to greet the train. Earl Packer, our chargé d'affaires, offered to put me up. The hotels are all jammed, and I had been wondering where to sleep.

The trip was striking. We crossed some of the most impressive mountains I have ever seen, and then chugged for mile after slow mile through country almost inconceivably desolate, barren, bitingly rugged, remote, and empty. Now I understand why many Allied officers don't look with much favor to possible operations against Germany within Turkey. This is the only railroad, and there are no roads at all. To move even one armored division from the Syrian frontier to Ankara might take six weeks. Anatolia is no place to put an army into.

At the village stations, where the train would wait for long intervals, I was fascinated as always by the way the Turkish alphabet has been Westernized. Buffet is *bufe*; police is *polis*; table d'hôte is *tablidot*; hors d'oeuvres is *or duvr*. The meals were quite good, and we washed them down with a light Turkish wine, called Kavaklidere. Half a dozen times we passed long trains on sidings, full of trucks, jeeps, and other *matériel*. My friends tell me that the Turks do not handle machines well. Who can blame them? A Turkish private may not know how to use a fountain pen or mechanical pencil, much less a radio. Officers, I was told, snitch radios from tanks to use them in their homes; they forget to drain water from new trucks, in freezing weather, and the trucks are ruined.

Most of our passengers were military or quasimilitary folk—though we all had to wear civilian clothes—and I heard much talk about military affairs in Turkey. The Army is a considerable force for reaction here; the old men hang on, and keep bright youngsters from being promoted. One anecdote pleased me, though I don't vouch for its authenticity: when a Turkish army mission visited Eisenhower in Tunis, its members were deeply chagrined because they had to walk up hill a couple of times visiting the front. High Turkish officers *never* walk! They are always mounted. But Eisenhower didn't have any horses.

Also much talk of espionage and counterespionage. The Germans may kill spies in Istanbul if they catch them; and I picked up some fancy melodramatic details which I don't quite believe. For instance the Gestapo may trail a man in a crowd and prick him in the shoulder with a heavy hypodermic needle. The German Embassy is a huge structure, extraterritorial and thus inviolate to search; and sometimes people are kidnaped, taken there, and tortured. The bodies may be chucked into the Bosphorus, or—a nice touch—they are bundled into mail sacks and shipped by Lufthansa plane to Sofia, where they are easier to dispose of. The British kill too. What the British like is to entice some unwary agent over the border into Syria. They are just as tough at this sort of thing as the Germans. I even heard sentences like, "But lately we haven't been killing much."

In Ankara Mrs. Packer made waffles for breakfast. I called then at the Embassy and met Brigadier General Richard G. Tindall, our military attaché, Joseph C. Satterthwaite, the press attaché, and Michael Cordozo who is in charge of Lend Lease. Satterthwaite took me to the press department of the Foreign Office, and at six I saw Knatchbull-Hugessen. Dinner at Karpitch's, a gaunt Russian restaurant famous all over the Middle East, with American newspaper colleagues and a Turkish press officer, Nuzhet Baba, who is a character. From him, I got my transportation up to Istanbul tomorrow night. The first law of life in this part of the world is that, instantly you get into a town, you lay your lines toward getting out.

The planes and trains are impossibly crowded, and it may take weeks to get a reservation on the Taurus except by payment of preposterous backsheesh, or unless you are very lucky, which I was.

Ankara has, I found, changed literally beyond belief. I was here last in 1928, and in those days it was a muddy village with the makeshift atmosphere of an American frontier town; primitive, strenuous, unkempt, full of scaffolding, and busy. (It rather impresses the Turkish officials, incidentally, when I tell them that I was here, in their capital, fifteen years ago, long before most of them ever saw it.) Today Ankara is a neat, well-planned, well-built small metropolis, with broad boulevards, streets with curbs and traffic lights, clean modern taxis, sturdy shops, and a distinct atmosphere of propriety and modernity; it seems much more "Western" than Cairo; it even has the benison of telephones that work. I remembered the hotel I stayed in fifteen years ago (if you could call it that), while inspecting the Ankara Palace hotel which is now the pride of the town; the contrast was impressive, though I found it a little sad that the Turks should have sought to imitate the accouterments of a western European hotel so closely, with showcases in the lobby containing everything from colorful men's haberdashery to sapphire necklaces to novels by Louis Bromfield. I wandered around the town, saw the splendid new university (co-educational—in Turkey!), and looked at the shops. They are full of stuff. Earl Packer tells me he can buy things here which were absolutely unobtainable in his last post, Dublin. I saw automobiles in the shop windows (but without tires), frigidaires, Scotch wool, electric irons, and all manner of small manufactured goods, much of it German. The Turks take from both sides. The prices are of course fantastic. The fact that there is so much German material in the shops makes the average Turk think that the Germans are better off in such things than we are.

I went into a bookshop and had the unique experience
of buying a *Völkische Beobachter*, a *Journal de Genève*, a
Corriere della Sera, a Vienna *Tagblatt*, a Paris *Journal*,
and the Moscow *Izvestia* from the same counter. I went
through these papers closely when I got home. It was
fascinating to look at the amusement columns. Moscow
was playing Tschaikovsky's "Demon" and "Anna Kare-
nina." The *Journal de Genève* had a substantial editorial
exactly like a thousand that I used to read in League of
Nations days, and the ABC Cinema was showing Greta
Garbo in "Ninotchka." The Paris *Journal* looked drear.
Its headlines were noncommittal, like *Les Événements
d'Italie*; there were no advertisements of amusements at
all. The Vienna theaters seemed mostly closed, and I
could not identify anything that was playing in Berlin.
But it struck me extremely that the *Völkische Beobachter*
was still printing with fair completeness the proceedings
of the New York stock exchange. It was strange to read
in the official Hitler paper that "Amer. Lokom." was
12⅜, and "Dup. de Nem." 144.75, with "Int. Teleph. A
ausl. Zert." at 14.50 and "Mongomery" (*sic*) at 45. The
Moscow *Daily News* (in English) had a leading article,
"Extraordinary State Commission Nails Hitlerite Fiends
for Hideous Crimes," and described an investigation that
may promise interesting developments. Also I picked up
copies of the German propaganda magazine, closely
modeled on *Life* and printed biweekly in separate German,
French, and English editions, called *Signal*. It is certainly
a handsome job. Each issue has half a dozen pages in
color that rival anything we do technically. But the intel-
lectual content was laughable. One leading article was
about the "Meatleggers" of New York; another, "The
Spider and Its Web," described the "interlocking" relations of the Air Transport Command and Lend Lease; a
third, called "A Secret Understanding," traced a gigantic
Jewish "plot" linking Litvinov, Baruch, Frankfurter,

Rosenman, Harold Laski, Maisky, Steinhardt, and Lozovski.

Joe Satterthwaite took me for a drive along Embassy Row, or Atatürk Boulevard. The Russian Embassy stretches for a hundred yards up a terraced hill, behind a handsomely kept grove; next door is the German Embassy, equally ample and impressive. Von Papen, however, does not use it except as an office; for some reason he prefers to live in what was the Czech Legation. The Austrian Legation, ocher-colored and built to resemble an Alpine châlet, is now the German consulate. Nearby is the house of Ribbentrop's sister, the wife of a German engineer, Jenke by name, who has been a resident in Turkey for many years; she is known everywhere simply as "Frau Schwester." The British Embassy is not so big or ornate as the German or Russian, but it is—of course!—climactically situated at the very end of the row, and on a smart hilltop. As always when I look at buildings like these I feel considerable shame that we, the United States, are so provincial; we starve our diplomatic service. The American Embassy in Ankara is a small, mediocre, unhandsome rented building altogether unworthy of a nation in a community where prestige counts.

We looked at the great bronze statue of Kemal Atatürk in the center of town; every town in Turkey has one, but this is *the* statue of them all; storks perch on it day and night, which is thought to be good luck. Next to this statue—the symbolism is perhaps significant—is the Halk Evi or "People's House." This is a kind of combined recreation center, public library, YMCA, and culture headquarters for adult education, closely on the Russian model; every one of the 40,000 towns and villages in Turkey is supposed to have one. Nearby is Kemal's grave, which I wanted very much to visit. But he is buried in, of all places, the Archeological Museum, an old-style Turkish building with a dome and Moorish windows, and nobody is allowed in. Diplomats lay wreaths inside when they assume posts in Turkey, but otherwise the building is never opened.

At lunch today I began to learn something about Turkish prices. They are so high as to be a kind of substitute for rationing. Sugar is 75 cents per pound, butter $1.30 per pound, milk 50 cents a quart. The only basic goods rationed are coffee, the shortage in which is a great hardship to Turks, and petrol. The coffee ration is 125 grams, or roughly a quarter-pound, every three months.

At Karpitch's during dinner, we met some of the Ploesti fliers who had forced landings and are interned here. The orchestra at this restaurant is Rumanian, and it seemed odd that these young Americans should listen so attentively to music played by people of the country they had just bombed.

Ankara, Saturday, August 14.—Gradually I'm hearing about the diplomatic complexities of life in a neutral capital. Allies and Axis do not, of course, speak. The *corps diplomatique* has two *doyens*. But the Turks have one official reception a year to which both sides must be asked; the room then freezes into two vast hostile groups, with young Turkish attachés trying to glide between. Normally the Turkish Foreign Office has two parties to celebrate every occasion, which doubles the entertainment bills. Neutral diplomats—the Swedes and Swiss and so on—get invited to both.

Occasionally in less official society there come fabulous contretemps. One evening in the grand ballroom of the Ankara Palace the wife of a British naval attaché and Frau von Papen got hooked together, in the middle of a dance, and for an interval no one could tear the gowns apart. At such events as funerals, the neutrals tactfully slip into line between Steinhardt, say, and von Papen, while everybody tries not to stare too glacially. A swimming party was held recently at Kemal's model farm, where the great pool is shaped like the Black Sea. As if by instinct, the Russians and British took their positions on the north side of the pool, and the Germans clustered on the west, so that the party duplicated real political geography. (The Sea of Azov in this pool is used as a wading place for kids.) The Turks on the whole enjoy Allied parties best. This is because we permit dancing; the Axis doesn't.

I saw several Germans today. One was in a bookshop. Somehow, before I heard him speak, I knew that he was German; he wore nothing distinguishing beyond a dark gabardine suit and heavy owlish glasses, but the German note he gave was unmistakable, something in the set of the shoulders or the way he prowled through the aisles of books. Then at the Foreign Office I met at the top of the narrow circular stairs a slight young man in well-cut slacks and a tweed jacket. He might easily have been English. There was hardly room for both of us abreast, and I said, *"Après vous, monsieur."* He said, *"Après vous, monsieur,"* and we stared at each other, guessing. Then, at the same instant, we both started down the stairs together, shoulder to shoulder but not talking. At the bottom he started to giggle and I laughed.

This morning I called on Selim Sarpar, the director general of the Press Bureau, and Nuzhet Baba. Very hearty, very direct, very jovial. A far cry from the dream world of Cairo. Then lunch at the Packers' to meet dignitaries of the town, among them a Canadian banker, H. Somerville Smith, who knows a lot about fields of Allied operations here that may not be written about. Later there was discussion of Turkish censorship. One Turk told me, "It's all right for you to write that Hitler is crazy, but don't say that *we* said so."

Off to Istanbul at 6:10 on the Anatolian Express. The train was full of friendly, modern-minded, and realistic Turks. Two were deputies, who spoke English perfectly;

one had been in business in the United States for years, and the other—like so many Turkish intellectuals—was a graduate of Columbia. A third, who was in charge of the American desk in the Foreign Office, was extremely eager to show his good will; he said, "Ah, you are the flower among nations." The two deputies were vigorously talkative. I asked if they thought Turkey was a totalitarian state or not; one replied, "We're not interested in isms; we're interested in results." He asked me what I would call it if all the political parties in the United States banded together in patriotic union, for the sake of the nation. I said it depended; we might call it Fascism. In reply the Turks quoted Lincoln. Turkey, they said, certainly represents a government "of" the people and "for" the people, but it is not yet governed "by" the people. They insisted that democratic forces are getting stronger all the time.

Here are notes on this talk as I took them: What's wrong with Turkey? Bureaucracy. Hangover from early days. Corrupt sultanate administration. "How long does it take to cash a letter of credit here?" A whole day! . . . "What we're after is food, shelter, cheerful surroundings, friendly greetings from a neighbor." Saw neat model farmhouses as we whipped by. Quite impressive. . . . Bureaucracy makes vicious circle. You educate folks, then they want govt. jobs; so the more you educate, the worse the bureaucracy gets. . . . Clumsiness. Not enough adeptness yet at modern techniques. But really there is great attention to educ. here. Budget for educ. greater than any ministry except natl. defense. Educ. free compulsory for five years, 9-14 (?). I asked about Turk. imperialism. Nonsense to think of it. "Hell, we don't want territory. What we want is to lick malaria, and get milk for kids!"

I had picked up copies of the foreign-language newspapers published here, and after dinner I thumbed through them. The British-subsidized paper is *La Turquie*. It is maddeningly fair. It prints the war news in parallel columns, *Communiqués des Allies, Communiqués de l'Axe*. Even the Russian news is set under twin heads *Selon Moscou*, and *Selon Berlin*. The chief Axis paper is the French edition of *Cumhuriyet*, called *La République*. Its chief object seems to be to make people scared and angry; it is full of details of the "criminal" Allied air bombardment of Germany, with intimation of worse to come. The *Turkische Post*, another Axis sheet, talks about Nazi "victories" in Russia, and stresses U-boat sinkings; its *feuilleton* is a dull piece about the centenary of Field Marshal von der Goltz. The *Journal d'Orient* is supposed to be financed by Allied or Jewish money, but its complexion seems mixed. Its main feature is a serialized life of Bismarck; also it has a syndicated piece today by Major George Fielding Eliot. *Istanbul*, another French-language paper, subsidized by Vichy, quotes conspicuously a round-up of the United States press, and says that an accord with Russia is essential to Allied strategy; its *feuilleton* is the memoirs of Caillaux. Finally, there is a miserable Italian rag, the *Beyoglu*. Its biggest story is an analysis of the Sicilian campaign by the German commentator, Sertorius.

Dialogue with a waiter in the *wagon*-restaurant:

"Have you any whisky?"

"What kind whisky?"

"Scotch whisky."

"We have Turkish Scotch whisky."

I turned in early, and when I woke up we were skirting the Sea of Marmora. It was very beautiful. It looked like the French Riviera but less well-groomed.

Istanbul, Sunday, August 15.—Ambassador Steinhardt sent his motorboat to meet me; all the great embassies have these boats, which are indispensable for getting around in this area. Ours, the "Hiawatha," is more modest than most. I'm going to live at the Embassy. We cut through the harbor waters, from Haidar Pasha on the Asiatic side, past Stamboul and Galata, to Pera on the actual continent of Europe. I watched it all with deep emotion and avidity. This is the most princely, sage, and glorious of all views I have known in the world. The Seraglio had a creamy early-morning glow, and the dome and minarets of St. Sophia and the Blue Mosque held a balance, a richness and maturity that were breath-taking.

Breakfast with the Steinhardts, and then on the boat again for a long excursion, near Prinkipo and the other bejeweled islets almost incandescent in the sunshiny water. Boarding the boat I gaped. The Ambassador had wondered if I would know his other guests. Two or three were among my oldest friends, like G. E. R. Gedye and George Earle. Also aboard were Cyrus Sulzberger of the New York *Times*, the most accomplished and promising young foreign correspondent I have met in years, and Robert F. Kelley, Steinhardt's counselor. Gedye is a colleague from Vienna, where he was the correspondent of the *Daily Telegraph*; later he represented the New York *Times* in Moscow, and I last saw him there the week of the Russo-German pact. It was startling to see Earle as a commander in the Navy; he is assistant naval attaché here. Formerly of course he was American minister to Vienna and Sofia, and governor of Pennsylvania. I hadn't seen him for six or seven years. It all made quite a reunion.

In the harbor we saw more than pellucid beauty. We passed Inönü's yacht, and close by was a German tanker with a hole blown through its bow. A Russian submarine got it in the Black Sea, but it had managed to limp back to neutral refuge. A mile or so beyond were two handsome dark gray Rumanian liners, the "Transylvania" and "Bessarabia." They were caught here when Germany invaded Russia, and they have never dared to run back through the Black Sea to a Rumanian harbor.

We had a picnic lunch while Earle and Gedye fished, going round and round an islet. Then in the evening we drove deep into the silvery Bosphorus. At the end there is a boom; no ships are allowed to pass at night. All around here the Turks have established a forbidden zone. We had a moon; first it looked like a thin slice of melon, then it became the Turkish crescent. Just as we were thinking of the symbolism there came an eclipse; no one had known that an eclipse was due tonight. But mostly I kept thinking of something else. Here we were, directly between Europe and Asia, and our searchlight kept playing on the American flag stiffly waving at our stern.

Istanbul, Monday, August 16.—Lunch with George Earle at Abdulla's, which my friends assure me is the best restaurant left in Europe. He told fabulous stories of his last days in Sofia, his encounters with Jugoslav spies and Nazi agents, his final talks with King Boris. All afternoon roaming bazaars with Earle—who knows every shop and trinket—and a young Persian, by name David Musa Zade. Later I had a good talk with Steinhardt, getting myself oriented, and then an hour with a Bulgarian deputy who has just arrived from Sofia. Half the work here is watching Balkan stories.

Dinner at Abdulla's with Cy Sulzberger, Frank O'Brien of the AP, and the ebullient Ray Brock of the *Times*. We went on to a night club called Taksim's. This is new since my time. It is attractive. The building is set in a grove near the Bosphorus, and the restaurant surrounds a large open-air dance floor, where there is a floor show. Then above is a smaller, more intimate dancing place, with an orchestra, loges and a bar. The moon looks down on you, and you look down on Istanbul. Taksim's is the gathering place for everybody. It is full of Hungarian blondes who may, or may not, be spies. Half the fun is wondering who you will be sitting next to.

"Now look down that aisle, but not too conspicuously."
This is Cy or Ray speaking. "At the first table, that's the
Polish military attaché. Behind him, he looks uncomfortable, is a Gestapo man; handsome son of a bitch, isn't he?
He's the German agent specifically assigned to watch
Americans, he's the American 'expert' of the Gestapo. Now
look: that's Bergery coming in, he's the Vichy Ambassador. Right next to him is a Lend Lease guy; watch how
they dodge each other. There's the Swiss minister, bowing
both to Axis and us; at that corner table, see the pretty
girl; she's Hungarian of course; the chap with the monocle
is British; a Turkish officer slapped him here last night.
Here comes the Bulgarian chargé; right behind him is
one of our folks, but he's very hush-hush; I don't know
what he does."

I hear that Messina is about to fall. Steinhardt tells
me there is no news whatever of an Italian peace offer
so far.

Istanbul, Tuesday, August 17.—I hear more and more
conflicting talk about the Turkish army. This is partly
because of the strict secrecy with which the Turks—like
the Russians—conceal knowledge of their military stuff.
To cite just one example of this secretiveness: the naval
attaché of a friendly power (the Navy here is subordinate to the Army) had to wait eighteen months before he
was allowed on board a Turkish warship. The Turks say
that they have a million men mobilized, but most non-
Turks think the number is nearer 700,000. The troops
are stubborn, fatalistic, and distinguished by what I hear
called "a suffering kind of courage"; they are hardy
enough and quite well trained, but their equipment is
pretty terrible. Most mechanics in Turkey are Greeks. Yet
the Greeks aren't allowed to serve in the armed forces
except as unskilled labor. Discipline, I hear, is capricious;
very strict in some cases, lax in others. Mostly the privates
are terrified of their superiors, but junior officers are terri-

fied too; they're afraid of being blamed and punished in case anything goes wrong.

Lunch at the Embassy, and at three we took the boat up the Bosphorus again, to spend the afternoon and dine with Falih Rifki Atay, a deputy once close to Atatürk and now the editor of *Ulus*, the most prominent Ankara newspaper. Many Turkish politicians were there—though officially no member of the Turkish Government "ever" leaves Ankara—among them the chairman of the Foreign Relations Committee of the Grand National Assembly. I don't know which I enjoyed most: the political talk, or a poker game that developed. Turkish poker is deadly serious. The deck is stripped to the 5's, and the minimum bet was a Turkish pound, or 55 cents.

What a wonderfully sumptuous post Istanbul was for diplomats in the old days! Or even now, for that matter. Not only do foreign governments maintain establishments in both Ankara and Istanbul; most of them have, or had, summer places near Serapia on the Bosphorus. Today we passed the German Embassy here—the third giant German Embassy building I have seen in this country; it's a handsome twin structure with red slate roofs, and though it is quite modern it reminded me of something out of Grimm. The Russian Embassy—as always, it seems to be right next door—has grounds that stretch for miles, literally, behind the Bosphorus shore. The Italian is one of the ugliest buildings I ever saw; and the French is painted a dirty rust-colored red, the color of dried blood; it was thought that this color would please the sultan, and no one has ever bothered to repaint it. At one point today we passed the old castle which marks the narrowest part of the Bosphorus; here the water from the Black Sea and Sea of Marmora meet in a churning twelve-mile current; and it was here that the Turks first crossed from Asia into Europe.

Istanbul, Wednesday, August 18.—Cy Sulzberger, who

is off to Ankara this evening, came to breakfast and shared
with me some of his wisdom about the Balkans. I wrote
a broadcast, and then had lunch with Lewis Thomas and
Hal Lehrman, the O.W.I. men here. Steinhardt took me to
see Saracoǧlu in the afternoon, and I dined at Taksim's
with General Tindall and MacFarland.

I learned at lunch that the most popular novel published
here in the past twenty years—called *Chaly Kushu* if I
took notes aright—describes a Turkish girl educated in
an urban normal school, who goes out into the incredibly
backward rural districts to live and teach. Thomas, who
knows Turkey exceptionally well, said that what was
significant about this was that it was so popular. It
reflects what everybody thinks everybody ought to do.
The shortage of teachers is one of the gravest problems
of modern Turkey; it is appallingly difficult to get bright
young men and women out of the towns, into the remote
hinterland. All the young folks want, of course, to move
into Ankara or Istanbul.

Thomas talked about the religious situation. Kemal,
as we all know, did his best to abolish every trace of Islam
in Turkey, to establish a lay state. He was successful in
that religion is no longer a political issue of any consequence; yet people still pray, Thomas says. In fact, when
Atatürk died, children asked their teachers *how* they
could pray for him; and a mosque was actually built at
the site of his mother's grave, which probably made the
late dictator turn in his. Inönü himself presided at its
dedication.

I have a good talk with Steinhardt almost every day. He
doesn't give me any definite appointment, but any time
he has a spare ten minutes he's willing to squeeze me in
and let me ask questions. He is tireless and expert.

Istanbul, Thursday, August 19.—I wrote a story about
Saracoǧlu. Then a confused and busy day. I haven't even
had time to walk down the Grand Rue de Pera. Gedye

gave a lunch for the Steinhardts. Bright talk about how, legally, we are going to punish Axis criminals after the war; the Ambassador had sound ideas. At four I had a session with Burton Berry, our consul general, who is in charge of gathering Balkan information here. At six, tea at the Park Hotel. This is a formidable new structure, the most fashionable place in Constantinople and packed with Axis. But a few of our own people live at the Park now. One of them jibed, "The Turks really must realize now that the Germans will lose the war, because they're letting *us* infilter into the Park!" At seven, I called on a bright young man named Musifer, the engineer in charge of the local radio station; he was educated at the University of Michigan. Then a farewell dinner for Ray Brock at Taksim's. Among the guests: Sam Brewer of the Chicago *Tribune*, very astute, and Eleanor Packard of the UP, who has the deepest laugh I ever heard in a woman.

Gradually I'm getting accustomed to the extraordinary prices at Taksim's. A small drink of whisky is a flat two dollars American; a bottle of French champagne (a few survive) is $40. Mostly we drink Turkish cognac. It is, as a friend of mine once said in Vienna, very "spiritful." Brock has worked out an arrangement with the maître d'hôtel whereby we buy at cut rates. Even so, it costs 40 Turkish pounds a bottle, or $22.

Istanbul, Friday, August 20.—This was my broadcast day. It was weird. The equivalent of my New York time, 10 P.M., is 5 A.M. here. The Turks were completely co-operative even at this unearthly hour. There is no proper outlet in Istanbul, and so the technique is to talk over the telephone to Ankara, where the stuff actually goes on the air. Apparently an engineer has to be stationed every hundred miles or so along the line, to crank up the apparatus so that the voice will go through. Of course, too, the script has to be censored; and the censorship is in Ankara, not here. So I had telegraphed my script down to Nuzhet Baba, and he telephoned back to approve it, with a few minor changes. Meantime I had exchanged half a dozen wires with New York (at something like 75 cents a word, since Turkey has no deferred rate) to check on times and cues. And again today I explored the whole setup with Musifer and his engineers. I got to the studio at about four, and we raised Ankara on the wire. I had to begin by blindly guessing when the New York commercial would stop, because a last wire from the network didn't arrive in time. Everything seemed fine when I finished. Except (we found later) there were sunspots that morning, disturbing the atmospherics, and not a word got through.

The rest of the day was comparatively tranquil. I dined alone at a Russian restaurant called the Regence, the first lunch or dinner alone I've had in about six weeks, so it was quite a luxury. Years ago this restaurant was known as the Turquoise, and I had a New Year's Eve dinner there in 1928 with someone I am very fond of.

Istanbul, Sunday, August 22.—Into the boat, and up the Bosphorus to lunch with A. V. Walker, the head of Socony Vacuum here. We docked near the old Austrian Embassy, and it seemed strange to walk underneath a huge swastika. Jim Linen and George Britt of O.W.I. have arrived, and they made part of our group. Walker, like all big oil men, knows a lot; he talked mostly about Bulgaria and also *Varlik.* Late in the afternoon we crossed over to Asia, and had drinks in the Standard Oil rest house. Then into town with MacFarland, and dined at Abdulla's with Sam Brewer and a Hungarian friend whom I once knew in Budapest and who works here under a different name.

Talk on why the Turks are xenophobic. I had heard from several people, among them Somerville Smith in Ankara, that the root reason was the old regime of capitulations. But Brewer doubted this. He said that the Turks have always been contemptuous of foreigners, and that they gave them their own consular courts—in pre-Kemal days—in order not to be bothered with them.

At the Walker party a Polish lady was present, who told of unimaginable horrors when she was interned after the Russian occupation of eastern Poland. The Turks seemed to like this, I felt. Also among the guests was a wonderful old British admiral, by name, Kelley. He is well over seventy, and looks to be fifty-five. Winston Churchill sent him here when he, Churchill, was First Lord, because the Turks like *old men*, and Kelley was a friend of Marshal Cakmak, the venerable boss of the Turkish army. I thought this was a nice example of British foresight and astuteness.

Something occurred to me today: anything broadcast to the United States from Turkey reaches America without benefit of American or Allied censorship; this must be almost the only place in the world where this is true. Newspaper dispatches are, of course, censored in New York or Washington as they arrive, before publication; but there is no mechanism for stopping anything once it is on the air. (Anywhere else, of course, radio broadcasts are censored before they are transmitted, but, since Turkey is neutral, no Allied censorship exists in Ankara or Istanbul.)

Gedye tells me that a close friend of ours who was once the Vienna correspondent of an important American newspaper is now here, working for the chief Nazi news agency. I wonder if I will run into him. If Gedye sees him, they cut each other. But the Germans are, on the whole, encouraged to mix with us, if they can; they hope to pick up information that way. We, however, do not "mix" except in special circumstances. If you see an American or Briton with Axis folk, it means he has orders to this effect.

Istanbul, Monday, August 23.—Good talk this morning with Ahmet Emin Yalman, a Columbia graduate and the publisher of the newspaper *Vatan*. Then I shopped awhile, and at lunch met Muvaffak Menemencioğlu, the brother of the foreign minister and head of the official Anatolian News Agency. The Steinhardts had a dinner party for Linen and Britt, and I met another well-known Turkish editor, Dr. Esmer of *Ulus*, who also went to Columbia. One thing in a personal sphere struck me at dinner; I happened to sit between two Americans, Dr. Luther Fowle and Dr. Shepheard of the American hospital here, and found that both have sons at Deerfield Academy in Massachusetts, where my son goes too. Three Deerfield fathers in a row, 6,500 miles away in Istanbul!

From the Turkish editors I get the same prevailing impressions (which I have tried to sketch in the preceding chapter). They are emphatically pro-Ally; they want to keep out of the war as long as possible; they fear Russia. Someone suggested tonight that the Turks might achieve both of their supreme ends in foreign policy, (a) get a place at the peace table as an ally, without fighting, and (b) fend off the Soviet Union, by the single and simple expedient of letting the Americans and British into Turkey as an interim occupying power.

After the party, a long discussion with the Ambassador, Britt, and Linen. It centered on why our campaign is being handled so slowly in Italy. Three ideas: (1) Hesitancy on our part to take serious casualties. (2) The complexity of modern warfare, and the extreme difficulty of amphibious operations. (3) American worship of perfection. We hate to improvise; we don't go into anything until every smallest detail is absolutely ready and right. Someone told a nice anecdote—apocryphal I am sure—about a great airfield we built in an emergency but which we did not use for some weeks because the Coca-Cola machines had not been installed.

Cedric Salter, a British correspondent here, told a story about Duranty tonight. Someone said to Duranty reprovingly that he was not taking care of himself properly, whereupon Walter replied airily, "Oh, I die as I please."

Istanbul, Tuesday, August 24.—Today I called on Walker, at the Socony Vacuum offices, and then had lunch with George Earle. Dinner with Lehrman and Thomas of O.W.I., and on alone to Taksim's. I had mentioned to the proprietor that Jack Benny was in Cairo, and the Turks would love to have him here. They asked me how it could be managed, and I said the choice was simple; to get Benny to Istanbul would either cost them (a) Turkish neutrality, or (b) $10,000 per week.

Interesting experience late tonight. I had a two-hour talk with the young German who is chief of the "American" section of the Gestapo. We met way out in the wilderness somewhere. I think he wanted to "give," that is, sell out, and he thought I might be useful as an intermediary.

Istanbul, Wednesday, August 24.—Wrote two stories for N.A.N.A., and then a revised version of the broadcast that didn't get through. Then a talk with Earle C. Taylor, the commercial attaché. Also I have been asking Steinhardt about economic matters. Turkey is, of course, a peasant country, but industrialization is increasing all the time. Here, as almost everywhere in the world, the prevailing stress is toward state control, etatism, and the like. I collected a mass of stuff, which I will probably never use; one of the dismaying things about journalism is the enormous amount of material you accumulate, and which somehow, at the end, never gets into print. The government controls a number of banks here, and these, in the familiar Central European pattern, own or control the new mushrooming industries; so the government is itself represented in sugar, textiles, steel, paper, leather, glass, and, most important, mining. I heard it said: "The country isn't quite as state capitalistic as the government

would like it to be, but the government controls everything worth controlling anyway."

Lunch with some British friends at Abdulla's. Near us
was a group of "probable" Germans. They had a bottle
of actual Scotch on their table. "Of course they're German," said one of us. "Only Germans can afford Scotch
whisky."

In the evening, after a farewell dinner to the Steinhardts, I met some Czechs. "To Prague!" they kept saying. "To Benes in Prague!"

Istanbul-Ankara, Thursday, August 26.—Up at six,
and into the boat with Steinhardt and Kelley for the last
time. I looked at the incredible beauty of the harbor once
more, and wondered when I would see it again. Being
here has made me as fond of Europe as I've ever been.
Jim Linen caught the Taurus with me, and we pounded
on the rails all day to Ankara. Cy Sulzberger joined us
there; a crowd of all our friends had gathered to see
him off. Cy jubilant, because he has just got a long series
about *Varlik* through the Turkish censorship.

Chapter XIV

The World of the Middle East

D URING the last week in Istanbul, I spent an hour or two each afternoon talking to people who knew Central Europe and the Balkans well. Most of these were Americans, experts in the field, who use Istanbul as a watchtower. I tried to find out what was going on in the Axis satellites first—Hungary, Rumania, Bulgaria—and then in the occupied states, Albania, Jugoslavia, and Greece.

As far as the satellites are concerned I came away with one main conclusion. Strange as it may seem, it appears that the rank and file of people in these countries are on *our* side. The paradox has arisen that most of them, though German "allies," hope for an Allied victory; I even heard it said that they "pray" for Anglo-American invasion of the Continent as soon as possible, to deliver them from their Nazi masters. In other words the German Fortress—at this end of Europe at least—is filled with people who want us, their "enemies," to win. Above all, most of the satellite peoples do not consider the United States an actual enemy. They think of their war against us as largely a "paper war."

I was surprised to hear that neither Hungary, Rumania, nor Bulgaria, are as yet formally "occupied" by Germany. I had thought German troops filled them. But this isn't so. There are no German garrisons in either Hungary or Bulgaria; the only uniformed Germans in Hungary are technicians, personnel on landing fields, and the like, and in

Bulgaria some submarine crews at Varna, on the Black
Sea. In Rumania, it is true, there are some German troops,
but most of these are survivors from the Russian front,
sick or wounded men whom it is cheaper to feed in
Rumania than in the Reich. But Rumania is not formally
"occupied." Twice, in fact, the Rumanians have refused
German requests to increase their garrison, first after the
Hitler-Antonescu conversations in April, 1943, and then
following the Ploesti raid. The Nazis wanted to send an
armored division into Rumania as a "reply" to Ploesti.
The Rumanians answered, "What good is an armored
division against airplanes?"

The main reason the Germans do not heavily encrust
the Balkan satellites with troops is, of course, shortage of
man power. But also there are political reasons. Germany
likes to consider Hungary, in particular, its first "ally,"
and the propaganda value of this alliance, such as it may
be, would obviously be lost if the Nazis were forced to
take the country over. You shouldn't have to occupy "loyal
allies." Also, German occupation of Hungary might pro-
voke serious resistance; Hungarian partisans might rise,
which could involve more German troops than Berlin
cares to spare. Finally, it might deprive the Nazis of
Hungarian raw materials which they now get without
fighting.

I heard evidence from many sources of widespread pro-
Ally sentiment in the satellites. Bulgaria is a special case,
because Bulgarians are 90 per cent pro-Slav and pro-
Russian; Hitler has never been able to make the country
declare war on the Soviet Union. Such a declaration would
probably cause the collapse of any Bulgarian government.
Also the Bulgarians are moderately pro-American and
pro-British. Newspapers in Sofia print conspicuously announcements of broadcasts by Roosevelt and Churchill,
even now. As to Hungary, it seems more pro-Ally than
pro-German; Budapest has the atmosphere of a neutral

capital. The radio is quite free, and anybody can listen to anything. The best selling book in the country is, believe it or not, John Steinbeck's *The Moon Is Down*, which tells people of an occupied country just how to resist the Germans best. And such a Russian novel as Sokholov's *Quiet Flows the Don* is having wide popularity there. One Budapest newspaper dared early in the summer to assert openly that the Hungarian peasant has only one chance for a real future—an Allied victory—and a new liberal paper, the *Magyar Nemzet*, prints American and English *feuilletons* almost exclusively. All the Left Wing papers in Budapest are, in fact, more vocal than they have ever been before, and a kind of liberal Popular Front is being permitted to emerge. The reason for this is curious: Admiral Horthy, foreseeing the days of German collapse, is now giving as much encouragement as he dares to the Left, in order to have a counterbalance against the extreme Right which is still pro-Nazi.

The period of bitter and outspoken hatred of Germany in Hungary began with the battle for Voronezh in Russia last spring. Hungarians say that the Germans withdrew on both flanks without warning, thus leaving them as an exposed rear guard; they were slaughtered wholesale, while the Germans got away. Hitler flatly asked Horthy for more troops in April, 1943. Horthy refused.

Why, in view of all this, does Hungary not desert the Axis, and sue for peace? For one thing, it has acquired territory from Rumania and Jugoslavia, and in the event of surrender it would presumably have to disgorge this loot. Again, the Germans are close by and still powerful—the Gestapo is active everywhere—and they can exert enormous pressure on Hungary, a weak and exposed state. Horthy's basic line of policy is to try to keep Hungary from becoming another Jugoslavia, *viz.*, a battlefield.

Rumania next door is shivering with apprehension.

The Rumanians know that the Russians will take Bessarabia and Bukovina back, and that their Transistrian province (near Odessa, which they administer jointly with the Germans) can never be held. As to Transylvania Hitler divided that province between Rumania and Hungary, giving Hungary three-fifths; and the Germans still attempt to hold both Hungary and Rumania in line by threatening to give more of Transylvania to the other.

The Germans are unpopular in Rumania; only one movie house in Bucharest shows German pictures, and the leading play of the season has been "Anna Christie." There is very little anti-Allied material in the press, except in papers overtly subsidized by the Germans. When Hitler met Antonescu, the Rumanian dictator, he inserted into their joint declaration the pledge that Rumania would continue to fight not merely against the Soviet Union, but against the "Western plutocracies." This created much excitement, and the peasant leader, Julius Maniu—who still holds considerable power—went so far as to address a formal "protest" to the government. After Ploesti, sentiment against the United States might have been expected to rise. But it turned out exactly otherwise; the fact that we bombed them soundly raised our prestige with the Rumanians, and the Ploesti fliers who came down on their territory were well treated, so I hear.

Of course the basic orientation of Rumania has always been toward France. When the French collapsed, Rumanians were bewildered, and ever since they have felt anchorless and forlorn. Whatever we do to help France, will help us in Rumania too. A unified France on our side will produce good repercussions in Bucharest as well as Marseilles.

The chief obstacle to Bulgarian surrender and desertion of the Axis is that the country would lose much territory by so doing. The Bulgars got the Dobrudja from Rumania in the summer of 1940; then after the breakup in Jugo-

slavia they took the bulk of Macedonia, including a slice
that belonged to Greece. Thus their full territorial aspira-
tions were achieved at last; what the Bulgars had dreamed
of for fifty years had happened. We do not, presumably,
recognize these Bulgarian conquests; therefore we are in
the awkward position of trying to seduce the Bulgars out
of the Axis with one voice, while also telling them that
they must give up what they have gained. Another aspect
of the problem has to do with the U.S.S.R. The Bulgarians are, I've just said, at least 90 per cent pro-Slav
and pro-Russian; but this does not mean that they want
the Soviet Union to take over the country or that they
are 90 per cent communist. One estimate I heard is that
the country is 5 per cent pro-Fascist (the officer class
which is the ruling clique), 35 per cent pro-democratic,
60 per cent communist. What many Bulgars fear is that
if they drop out of the war, the country will be torn by a
revolutionary struggle between anti- and pro-communist
forces, and that it might be "absorbed" by Russia.

Germans are not much in evidence in Sofia—except
Gestapo—though German pressure is considerable. The
people, by and large, are so friendly to Americans that
the well-known American college in Sofia was permitted
to function even after the declaration of war against the
United States. One story is that the Bulgars made war
on us as a sop to Hitler, since they had refused to declare
war on the Soviet Union. Another aspect of Bulgarian
policy is worth noting: that every living Bulgar would
take arms and fight to the death to keep the Turks out
of the country. If the Allies should use Turkish troops to
assist an invasion of Bulgaria, it would almost certainly
drive the country straight into the arms of the U.S.S.R.
Bulgarian communists are, by the way, strictly nationalist;
they do not talk in terms of affiliation with the Soviet
Union, but only of a future *Bulgarian* communist state.

Preoccupation with Russia is of course a dominant

factor everywhere in the Balkan area. Many Hungarians
and Rumanians and Bulgars hope for an Allied victory,
as I have said; but they want this not only so that we
may deliver them from Hitler, but because then—they
think—we may "save them from the bolsheviks." Fear
of Russia is almost as pronounced in Bucharest as it is in
Istanbul. And the Germans do their best to play up the
bolshevist bogey as a device to keep the Balkan states
subdued.

Do the Russians want revolution in the Balkans? Most
of the well-informed people I met in Istanbul thought not.
They suggested, in fact, that the dynamics of this whole
issue have changed. Whereas in former days bolshevik
agents might have provoked subversive dissension in
various countries, hoping thus to manufacture a communist conspiracy or uprising, nowadays there is much
more possibility that the countries themselves will independently adopt communist or semi-communist forms of
government, and ask Russia to take them in. The shoe is
on the other foot. It is no longer a question of Bela Kun,
say, being sent from Moscow to Budapest; it is a question
of some latter-day revolutionary arising in Budapest and
asking for sustenance from Moscow. I mention this quite
without consideration of the indisputable trend in Russia
itself toward the liquidation of international communism,
the abolition of the Comintern and so on. Purely from
the point of view of the Balkans themselves, the situation
has vastly changed. This is partly because of the enormous
irrigation and fermentation in social thought the war
has produced, partly because the evolution of Popular
Front, Leftist-peasant movements in the Balkans is an
inevitable concomitant of the economic realities of the
region. Also the upswing of revolutionary or semirevolu-
tionary tendencies is the result of repression by reactionary governments, as in Hungary, and because the best
underground organization, which survived and fought

the Nazi terror with most tenacity and endurance, was almost always the Communist party. Finally it is the result of the enormous polarizing force of Russia itself, especially since the massive German defeats at Stalingrad and in the Ukraine. The little countries are drawn to Russia, their nearest great neighbor, as to a giant magnet.

Turn now to Greece, which is a course in a different category than the satellites. Greece, like Jugoslavia, is an ally which the Nazis have temporarily overrun, and the situation there is painfully complex. In Cairo, as we know, King George II heads the Greek Government-in-exile; within Greece, at least two guerrilla organizations with powerful civilian support have brought the country to the verge of civil war.

In general, everywhere in Greek circles, I found vivid opposition to the king and the official regime. This is based on a number of factors. As I heard it put somewhat cruelly, "Well, George isn't a Greek, and anyway most Greeks don't like kings." And I heard a purported remark which George's father, the fate-smitten Constantine, is once supposed to have made to his son: "Never forget that you're not Greek, and never let the Greeks remember it." The Greek royal house is, of course, German in origin; and it has not helped King George's popularity that his brother and presumptive heir, Prince Paul, married a German princess, and that his sister married an Italian. Be that as it may, other than dynastic considerations have more concrete bearing on the situation. What all anti-royalist Greeks resent most is that George returned to power in Greece (November, 1935), under a pledge to restore constitutional government. All the republicans, all the forces representing democracy in the country, said in effect, "Give him a chance." Within nine months, on August 4, 1936, the king dissolved parliament, and turned the government over to a Fascist dictator, General Metaxas. Perhaps the king's hand was forced by circumstances beyond his control. But people have not forgiven him that his country was ruled until Metaxas died by a clique of what were called the "August Fourth" military reactionists.

The situation today is that George is not boss in his own house. He behaved with the maximum of courage and resource during the German invasion in 1941; he stuck it out in Crete to the very last, and only barely escaped with his life. Nevertheless, things have not gone well. For a time George's government—recognized by the Allies and supported powerfully by the British—sat in London. In March, 1943, came the curious and little-known mutiny or "revolt" of the Greek army in Syria. This revolt was, in large measure, simply a gesture of irritation and impatience by Greek troops stationed in the Levant that they were not being used. But also it had profound political overtones. It was, in fact, made by republican officers, behind whom were the rank and file of soldiery, as a protest against the royalists. The revolt had to be put down by force. Then in August came a counter-revolt, made by royalist officers; its leaders were arrested and interned. They were Metaxas' survivors, "Fourth of August" men.

As a result of the March imbroglio two things happened. First, George and his government moved to Cairo, to be nearer the scene. Second, the king liberalized his Cabinet. In fact—strange paradox—the Cabinet now contains no fewer than four professed republicans, among them Sophocles Venizelos, the son of the late great republican leader. The four have, moreover, the key posts, except the prime ministership; they hold the portfolios of vice premier, war, navy, and aviation. The prime minister is Emmanuel Tsouderos; he is known as a "moderate" republican, having been a Venizelist deputy from Crete for many years.

Pressure against the king became so great in the summer of 1943 that, largely on British advice, he made a radical new declaration of policy. What the king wants is a chance to return to liberated Greece at the head of his army. Then, if the country says so, he is willing to get out. The new declaration is a pledge to appoint a coalition ministry representing all parties which, after liberation, will hold elections for a constituent assembly. This assembly will decide finally whether Greece shall be a republic or a monarchy, and the king promises to abide by its decision. In other words the king has consented to let the people choose as to the future of his person. But this has not quite settled the issue. Because the republicans say that the king must not return to Greece until *after* the elections; they fear, of course, that he will influence them. And George wants to be there.

Inside Greece the two main guerrilla parties are both anti-royalist. There is good reason for this. The bulk of the Greek army did not escape after the Nazi invasion. Only a handful of officers and the rich managed to get out. It cost money to get out. So the soldiers and peasants who remained in Greece, who have been enduring the most savage hardship ever since, who have seen thousands upon thousands of their countrymen dying of starvation, have no great fondness for the royalist émigres living in comparative comfort abroad. This brings up a point that will, I think, play a considerable role in the future, not merely in Greece (and in Jugoslavia) but everywhere in Europe. The great political cleavages are apt to take on a new form. It won't be so much a question of Left versus Right, say, or of socialists versus conservatives, or townsmen versus the peasantry. It will be a new and more fundamental cleavage between those who got out, and those who stayed in; between those who lived in safety abroad (though devoted to strenuous patriotic activity) during the war, and those who did not get out: those who fought and labored and suffered *at home,* directly under the Nazi hammer.

The Greeks are tremendously pro-American. They would like to see the United States take a pronounced role in Balkan affairs. Partly this is because they think we have no ax to grind, and that we may be a counter-weight to future British (or Russian) influence.

This raises another point. In Greece as in Jugoslavia the partisan movement, closely interlaced with agrarian communism, apparently grows stronger all the time. And the United States and Great Britain will, sooner or later, have to decide with sober responsibility what attitude to take toward these partisan or Popular Front movements all over Europe. Once they are genuinely rooted in the people, they cannot, I am convinced, be overcome except at a grisly cost in good will and perhaps bloodshed. Surely what happened in France points up the issue: the more we sought to support Giraud, the stronger De Gaulle became. If we continue obtusely to follow a Metternich policy and support reactionary forces, we will inevitably help produce exactly that which we wish to prevent—revolution. Because, as prospects of Allied victory become brighter all the time, the people of Europe who have been oppressed by Fascism are bound to break out against it.*

One more word. If this is not a war for peace—in the Balkans and everywhere else—I do not know what it is. Yet there can be no peace if the United States removes itself from the world as it did in 1919. Everywhere in this area I have found deep apprehension that, once again, we may walk out of the peace. In order to keep the United States in the peace we have to do two things: conquer hatred, and conquer fear. And let me repeat: this is a war *for* peace. If we do not finish the job this time it will

* As this book goes to press there are signs that the worldly and realistic British, on military as well as political grounds, see the way the wind is blowing, as witness their shift in support from Mihailovitch to the Partisans in Jugoslavia.

have turned out to be the silliest war in history, because one new giant fact emerges from every development, every event: without United States participation, there will be no peace.

Aleppo, Syria, Saturday, August 28.—We pulled in at about 7 A.M. Trip not too bad. For some reason bedbugs, even the choice variety on the Taurus Express, do not like me. The RAF offered us a lift to Beirut, but we decided to go by road instead, to see more of the country. We piled into two cars, the State Department station wagon, which our couriers use, and another in which Barclay Hudson, the O.W.I. man at Beirut, met the train.

All day on the road, through territory I have not seen since 1929, when I had a trip in Syria with Vincent Sheean. We paused for a moment at the fine old town of Homs, and had lunch near the spacious ruins of Baalbek. I remembered Mount Hermon; it still looks like a tiger, striped with snow. We passed a number of British and Greek camps, all very neat and efficient, and I was impressed by the tremendous attention paid to malaria control. There are huge signs along the blanched roads, warning troops where not to pitch camp.

I put up at the Hotel Normandie, Beirut. Steamingly, swelteringly hot. Drinks with Sulzberger and the British PR officer here, the amiable Captain J. P. Henderson. Then dinner alone in a French restaurant across the street. The headwaiter asked me to write a letter to his sister in Chicago, from whom he has not heard in seven years. I walked a bit in what seemed to be a comedy blackout, and then wrote a story about Hungary which Cy offered to take to Jerusalem and file.

Beirut, Lebanon, Sunday, August 29.—This is Election Day, and I began to hear about Lebanese and Syrian politics from breakfast on. But I managed to squeeze in a quiet swim in the broiling sun, and then had lunch with George Wadsworth, our diplomatic agent and consul general here, an old and valued friend who loves his job and has encyclopedic knowledge of the region. I asked him a question, "Who really runs this place?" He replied, "Do you want an answer or a speech?" I said whatever he chose. He said, "The answer is that the French run this place. Now to explain that answer I must make a speech." Then he talked with the utmost discrimination and detailed exactness for an hour.

Dinner with Major General Sir Edward Louis Spears, who holds a double job: he is British minister to Syria and Lebanon, and also head of the "Spears Mission," the liaison mission between British and French. His wife is Mary Borden, the novelist. Driving up to his house I had noticed more signs of the election—young men haranguing crowds, trucks pounding through the streets, and so on. I asked what the election was "about." Every face at the table drooped in a tragi-comic manner, and everybody said that this would take a long time to explain. Spears has been here since 1941, I believe; he was formerly an M.P., and is one of Churchill's closest friends. Also he is known in local circles as the "creator" of De Gaulle. He went to France on the last desperate British mission there, before the collapse at Bordeaux, and he was largely responsible for getting De Gaulle safely out of the country. His present post, Syria, has made a mountain of trouble. Most people tell me he has handled it very well; some think he has "coddled" the French too much.

At lunch we heard that King Boris of Bulgaria is dead. This struck me sharply, because before I left Istanbul I wrote a brief Bulgarian story which began, "Competent observers here think that the situation in Bulgaria next door is coming to a head so rapidly that it may reach explosive climax before this dispatch arrives in New York." And my guess is that this story will have reached New York only today.

Beirut, Monday, August 30.—As a matter of fact the Syrian political situation has not changed basically since I was last here. Predominantly, it is still a struggle between the French who want to hold onto the mandate at all costs and to the bitter end, and the Syrian and Lebanese nationalists who hope to get rid of French control. But since the war this struggle has naturally become exacerbated, and now it is even more dangerously complex and intertangled than before.

The curse of Syria is, as everyone knows, sectarianism. There are at least twenty different religious cults in the country, most of which want their own special political representation. For years the French kept the country divided into five separate areas; this was done partly to correspond to the natural fragmentations, partly to make the country easier to handle by splitting and subdividing the Moslems. The Christians are mostly concentrated in the Lebanon, which has a large Moslem population too. But the overriding point to make is that almost all the Lebanese and Syrian groups, of whatever creed, are now dominated by a single aspiration and emotion, their desire for authentic independence. Lebanon and Syria want to be completely independent sovereign states

They claim, moreover, that they have a juridical basis on which to ground this hope. In 1941, following German use of Syrian airports in the Iraqi fighting, the British and Free French ousted the Vichy French from Syria, after five weeks of bitter fighting. Thereupon, General Georges Catroux, the French commander-in-chief and now one of De Gaulle's top men, formally proclaimed the independence of Syria and the Lebanon. This statement was categorical. But ever since the French have sought to wriggle out of this pledge and whittle it down. A long and viciously angry period of political bickering began, leading to the elections which took place yesterday. Twice this year the French have ousted the Chief of State in Lebanon by peremptory methods; the "country" has had three different presidents since March, which has made popular feeling intensely bitter.

Things are so mixed up that mention of any particular issue leads to hours of complex discussion. For instance Syria, with its capital at Damascus, stands all-out for complete independence, without qualification. But most Christian Lebanese want "complete" independence plus a certain measure of foreign protection, because they fear the Syrians. The Moslems want to break up the Lebanon. And some Lebanese would prefer a rump-state, exclusively Christian. The French of course take advantage of such frictions. Also they exercise autocratic financial control over both states. The British line has been generally to play with the French, but with full attention to the explosive potentialities of Arab nationalism. For instance it seems to be the British view that although France has "proclaimed" the independence of the Lebanon, the French should retain their mandate until the League of Nations itself terminates it. But the League is extinct politically, and could not terminate the mandate if it wanted to. At the same time the British have also done their utmost to wean Syria and Lebanon toward free elections. But the result of these—if they mean anything —can only be the end of French power. So the British line, like ours, is a kind of straddle.

Basically, of course, British policy looks further afield. What the British want fundamentally is (a) to encourage development toward a broad Arab federation in the whole Middle East, and (b) to keep the area quiet under British influence, so as to preserve the security of imperial communications, and avoid trouble in other Arab states.

The French delegate general is Jean Helleu. I'm told that he was appointed some years ago to be Vichy minister to Persia. He applied, however, for a job with De Gaulle, who turned him down. Then Vichy promoted him to be Ambassador to Turkey, whereupon De Gaulle took him in.

The American point of view is to work for tranquillity and a decent settlement. We recognize that Syria and Lebanon have a kind of "limited independence," which they cannot exercise fully on account of the exigencies of war. Unofficially we promise them—not full independence —but support of their desire for independence, when the war is won.*

As far as military affairs are concerned the Lebanon, like Egypt, impressed me as being something of a backwater. The headquarters of the British Ninth Army are here, and many French troops are in evidence; they are, however, mostly Syrian or Senegalese; there are very few French *white* troops. Beirut, like Cairo, is valuable as an entrepôt and a training center; also it could be the fountainhead of a new route of supplies further east, and to Russia. There is a good deal of attempted espionage by Germans here—I even heard rumors of Nazi agents being dropped by parachute—and every once in awhile the frontier to Turkey is declared "closed."

Dinner tonight with Captain Henderson and two British officers, one navy, one army. We went to a Russian night club, full of French. One young Frenchman kept saying he was "a veteran of the last war." I did not understand until I realized he was talking about the war in France, 1939-1940. Another French officer got very tight. He kept singing and shouting, "I believe in France! To hell with communism! It happens that I am a royalist! But to hell with royalism too! Vive Stalin!"

A young man of neutral nationality came in. My com-

---

* In November, 1943, all this came to angry climax. The Lebanese nationalists, having taken power, voted to remove all French controls. M. Helleu lost his head and forcibly dissolved the nationalist chamber; several days of rioting took place. In December it was announced that the French would surrender to the "Syrian and Lebanese governments all legislative and administrative functions."

panions looked embarrassed. They had been guests in his house the week before. But now they have been told that he is "suspect," and perhaps an Axis agent; so they had to cut him without being able to tell him why.

You could fireproof a building with Syrian matches, which are made of the most uninflammable wood I ever saw.

Cyprus, Tuesday, August 31-Wednesday, September 1. —Pat Henderson suggested that I fly over to Cyprus for a day, and he fixed up the transportation. I've never been there, and so I was delighted. But when we arrived at the Beirut airport I wondered if I were not mildly out of my mind. The plane was Egyptian, built in the middle 1920's; it was a 4-motor job, tied together somehow, and it looked like a child's toy; the motor housings seemed made of rough plasticine. No wingflaps, no landing brakes, and wheels that didn't retract. But it flew nicely—we just skimmed a camel taking off—and even though we were traveling over water in what was indisputably a land plane, I did not worry much. One of the passengers was a fat Egyptian lady with two stout children; every time a child was sick, which was often, the party of three walked back to the toilet; this pushed our tail down and almost made us stall; the pilot, Captain Yehia Lotfy (who told me he has done 3,500 hours) would hold onto the controls with one hand, and with the other try to make the lady and children stick to their seats. Far cry from a C-54!

Arrived at Larnaca, one of the Cyprus airports, at 2:45 P.M.; we were told that we would drive to the summer capital, Troödos, two hours away. Actually the trip took almost four; Troödos is up in the hills, above 6,000 feet. We rose from the hot and dusty coastal plain, which looks like Syria, to pine woods that look like Maine. All the flat places are filled with obstructions, to prevent enemy landings by glider. Boys sold apples on the road; we saw signs in English, Greek, and *old* Turkish; and I learned that the

native population suffers unanimously from an illness
known as Cyprusitis, or the desire to do nothing.

Captain W. Byford Jones, the PR officer, was waiting
in a mountain camp at Troödos, and we dined with the
governor, Sir Charles Woolley. Again I was impressed
admiringly by the superb British talent for living as Brit-
ons anywhere; this "governor's cottage" might have been
a rectory in Hampshire. Its freestone walls were remarkable, colored alternately a bright dark blue and a clear
lucent red; and it happened that these were exactly the
colors of the sunset, which was approaching. The governor took me for a walk. We hiked along an edge of rock,
above a solid foam of clouds. Far below, between Paphos
and Limassol, was the place where Venus rose from the
sea. And I thought of lines from James Elroy Flecker,
of "black Cyprus ringed with a lake of fire." The governor explained the difference between a "Cyprian" and a
"Cypriot" as we walked, but I'm afraid I didn't quite
understand. Then to dinner. There was a splendid wood
fire burning. Along with the entrée came an alert; the Germans raid Cyprus from Rhodes every once in awhile; but
nobody bothered to get up. Then—of all things—we listened to the BBC relaying a speech of Mr. Churchill's
from Quebec. I don't think I've ever felt the power and
immediacy of radio in more dramatic or picturesque surroundings.

The next morning Byford Jones drove us down to the
airport, and I caught the same Egyptian plane going back
to Cairo. The pilot said that an aircraft of this type was
hard to handle. "It is like a cold woman: not responsive
to controls."

The story of Cyprus—another island bastion of the
type the wonderful British have scattered all over the
world—is the story of an island that thought itself
doomed, and then escaped death. When Crete fell in the
spring of 1941, everybody assumed that Cyprus would,

of course, go next. The island was virtually defenseless. But the Germans did not attack. The British got to work and in a miraculously short time Cyprus was in a position to defend itself. A big garrison moved in, and airfields were built everywhere. Now Cyprus is not only fairly safe from attack; it could, like Malta, turn the tables and become a springboard for offensive action against Rhodes and the Axis-held Dodecanese. Rhodes is, however, about three hundred miles away, which makes Cyprus too far distant to be wholly satisfactory as a fighter base. The enemy is very curious about what we are doing on Cyprus, and reconnaissance planes come over—very high—to investigate. They don't get through very often.

There is an interesting political problem here. The population is four-fifths Greek (the minority, which makes little trouble, is mainly Turkish), and they stand overwhelmingly for what they call "Enosis," or union with Greece. During the early phase of the war, even when the Nazis invaded and took Greece, the stubbornly nationalist Cypriots were very cool to Britain. Now, however, as it is clear that the Allies are going to win the war, the temper has changed somewhat. The nationalist leader is the head of the Greek Orthodox church, and he swerved to a moderately pro-British stand some months ago; so did the leaders of Akel, the labor organization, which had been very anti-British and anti-war. Very few Cypriots speak English, incidentally. The islanders still call the period 1932-1942 the "black decade"; there were serious nationalist riots, and the British had to take repressive measures. Most of these have now been lifted.

Then I heard the story of the Hungarian glamour girls of Cyprus. When war came, about forty-five young cabaret dancers from Budapest were working on the island. They could not get out, of course. Since then, about fifteen more have strayed in from Turkey. They are technically enemy aliens, and they must report to the police three times a week, but such is the remarkable elasticity of political and human nature that they have become socially *élite*; in fact they dominate the unofficial life of the island. They are chic and pretty, and they set styles for everybody; the Greek and Turkish women copy their clothes and the way they do their hair; they are the undisputed after-hour queens of the British colony. These girls can, at a hundred yards, identify any kind of uniform, and they know the exact pay of every category of officer. Over all the Middle East they have become famous. Regiments come and go, and officers carry legendary word of Fräulein Lili or Fräulein Kathi to Bagdad and Khartoum and Basra and beyond. Some of the girls have fine Scots accents now. They have transformed Cyprus from a beleaguered and somewhat arid island into an arbor of romance; they have made good the legend that Venus was born here. . . . When Hungary declared war on Britain, all the girls were told that, for the sake of propriety, they would have to shut up shop. But the ban only lasted three days.

Cairo at 7:15 P.M. after a long and tedious flight. I was too tired to call anybody up, and I worked awhile and went to bed.

Cairo, Thursday, September 2.—The hotel is in a fine frenzy, and so is everybody else, because there happen by odd chance to be three Gunthers registered. One, a treasury official, carries my first name too; he wired Kirk from Teheran and the minister wondered how on earth I had got there.

This afternoon I had talks with several extremely nationalist Egyptians; they were so violently anti-British that they prejudiced their own case. They used the word "Quisling" to describe Egyptians friendly to Britain, which startled me. Of course—so they say—they hope that the Allies will win the war. The Axis is "the enemy of humanity." But, they add, British rule "is almost as bad." Every time that Mr. Roosevelt says something encouraging about the status of the future world, Mr. Churchill takes it back the next day. Yet—they all insist —they are "loyal." I asked why they did not demand a better price for their loyalty. They replied that it was not a question of price, but of *right*. And they talked of fifteen million Egyptians being "slaves."

It is Ramadan just now, the month-long Moslem holiday. So all the waiters and taxi drivers have gone to pieces. No Moslem may eat or drink or even—strictly speaking—swallow his own saliva between dawn and sunset during the long days of Ramadan, and their nerves naturally give way. So do ours.

Grant Parr of NBC is away, and his assistant, G. E. Janssen of the American University here, is helping me fix up a broadcast which I must do at the unearthly hour of 5 A.M. (But again, as in Turkey, it didn't get through.)

Calling at one of the American offices here I heard an odd little story. An infantry captain said that he had just chanced to run into his own son, who is also an infantry captain, and whom he had not known was within a thousand miles of Cairo.

A British friend, a civilian, told me tonight on Shepheard's terrace that the Allied invasion of the Italian mainland will begin tomorrow.

Cairo, Friday, September 3.—Years ago, in a series of articles about Egypt for the Chicago *Daily News*, I wrote that the struggle for power here was triangular: between the British, the Wafd or nationalist party, and the king. This still seems to be true, though with certain modifications. The British have an Embassy in Cairo now, not a Residency; the Wafd has had a series of upsets and rebirths, and the king is a different king; but the permanent realities remain much the same.

All Egyptian politicians are anti-British, except outright tools. This is the first rule of life in Cairo. The only differentiation is *how* anti-British they are. Until 1936, when the Anglo-Egyptian treaty giving Egypt qualified independence came into effect, all political parties in Egypt had the same policy. There was only one platform: Independence from Britain.

For many years the two leaders of the Wafd were Nahas Pasha, who is at present prime minister, and his close friend Makram Ebeid, a Copt. Now these Wafd chieftains have quarreled venomously, following a scandal that ripped Cairo asunder. Makram was for a time minister of finance under Nahas. Then he was dropped from office, and he presented a petition to the king in the form of a "Black Book," detailing various scandals in which he alleged Nahas to be involved. People thought that Nahas could not weather this crisis. But he did weather it, and Makram, after being expelled from the chamber, retired out of public life. This story would not be worth telling except for a reason. The reason is that any quarrel between Egyptians always plays into British hands.

After the treaty in 1936 the tenor of Egyptian politics changed subtly. Egypt was now "independent." So the Wafd—which under Nahas had always screamed for nationalism—lost its chief *raison d'être*. But the fact that British troops remained in the country was, of course, a restriction on complete Egyptian sovereignty. So the various parties developed a double policy: if in power, they supported the treaty; if out of power, they attacked the treaty as strongly as they dared, urging further progress toward an independence more complete. But when any party, such as the Wafd, got into power, it had to stand by the treaty, because without the treaty it was helpless. Moreover the treaty, a binding obligation, could not be disavowed. So it developed that the opposition became more and more nationalist: the only way to attack the government was to attack the British too, since they had become intertwined. The government, analogously, had to be pro-British. The general rule nowadays is that when opposition becomes too obstreperous, it mysteriously gets absorbed "into" the government. All manner of Egyptian politicians, once violent nationalists, are now pro-British within the government fold. Nahas is a conspicuous example.

When war came in 1939 the prime minister was an independent named Ali Mahar. The Wafd was in opposition. Ali Mahar was a palace man; he was a close friend of Farouk, the new king, and chief of the royal Cabinet. Ali Mahar is the only exception to the rule that prime ministers become progressively less and less anti-British as they solidify themselves in office. He became a nuisance after awhile and the British had to get rid of him; the relationship between Britain and Egypt was inevitably strained under pressure of the war, especially after Italian entrance into hostilities. (The late king, Fuad, was educated in Italy; the palace was full of Italians, and Fuad was generally regarded as being pro-Italian. This, incidentally, is not true of his son, Farouk.) Ali was removed as prime minister, and eventually interned.

Early in 1942 Nahas became prime minister. Almost to the moment of his appointment, he had been making fiery anti-British speeches. But the British decided that it would be a good thing, given all the circumstances, to let the Wafd come back into power; it was the most popular and best organized party in the country; it could best keep the bulk of people in line, and doubtless it would be chastened by the responsibilities of high office. By making Nahas prime minister the British could shut him up. But there was an obstacle—the king. Because the palace felt that the Wafd, in power, would become *too* pro-British, and moreover the king didn't like Nahas; he wanted to rule as well as reign. As a result came the most picturesque crisis in the history of modern Egypt, on

February 4, 1942. The king found himself subjected to a very direct form of pressure, and the British Ambassador—with tanks in the palace yard—"suggested" to him that Nahas become the next prime minister. Since then the king and Nahas have scarcely been on speaking terms, and Nahas has played the British game to the hilt.

This has been a lively day. I had talks with several of our O.S.S. men, with Russell Barnes of O.W.I., with Colonel Stephens, the British censor, and with R. G. Casey, the minister of state, whose job is to be a kind of super-co-ordinator, responsible to London, for the three British armed services. I called on Philip Astley to say good-by, and had lunch with Kirk; he told superb stories of his ceremonial visit to Ibn Saud, the king of Saudi Arabia.

At 8:30 P.M. Lieutenant Commander Atif of the Egyptian navy picked me up, and we drove out toward Heliopolis. We sat on the terrace of the Heliopolis club for awhile, and after half an hour King Farouk walked in. He was quite alone; he sat down informally, and we talked till midnight. Again I was impressed by this young man's hearty good humor, restlessness, and enormous physical vitality. When he laughed, with echoing gusto, the whole terrace shook; people at other tables glanced at us, but paid no overt attention; the king's powerful informality of manner is well known. His talk covered a lot of ground, from how he loves milk shakes to how he hates cats, from Ibn Saud to Ginger Rogers, from psychoanalysis to the Dardanelles, from Willkie to his father to Mr. Roosevelt. Above all Farouk—who was perfectly discreet about the British and about internal politics—was interested in what role the United States would play after the war. I did my best to reassure him.

I heard a nice story about Eisenhower today. When he was making up his staff, just after he received the supreme command, a subordinate officer presented him with a list of names, all marked with an "A" or "B."

Eisenhower asked with his realistic, cheerful voice: "What are those A's and B's for?" His aide replied that these denoted whether the officers available for appointment were American or British. Eisenhower said, "Print the list over again without the A's and B's and then I'll make up my mind."

Chapter XV

The Wings of the A.T.C.

Cairo, Saturday, September 4.—I reached Heliopolis at about 9 P.M. I didn't know finally that I would get off tonight until four this afternoon, so the last three or four hours were insanely complicated. There was no phone in my room this time, and anyway nobody can ever get anybody else on the phone in this city. I had to go out to a corridor booth every hour to try to get through to the A.T.C. to find out when I was sailing. They make up the priority lists at the very last moment. Each call took six or seven minutes. The switchboard girl does her best. She must have nerves of corduroy. I had asked Cy Sulzberger and his wife to dinner, also Bob Parham, and I tried to call them to cancel it. I had two stories to write for next week's broadcasts, and I gave them to Janssen to clear through censorship. Then I packed. Kirk had told me it was essential to leave a card at the palace and Janssen drove me there. I cashed some money and paid my hotel bill. The Sulzbergers popped in just as dusk fell sharply on the terrace; we clustered into a group with one of the Ploesti fliers. Then I was infinitely pleased to see General Beaumont-Nesbitt grope through the dimout; he had called to say good-by. We all had a drink or two in the darkness, and then it was time to start. I drove to Heliopolis in a dilapidated taxi, and had a moment of pure panic thinking that the driver, who knew no English, had not understood where to go. He kept taking odd turns and gesticulating. The A.T.C. had said 9 P.M. sharp, and I didn't want to miss a trip to the United States by being five minutes late. Our blue headlights prodded through the dark streets. I felt for my gear and wondered if I had forgotten anything. I hated to leave my steel helmet behind, though I had never bothered to wear it in Sicily and in fact had never used it except to flush out a dirty can.

They wouldn't let the taxi through the gates at Heliopolis. In shadowy darkness I felt my way to the nearest building, and inside were lights and a telephone. The A.T.C. hangars were a couple of thousand yards down the field. Yes, they would send someone to the gate. Then an American jeep drove up. The corporal said he thought he could find the hangar and he gave me a lift.

When I reached the A.T.C. office I knew I was among friends again. The dispatching officer had bright red hair, and I wondered why all dispatching officers are, apparently, redheaded. Cheerfully he checked my name against his list and made out my ticket. But the whole atmosphere of this take-off was dim and confused. Even the sergeant behind the desk wondered why I was taking the southern route, and I had the impression that I could have got on a northerly plane if I had asked. Two or three days before I had told General Brereton that I wanted to return across Africa, no matter how long it took; I wanted badly to see our airports there and cross the South Atlantic. Brereton, it happened, was returning home this week end and he offered me a lift in his ship which would fly north and reach New York in about sixty hours. He thought I was mildly crazy when I said No. Now I discovered that Brereton was actually taking off in a C-54—with seats!— this same night. And I noticed how the passengers were stratified. Those to go on the 54 were almost all field officers; they looked very aloof, polished, and superior. Their uniforms seemed excessively smart and neat. They made their own cool little group. Those of us flying south by slow freight included much younger officers—kids in fact—technicians in rumpled shirts, and sweating civilians. I felt as I had once felt crossing the Atlantic by sea. That snooty group up there was first class, and I was steerage.

Our plane, a stripped DC-3, was on the apron just outside the office. Mechanics with flashlights were crawling over the starboard motor. It was now ten o'clock, and soon it became eleven. There was no passport examination, and only the barest minimum of customs control; I showed what few papers I had, and everybody was patient and polite. In the control room I met our pilot. He was First Lieutenant Donald Whaley, twenty-one years old, born in Wisconsin; recently he had been promoted from flight sergeant, and he had never even seen a DC-3 until he got to Africa a few months ago.

The half dozen youngsters in the control room—most of them under twenty-five—impressed me vividly. None had ever been abroad before; now they were flying daily between Cairo, Khartoum, Bagdad, the Persian Gulf, Ethiopia, and God knows where else. They never knew what their next trip would be; they took it all as a matter of pure routine; they drew a ticket and jumped continents as I might cross a street. I tried hard to catch their small talk, to remember just how they expressed themselves about their flights, their ships. Always the shoptalk of pilots is superb. But I was too tired tonight to remember much. "Well, he just mushed her off . . ." "How many horses does she pack? . . ." "That was the lousiest four-motor job we ever had to work on. . . ." "Don't kid me, if you hit anything with that kind of ship, you fry." Now the sergeant who was apparently charged with seeing our ship off the ground, kept repeating to Lieutenant Whaley, "I'll lead you out with my jeep, you can follow my small lights; you can see by my lights, then I'll squat just behind you when you run her up."

One lad came in with what looked like a hamburger on a roll. Six others leapt at him. "Boy, what I wouldn't give for a steak sandwich!" "The biggest dry martini I ever had was on Forty-second Street." "Two pairs is the most difficult hand to play, but oh boy, when you have two small pairs and no one calls you . . ." They liked to play poker but a gang that met regularly in Khartoum had had to give it up, because it wasn't "friendly" any more. One corporal put his head on his crossed arms. He was irritated and sleepy. He started to mutter in what was almost a cry, "When will it be over? When will we get home again?" He turned to me, "Do you think we ever *will* get home again?" But what most men want is not so much actual leave, as to know exactly *when* they are going to get leave, if any.

We took off a few minutes before midnight; when everything got shaken down, we were only four passengers. Two were youthful air force officers from Tunisia who were going home to learn to fly. One was the first American private to land in Greenland; now he was a captain at twenty-two. The fourth passenger was a civilian who had injured his hand in an accident at Asmara, in Eritrea. He was being flown home for treatment; his hand, bulging around the cast, was bright purple, and the size of a pushed-in football. The plane was full of crates. We each had two or three buckets to ourselves. If you put your shoulder in one bucket, and are approximately the right size, your behind fits in the second bucket down, more or less.

We arrived at an airport near Khartoum at 6:15 A.M. For two hours it had been cold and fairly bumpy. The pilot said when we got off, "Whew, that rainstorm was certainly a beaut." But I had slept through most of it. We walked in to breakfast. I hadn't had anything to eat or drink—not even a sip of water—since leaving Shepheard's yesterday.

An Airport Near Khartoum, Sunday, Sept. 5.—The A.T.C. is always careful, and when we disembarked from our ship, No. 1003, the pilot said he "thought" a fifty-hour check might be necessary; after every fifty hours of flight these ships are meticulously gone over. So we went to bed. Travelers at this airport as at others operated by the A.T.C. are assigned bunks for which they pay one dollar per night. Meals are fifty cents each. The camp, beautifully organized and maintained, is a series of clean whitewashed one-story buildings spread in a broad rectangle near the landing strip. The officers' mess has a wide veranda, with double screen doors, and a softdrink bar with a giant white refrigerator. There are comfortable rocking chairs and miniature air-mail editions of American magazines, most of them several months old. I had very little sense of being in the Sudan, except for the black servants with their scarred cheeks. Otherwise we might be in camp in Maryland or Texas. . . . Transients are not permitted to drive in and visit Khartoum, though I might have wangled permission if there had been time. We talked about how big the backlog is at Accra; that is, how many passengers are piled up there awaiting the trans-Atlantic hop. My priority is a No. 2, so everyone says I will whisk through fast.

We woke up at about noon, and in the middle of lunch the dispatching officer told us we were taking off at once. We have a new pilot, a veteran of the civil airlines, with a keen, kindly, seamed face, Captain F. T. Pipkin of Independence, Kansas. The ship has been reloaded. Two immense barrels of Pepsi-cola are strapped forward, and in the tail is a mass of captured German equipment carrying the same priority as mine; it seems to be a mortar going to Washington to be inspected. I liked the way Captain Pipkin tidied up the ship. He adjusted the ventilators himself, scrupulously made our ladder fast, saw that all the cargo lashings were secure, and even checked the rubber disks in our windows, to see if they were snug. We took off at 2:02 P.M. I stretched out on my overcoat and tried to read with a 200-pound German bomb as a pillow.

Now I did begin to get a sense of Africa, though we flew very high, too high to see any game. Pipkin has flown this route a hundred times, and has never seen a living thing by day. But at night you can often spot native campfires, called "baboon" fires; this is baboon country and the fires keep the animals away from villages. I have never seen more empty and desolate country. The earth is flat and reddish, with lines of green that look like scum in a bathtub. This green scum always appears in the rainy season; three months from now the whole area will be parched. I kept reflecting on the extreme emptiness of the landscape. Surely the most remarkable thing about the earth is that so much of it is so little used.

We flew through a vicious little storm. For a moment we could not see our wings from the windows directly over them. Then after an hour or so the character of the country changed. It became more rugged, more variegated, with cold-looking boulders, purple blotches of valley, and knots of green trees. We were nearing French Equatorial Africa, but I had no feeling of jungle. Every time I have ever flown over jungle, even in Brazil, it looks like Montana. Once in India I inspected some jungle on foot, and it reminded me of nothing so much as a sylvan back yard in Connecticut.

I left Cairo a day after the Allied invasion of the Italian mainland began. I felt a twinge of regret that I was not part of it, especially since my Eighth Army friends must have been in the first landings. That morning, on September 4, an officer on Shepheard's terrace told me that American forces had landed in France. I saw no reason not to believe this, but somehow I doubted it. Last night and again this morning near Khartoum people kept on mentioning the reported landing as an accepted fact. "Have you heard the news?—we've landed a big force in France." How do rumors like this originate? I can understand how they spread, but I have always been curious as to the precise manner of their inception.

We crossed a river, twisting, lurching, and getting lower almost with the rhythm of a man coughing; the river was full of loops and the color of a moist dirt road. Pipkin—so careful but like all A.T.C. pilots anxious to be on time—didn't like the weather ahead and he was landing at a small field to pick up extra fuel. We shivered getting out of the plane. I swear I don't understand it. The further south we are, the colder it seems to get.

Airport "E," Near Lake Chad, Sunday, Sept. 5.— Landed at 5:58 P.M. A young captain took us into his mess, and gave us a snack showing the wonderful contrasts implicit in this kind of travel: it consisted of gazelle sandwiches *and* indisputably American apple pie. The gazelle tasted like well-done veal. On the veranda a little later the captain said, "It's 6:32, and it's going to rain now." And suddenly it did begin to rain. Great globs of it streamed down. The captain went on, "I know it rains every day at about six-thirty, but just the same you cannot forecast African weather. Last week we had an inch and a half of rain in forty-eight minutes with a seventy-mile wind." We watched the rain pile up like a lateral waterfall, and one of our passengers started to holler, "Rain! Rain!" It was the first rain I had seen on the ground since leaving New York.

Now this airport fascinated me. This was nothing but jungle a couple of years ago. We carved it out of waste. And although this is a minor installation it includes machine shops, sturdy quarters for several hundred men, a weather station, a good landing strip. Here right in the middle of Africa, isolated from the entire world except through the sky, is an American nucleus of aerial communications, a ganglion built by our guts and enterprise and operated in as taken-for-granted a manner as if it

were in Peoria, Illinois. Moreover this airport is one of a
dozen in the neighborhood. I looked at Pipkin's charts.
He had a choice of five fields in this immediate vicinity.
This airport "E," tiny as it is, is a link in the great chain
New York-Miami-Natal-Accra-Khartoum-Cairo-Teheran-
Karachi-Delhi-Calcutta-Chungking. It is on the main
trunk route across Africa. But airport "E" is only part
of the picture. Last summer it seemed that Rommel would
take Cairo. So another lateral route across Africa was
built further south, and it too spans the continent and
points its invisible path to India and China. In the past
two years we have netted Africa with airports and landing
fields. What will they be two years from now? Grass?
Will they go back to the jungle whence they came?

Our camp here is built inside the zareba, or enclosure,
a fence of matted twigs that surrounds the whole airdrome. One evening this week a cheetah got inside. The
native huts are round, about fourteen feet in diameter,
made of mud, and with overhanging thatched roofs, so
that they look like Balinese hats. The natives are friendly
—and very curious about us—and we do our best to cul-
tivate their good will. On the bulletin board I read notices
warning American troops to respect African customs, to
be careful of native susceptibilities, and "not to toss coins
at Negroes." "Due respect will be accorded the native
population." "Undue familiarity with the local citizenry
is undignified." "Sarcasm will not be directed against
natives." And so on. By and large it seems that the
attitude of our men is mostly one of amused contempt, and
the Americans are much easier on the natives than the
British, I was told. An officer said, "I'm inclined to think
the British idea of harsh treatment is right, and I'm as
democratic a guy as anybody." This was perhaps because
he was irritated at the laziness and shiftlessness of the
Sudanese working for him. "Instruct one of those big

bucks to go around camp and pick up bits of paper and he won't know how to do it."

We walked out and saw the planes line up. At one end of the field a squadron of British Baltimores was awaiting ferry, together with a dreadful-looking four-motor job that people insisted still operated as a transport carrier. I would not have flown in it for anything. Just beyond the zareba a group of RAF ferry pilots were dismounting cool-looking horses. They had been hunting, and they looked like a picture out of an English novel describing a Northumberland countryside.

Back at the base camp, I marveled again at the pro- digious amount of planning, technical adroitness, and sheer human effort that must have gone into this installa- tion. The transport problem—even for such a small airport as this—is appalling. Everything must come in by air. And what does an airport in Africa need? Not even counting the gasoline and machinery, I listed a few objects. Heavy scales. Maps. Weather balloons. Meteorological instru- ments of all kinds. Radio transmitters. Desks. Typewriters. A telephone system. Cargo loaders. A small derrick. Ice- boxes. Complete kitchen equipment. Nuts and bolts. Toilet paper. Stores for the PX. A machine shop. Paper clips.

Our host took us to the plane. He brushed a fly off his nose, and said to me briefly, "You might write something about these goddamned flies."

Captain Pipkin was in a hurry now. It was 7:02. We piled into our ship, and took off in the driving rain, which presently became a sunset.

I picked up an old *Reader's Digest*, and, just as darkness fell, by odd coincidence I came across this passage from Alma Heflin's "Adventure Was the Compass":

It was never a pilot who started the idea that night falls. A pilot knows that it does not. It oozes up out of the ground, fills the hollows and low places with purple pools of shadow that spread and rise to the tops of the trees and the houses.

Long before the sky has darkened, the world below is swimming in night. And then finally darkness begins washing up over the sky from the east, climbing over the zenith, closing down at last over the final gleams of the sunset. . . . Below the plane, lights map the towns, race along the roads, accenting but not relieving the blackness, for darkness clings to the ground. Whatever light there is clings to the sky to the last.

Airport "M," Nigeria, Sunday, September 5.—We arrived here at 10:31 P.M. Pipkin had estimated 10:29 so he was two minutes off. I am beginning to feel it has been a long flight since Cairo. By local time, which follows Greenwich, it is only 7:30, and so three hours are added to our day. We took off again, with a new pilot, Captain W. W. O'Neill, an Oklahoman, at 8:35. I was sorry to say good-by to Pipkin. I fell asleep almost at once. The co-pilot woke me in about twenty minutes and said we were returning to "M" to spend the night there. Some minor motor trouble had developed—of the kind inevitable on a run like this—and we needed a bit of repair.

The dispatching officer looked the board over. There were two more westbound DC-3's coming in during the night; a nice tribute to the general smoothness and efficiency of A.T.C. operation. In every station, a large blackboard shows the movement of every ship, its total weight, what cargo it carries, and how many passengers with what priorities. So it was easy to see if we could pick up another lift. We decided to stay the night in "M." We piled into a new station wagon, and drove six miles to the base camp near town.

While we were waiting—in a comfortable mess known as the Pig n' Whistle next to the landing strip—an enormous C-54 taxied up, and I looked at it with some envy. And as always I felt the intense thrill of seeing a really big aircraft glow into the darkness, unload its passengers, and prepare to take off again. This ship was going through to China, full of "rank," officers with very high priorities.

The scene is always about the same; the crew slipping out tired but bearing their responsibilities with cocky shoulders; a dispatching officer in a raincoat and the water sliding off his cap; the mechanics cautiously prodding with flashlights; the co-pilot gassing the ship and the navigator making his report; the sense of illimitable distances overcome, and time shriveling; the sense of the magnitude of the earth, and magnitude of men drawing lines across it.

"Hello, Hal!"

"H'are yuh, kid?"

"Well, Ralph, old man!"

These are the radio operator, the co-pilot, and the engineer of two ships meeting. They are pals. They have had utterly no idea they will run into one another in this place, and they may not have met for months. Tomorrow they will be off on their separate ways to Ascension or Kunming. They walk down the field arms across shoulders. And they look like college sophomores. When will they meet again?

I would not have missed the ride into town for anything. I certainly knew that I was in Africa then. There is no blackout problem here, since no lights exist to put out; we drove down a twisting muddy lane in absolute darkness, sloshing through puddles and bending through the bush to get around streams. Along the road—I gazed in astonishment—we could just see files of tall white-clad natives, carrying spears, who patrolled the jungle road. They looked like something out of *African Game Trails* or Rider Haggard.

Pilots like "M" better than any other stop on the line, and it was easy to see why. We came to a camp much like that near Khartoum. Dinner was baby shrimps, fried chicken, mushrooms, pie, and ice cream. When these camps were first set up, by Pan-American, they were equipped with large stores of canned goods; at "M" passengers may have delicacies that disappeared long ago from the shops of New York. The camp doctor sat at our table. He has not had a case of malaria in three weeks, and no gonorrhea for two and a half months. The wonderfully elaborate double screen doors I see everywhere serve their purpose in keeping mosquitoes out and thus keeping malaria down. The American army doesn't take much stock in atabrine, so far as I can see. This is the yellow pill, a substitute for quinine, that is supposed to be a prophylaxis against malaria. The British take it religiously, but they get malaria just the same. The British do not screen doors carefully. We do. And we don't get malaria so much.

The doctor loved his plant. He was a hard-boiled officer with a harsh voice but his eyes softened and gleamed when he talked about what he had. Here in the African jungle —with leopards two hundred yards away—his tiny operating room was air-conditioned! "I have the sweetest, the sweetest, the sweetest, the sweetest little hospital you ever saw."

I asked how we were getting along out here with the British. When we came—this is a British colony—English officers took the lead in being friendly; they deluged the Americans with invitations to their clubs, and so on. At first the Americans, shy, were standoffish; our senior officers had to persuade the juniors to mix. Apparently the chief British complaint is that we spoil the natives by giving too much "dash," i.e., tips. One officer wondered about the future rights to these new airports. Another answered him, "Oh, the British don't care; they figure that in the long run they'll get 'em anyway."

We filed up for billeting. I turned in at about 11 P.M., which by Cairo time was two in the morning. We have been en route just twenty-two hours.

Airport "M," Monday, Sept. 6.—Up at 2:30 A.M. local time. We checked out (everybody so casual and efficient) and had breakfast on flapjacks. Drove off in our station wagon at about four, in a ghostly light. The file of tall white-clad Negroes with spears still lined the road. The car stopped suddenly. Our native driver bounced out. Another black lad jumped in out of the darkness, and took his place. He came right in from the embracing lonely darkness. There was no explanation, and we all stared at one another.

Captain O'Neill took us off at 5:02 A.M. in a C-53, a cargo ship with double doors; its bucket seats are of a different type, square and if possible even more uncomfortable than those in a 47; but we have a wooden floor, which reduces vibration and makes the flight quieter.

A thin lad across from me said painfully, "I ain't got no meat on my ass. Jesus, I can't hardly sit down no more."

Kano, Nigeria, Monday, Sept. 6.—We landed here a little after seven. Mechanics looked over the plane, and there may be some delay before we get off. I still marvel at the unceasing care everybody takes to insure smooth, quick, safe operation.

Kano is a famous "walled city" but I must say the walls did not impress me much; somehow I had visualized immense towering structures. But Kano's walls are not more than twenty feet high, built of crumbling tawny-ocher mud. We went into the Moslem quarter. I was enchanted by the riotous color of the women's cotton dresses; I was depressed by the poverty, the filth, the disease. These Nigerians are very tall, coal-black, with thin legs and a handsome bearing. The women carry babies strapped over their behinds, and when they are pregnant too—as most of them seemed to be—the effect is startling. We saw lepers; vultures skidding over garbage; pickaninnies squatting on low bridges and defecating into the water; huddled families inside caves; a European cinema; long lines of women going to market; kids on bicycles. The cattle seemed scrawny, and eggs were two cents a dozen. Much of it reminded me of India; all of it reminded me that the two major problems of areas like this are education and health control.

No one could possibly resist looking at the wonderfully built women. My guide said, "See the headlights on those girls; aren't they terrific? But their faces are rather ugly, don't you think?"

Back at the airport around nine, we were told the plane would not be ready till noon. Then, after lunch, we fiddled through magazines, sipped Coca-Cola, and inspected python skins next to Hershey bars at the PX. Late in the afternoon No. 1003 limped in, and she too went into the machine shop for minor repairs. So two different DC-3's were stalled in Kano. The dispatching officer, a kid from Connecticut who had graduated from one of the best private schools in the world two years ago, said he had never known this to happen before. We looked over our ship and also No. 1003 with some attention. Men were hanging like flies underneath their motors. Around the nose was an enormous contraption—a novelty in this part of the world—whereby motors can be changed behind a weatherproof screen. A mechanic grinned, "Do we wear 'em out by repairing 'em too much?"

All this being said, let me add at once that of all ships I have ever been lucky enough to fly in, the sturdiest, the most foolproof, and the most reliable is the DC-3. And if DC-3's do get grounded occasionally, I certainly have no objection to the care taken to see that they fly again safely. The affection of pilots for these DC-3's is touching. They slap them on the sides like horses. All pilots I have ever met love and trust them. I have talked to pilots who have crash-landed them on twisting roads in this part of the world with hardly a scratch; with pilots who have put them down, at night, on patches of grain and braked them to a safe halt by letting them pitch forward on the nacelles.

We walked down the strip near the RAF station where

long lines of Hurricanes and Baltimores were waiting. Our men are giddy with consternation at the way some of the British fly. They hop into a ship and off they go, with very little of the painful, meticulous checking and probing we think essential. "Why, they take off without a run-up!" I heard it said. But everybody admired deeply the airworthiness of almost all British ships. The British choose a few good models and concentrate on them, sticking with them, whereas we are forever experimenting fussily to find something new. The United States has never produced a heavy bomber to match a Lancaster or a fighter comparable to a Spitfire. Yet, some of our ships are greatly loved. At the extreme end of the field Captain O'Neill showed me a Douglas Havoc. It was so new it might have been wrapped in cellophane. O'Neill had been shot down once flying a P-40 near Alexandria. He looked at the Havoc and his mouth watered. "How I'd love to be flying *that* baby!" he kept muttering.

In general, I found, our pilots dislike P-40's and P-38's. One reason is that it is very difficult to bail out of a P-38; the double tail may cut you in half. They respect the new Thunderbolts (P-47's), but think them heavy; they are full of admiration for P-51's (the new Mustangs); they think A-20's (Bostons) are absolutely first class, Mitchells pretty good, and Marauders indifferent. As to big bombers, B-17's are splendid ships from the E model on. Pilots have sharp difference of opinion about B-24's (Liberators); they like the tremendous range and bombing power of this ship, but they find it the most difficult of all American planes to fly. Liberators are hard to load, "full of tail," and murder to handle in bad weather.

The pilots I talked to—all along the line, not merely at Kano—have great respect for Messerschmitts. An Me-109 can outrun, outclimb, and outfight a P-40 any time. Of course they are not so good against P-47's. The Messerschmitt has a gadget whereby the motor can be dismounted by the turn of four screws, and a complete motor change effected in twenty minutes. We have nothing like this; our planes are infinitely more complex. An Me-110 turns more tightly on one wing than on the other, which is its chief vulnerability; you can fight them if you can spot how they're going to turn. . . . No pilot I ever met, British or American, had much good to say of Lockheed Hudsons. They have a drastic tendency to ground-loop, and Venturas are difficult to take off. Almost all pilots admire the C-54, now that its hydraulic system has been perfected. Most pilots dislike the C-46 (Curtiss Commando) because it often has ignition trouble and is exceptionally heavy to fly.

By six it was clear that neither of our stalled DC-3's was going to get off that night. But—service!—I was told that another DC-3 was coming in that I might take. The pilot who was to command this new ship worked out the weight over and over again. He had no slide rule, and he kept adding it up longhand. The ship was very heavy. I would be the twenty-eighth passenger. The pilot shrugged; he didn't like it. The ceiling at Accra, our next stop, was only 100 feet, and he wanted extra gas in case Accra closed up and he had to take her in somewhere else. If he took me, that would be so much less gas. Then an eastbound ship came in from Accra, and our pilot consulted its crew about the weather there. He decided to take a chance. The new DC-3 arrived, and my bags were put aboard.

We had supper in camp while a thunderstorm split the sky. I flipped a ride back to the hangars, and the young officer from Connecticut told me that still another DC-3 was coming in, somewhat lighter than the one to which I had been transferred. So would I mind transferring once again? Then this officer said that he did not like to send me on this new DC-3 because the people in Accra would think poorly of him for having shipped me on a plane with *no* seats. I would have to sit on the floor, he said. I said I didn't mind. The ship came in; my bags were once more trundled out of one plane and into another —all this in total darkness—and I met my new captain, by name Alexander Jacy. He didn't waste any time at all. We were off at 9 P.M. before I could say good-by. I was the only passenger in this new ship. Its cargo staggered me—two enormous Pratt & Whitney motors. They filled the whole cabin, so that the buckets could not be let down. Forward were two crates of mica from China. The thunderstorm was more intense now, and lightning slashed through the southern sky. I squeezed down on the floor between the mica and the motors, their enormous weight bothered me and I hoped they wouldn't slip. We burrowed and slithered through heavy rain and sticky bouncing clouds. But when we got to Accra, with its 100-foot ceiling, I never knew it. I had been up since two-thirty this morning, and I was sound asleep on the metal floor.

Just as we were taking off at Kano and the pilot looked at the lightning his radio operator said to me quietly, "A captain has to have a damn good reason for calling off a flight on this here run. We have a colonel down in Accra that don't believe in weather."

We arrived at Accra at 1:15 A.M. A courteous and efficient public relations officer, Lieutenant Louis Fuchs, met me and took me in to breakfast, which made about the fifth meal I have had in this long day. I asked him if he could get me off, across the Atlantic, right away. He said that a Liberator was indeed preparing to take off, and that he could indeed squeeze me on. But, he went on, didn't I want to stay over in Accra till the next evening? I ought not to miss Accra, he insisted. It was the show place of the entire route. I balanced my fork, thinking. I was in a hurry, yes. But what did twenty-four hours more or less matter? Fuchs swore that the backlog was light, that he would certainly see me off within the next day, and that I might be lucky enough to get a ship with seats. But, he proceeded, the Liberator was right there waiting, and I could take it if I wanted to. I debated with myself another moment, and decided to stay over.

We went to Barracks A, and I was given a pleasant room to myself at the end of a long corridor. I had crossed Africa and reached the Atlantic in a total flying time of about eighteen hours.

Chapter XVI

Flying Home: Accra
and Ascension

Accra, Gold Coast, Tuesday, Sept. 7.—It's cold here.
I have used my overcoat as a pillow and to sit on and
sleep on in airplanes, but this is the first time I've worn
it on the ground. At breakfast—the jet black servants
wore white gloves—I met an excellent officer, Lieutenant
Colonel Gustavus Reiniger, and we talked about the
battle going on in Italy. This town, like Cairo, is buzzing
with rumors of an American landing in France. And all
of us want to know, Where is the American Seventh
Army?

Lieutenant Fuchs picked me up at about half-past ten.
He looked pale. He said he had had very little sleep. We
discussed plans. Then he interrupted himself quite casually, "Say, it's just as well you didn't take that 87 (Liberator) last night."

"Why?"

"It took off a few minutes after you decided not to fly.
There was something wrong with the turn-bank indicator
and the pilot came back. He couldn't get through the scud
and went into a hill just over there. All the passengers
were burned to death."

I didn't say anything.

The lieutenant added as an afterthought: "It's the first
four-motor ship we've ever lost here."

"Too bad," I said.

We made a comprehensive quick tour of the camp. This is really quite a substantial installation, the biggest A.T.C. establishment I have seen so far. It takes four or five thousand men to run it, and its equipment and facilities rival that of any major airport back home, La Guardia or Burbank; even the machine shops for special tools are air-conditioned. We crossed a landing strip where young pilots incessantly practiced take-offs and landings in DC-3's. I began to learn how much training a pilot goes through, above and beyond his previous experience even if that is thousands of hours, before he is permitted to take over an A.T.C. run. And this is only one of four major jumping-off-places for the flight across the South Atlantic. The traffic is tremendous, and will get more tremendous as the war goes on. Last night no fewer than seven Liberators, not including the one that crashed, took off westbound. The heaviest traffic is for China. Accra is already a king pivot in communications to the China war.

Lunch at the British club with Colonel Reiniger. One almost forgets that this is the capital of a "model" British colony; we operate here on a 100 per cent extraterritorial basis. But even so the British Empire is pervasive, indestructible, and homogeneous: lunch here might have been lunch at Brighton, at prewar Rangoon, or Gibraltar. The orthodox courses were served in orthodox sequence, and the food, though plentiful, was pale. The dry sherry was just what it should have been, and the coffee execrable. And I marveled at the tenacity, the lack of showmanship, the respectability, the faith in tradition, the atmosphere of indisputable rightness without conceit, that the British show—and have shown for generations—in remote and undeveloped parts of the world.

We bowed to files of old men in soiled tropicals, reading copies of the *Times* six week old, and went out to see the town. This is not called the Gold Coast without reason. There are some two hundred registered goldsmiths in

Accra, and we watched several of them work; one was beating out a ring to Colonel Reiniger's own careful specifications. We visited a big general store run by Indians, at which you could buy anything from Flit to elephant tusks; we looked at the shops of the trading companies and prodded through ramshackle bazaars; we bought brass ornaments in a very Maughamesque market.

These Gold Coasters are good folk. "When our officers arrive they think they are gorillas; they think they are animals. They are not gorillas. They are not animals," Colonel Reiniger said emphatically. The best of them are of the Hausa tribe, from the north. We visited a family, and I met two of the prettiest Negro girls I ever saw. Around us crawled babies carved of smiling ebony. All the grownups spoke English well, and it was hard to believe that we were not in our own Deep South. Indeed, the great-grandparents of these folk along this coast are also the great-grandparents of the Negroes of Texas and Alabama. From the kitchen I heard songs, low melodious chants. I wished that I were like Carl Van Vechten or Miguel Covarrubias, someone with admiring knowledge of Negro folklore, so that I might better understand.

"The British treat the natives like dogs." So I heard it said. We, on the other hand, as I learned all along the route, spoil them. When I got in last night Fuchs' last word was, "Don't 'dash' the houseboys." Many officers I met think that the American camps at Accra and elsewhere will have a profound effect on native life and culture; no one in West Africa is going to forget our double-screen doors and frigidaires, our high wages and—for that matter—our essential good will and friendliness. A few miles out of Accra is the Prince of Wales College at Atchimoto, one of the best schools in Africa. But it is the only one of its kind in the neighborhood, and there should be hundreds of such schools. I asked about West African nationalism. It is getting stronger all the time, everybody said.

Colonel Reiniger asked our driver, "What are you?"

"Me, oh I city boy."

The Gold Coasters classify themselves as bush boys or city boys. The city boys naturally consider themselves much superior. This driver was an intelligent and amusing youngster. I asked him the meaning of a word, and then the name of his particular tribal language.

"Ga," he replied.

"What?"

"Ga," he repeated, pronouncing it with a hard G. "Just the same word, sir, as one of your states." I was bewildered until I realized he meant Georgia; he must have seen the abbreviation "Ga" on some envelope. He thought it was pronounced hard and his language has the same sound.

I wanted to know what our troops did for women. "They go out into the bush," was the shortest answer I got. The most extraordinary pains are taken to satisfy other wants the men have, and particularly to counteract the terrible monotony which is the curse of life in a base like this. There are movies every night; some are shown here before they open in New York. The PX is superb, and I spent an hour or two in a good small library. The officers have a bar, one of the very few I encountered in any American mess; its huge wall decorations of Petty-Varga girls made the imagination rock. There was a limited supply of both rye and Scotch; the barman even went so far as to fill my flask which has lasted since Constantinople. . . . I asked Lieutenant Fuchs what the men wanted most. "Well," he answered sagely, "you can't wrap it up and put it in a box." Of course I knew the answer. What they want most is to get home.

I had dinner with Major General Ralph Royce, who was flying through to take Brereton's command in Cairo, and Brigadier General Earl S. Hoag, the A.T.C. wing commander. These two officers made splendid company, and I had American beef for the first time since leaving New York.

The contrasts of Africa are marvelous. When I got back to barracks I found my houseboy intently reading a Penguin edition of *Othello*.

Accra, Wednesday, September 8.—Up at 3:30 A.M. Lieutenant Fuchs called for me and took me to the airport. Flapjacks again, and coffee. I have had more coffee in the past thirty-six hours than in the previous two months.

The technique of getting out of Accra is something like this. Your priority is posted, and you go by rote. The ships are made up late each afternoon, and mimeographed copies are inserted on bulletin boards in each barracks. There is no use asking questions until these passenger lists are put up. Then you scan the lists eagerly to see what ship you are on—if any. Last night at about ten I found my own name on the ship due to take off at five this morning. Normally the ships take off at intervals of about an hour, at such times as will make a daylight landing easy at our next stop, the mid-Atlantic island of Ascension.

Now we were getting ready to take off. Our ship was a C-54, with seats, and I looked with delight at its enormous contour. A friendly FBI official went through my papers, and I weighed up. There was a large sign over the desk warning passengers that they must have a yellow fever inoculation, but no one asked me for my certificate. We climbed into the 54 at about five-thirty. Majestically the great ship waddled to the end of the field, and then there was a wait. One motor slightly rough. Pilots listen to these motors as a jeweler listens to a watch. We taxied back, and got out. We were told that we might get off by eleven, but if there were any delay beyond that we

could not take off today, since this would mean a landfall at Ascension after dark. A second breakfast, and we
hung around. It was a long wait till ten-thirty, when we
learned that the flight was postponed until tomorrow. The
A.T.C. prides itself on its promptness and dispatch, but
occasional delays like this are inevitable on a rough run;
the A.T.C. is never haphazard; it is seldom late, but
always prudent.

Late in the afternoon Colonel Reiniger rang up to say
that Italy had surrendered. We had a drink to celebrate.

Accra, Thursday, September 9.—Again Lieutenant
Fuchs woke me at 3:30 A.M., and again we drove to the
airport in the chilly dawn. This time we did get off, at
5:15. Almost at once, we were flying over an absolutely
solid foam of pure white clouds. The lad next to me said,
"Get out your snowshoes, boys."

Our skipper was Captain G. C. Gibbs, who has crossed
the Atlantic eighty or a hundred times in the past three
years; I have never known a more vigilant or careful
pilot. He made us wear Mae Wests all the way across. We
put down at Ascension just before noon, after a flight as
smooth as soap.

Ascension, Thursday, Sept. 9.—This little-known island
is really a remarkable place. "Why, if a crow tried to
land here, he'd break a leg." That was an early military
report about its possibilities as a landing point. Now we
have chewed and gouged out of the volcanic rock of this
islet, a naked dot of lava in the middle wastes of the
South Atlantic, one of the fabulous airports of the world.

I began to hear about Ascension a year or so ago, when
its use was one of the best kept secrets of the war. Now
thousands of travelers know about this essential pivot in
the great route from the United States to Africa, China,
and the East. Until very recently, censorship imposed a
dead "stop" on any mention of this extraordinary lump
of cinder; it was seldom referred to except by a curious

code name, and even that was rarely mentioned, and never printed. Now, however, the story of Ascension can be told.

The island measures 5 miles by 7, and it lies roughly halfway between the downward bulge of Africa and the outward bulge of Brazil; to be precise, it is 1,362 statute miles from Accra, 1,448 miles from Natal. Thus by flying a triangular course via Ascension, our ferry pilots and bombers can avoid the direct route across. Nonstop flights from Africa to Brazil, and vice versa, are, of course, perfectly practicable, and have been done thousands of times, but the alternative flight via Ascension gives a comfortable margin of extra gasoline, payload, and—safety. The island fills almost the same role in the South Atlantic that the Azores furnish in the Central Atlantic; it is a stopping-off place, a marvelously convenient midway station in the perilously long transatlantic run. It is God's great gift to the ocean fliers; a place where they can come down. Also, use of Ascension means that small planes with less range can now cross the Atlantic under their own power.

With its thirty-four square miles, Ascension is the loneliest and most isolated place I have ever seen on earth, or water. The nearest land is St. Helena, about eight hundred miles away; except for that, there is nothing but the inconceivable vastness of the Atlantic. Before the war, not more than one ship a year touched at Ascension; it was so tiny, so remote, as to be virtually forgotten. In some British records, the island is simply called His Majesty's "Ship" Ascension, and indeed it is a kind of unsinkable ship.

Discovered by a Portuguese sea captain on Ascension Day in 1501, the island remained uninhabited for three hundred years. Later the British took it over and built a cable station; today, it contains about seventy-five British subjects, including six or eight women. The only other population—about eighty people—comes from St. Helena.

There are no native islanders on Ascension. It is one of
the few places in the world that never had aborigines. No
one could live on this water-swept, sun-scoured chunk of
rock. So the British imported workers from St. Helena
for their cable station, on two-year contracts. Incidentally
Ascension was the first spot chosen for Napoleon's exile.
Then the British reconsidered, and chose St. Helena instead. Ascension was, they thought, *too* lonely.

Look at Ascension now. The whole island is swarming
with activity. Several thousand American troops comprise
its garrison; everywhere, you hear the accent of Iowa or
the Carolinas. We have built hangars, machine shops,
barracks, hospitals, rifle ranges, mess halls, storage dumps,
an overnight hostel for air passengers, and all the parapher-
nalia of a great new airport. There are four open-air
theaters on Ascension, and four baseball fields.

But the pride of the island is of course its runway.
British engineers who first surveyed it said frankly that it
could not be built. It was built. It was built in ninety-one
days. This is a record in itself. I have never seen a runway like it. It stretches seven thousand feet, scalloped out
of the side of a rust-colored mountain. Right in the middle
there is a sloping hump. Our engineers made the runway,
and it works; but they couldn't smooth down the hump.
No dynamite, no TNT, was powerful enough to blast
through the final shelves of that red volcanic rock, and
get the hump whittled down to level.

"Deadline is three-thirty," Captain Gibbs said. "If we
don't get off by then, we stay the night." He didn't
want to risk having to return in the dark. This is a runway you want to see very clearly before you try to land.

Pilots sometimes overshoot Ascension. Finding it, in
Max Beerbohm's famous phrase, is a little like the swift
threading of a needle from afar. There is a powerful beam
here, yes, but sometimes the overcast is thick and pilots
fly past, still on the beam, but not realizing they have

passed the target. So there are always two or three Aira-cobras powered up on the island, fast pursuit ships, and they take the air and fly the big transports in if the weather is bad, or go after them and haul them back if a pilot overshoots.

Ascension is quite near the equator. So the first thing I did on getting out of our ship was to put on an overcoat. It never fails. Every time I have ever been near the equator, I've been half frozen. But most of the time, I was told, the weather here is perfect; not too hot, not too cool, and with a permanent twenty-mile breeze. The few guidebooks which mention Ascension say that it never rains, but as a matter of fact it rains often, and the red cinder dust turns to mud.

Our guide was the base commander, Colonel J. C. Mullinex. He drove us off in his jeep. Later he talked briskly into the jeep's microphone, summoning another jeep by radio. A voice answered him, "Where are you, sir?" Mullinex laughed and a junior officer came tumbling out of a building. He had not known that his command-ing officer was just outside.

We visited Georgetown, the headquarters of the British community. There is an "Exile's Club," and a prison that hasn't had a client since 1925, and a big sign over a mildewed plaster building, GOVERNMENT OF ST. HELENA, which has an office here. We twisted through lava valleys, bounced over rock-strewn pastures, and looked upward at what is called "Green Hill," not very green. We saw the foaming beaches, where the swimming is as dangerous as anywhere in the world, and the guest house, now nearly completed, which is nicely situated on a sharp slope overlooking the sea. "Might as well give 'em a view," the colonel said.

The most conspicuous inhabitants of Ascension are the terns; thousands upon thousands of these birds, about the size of small ducks, squat noisily on the rocks. When big clusters of them assemble on the runway, they can be a serious menace to aviation. One flew into a B-17 recently, smashing through the window and wrecking the plane's radio. These terns lay literally thousands upon thousands of eggs. The birds are not edible, but the eggs are. We wandered over the cindery slopes, picking them up, tossing them away again.

Lunch was something special. The officers' mess at Ascension is a cafeteria. We had a good thick soup, baked frankfurters, a choice of four vegetables, a handsome salad with a cheese dressing, lemonade, cake, stewed fruit, and coffee. Every cubic inch of food, except the local eggs, must be brought in. Nowadays a supply ship reaches Ascension about once a month. Every ounce not merely of food but of clothing, gasoline, equipment, and munitions must be sailed in. There is no water on the island. Not one drop. Chemists purify the sea water, and make it fit to drink.

Near the long curving beach at the bottom of the runway I saw an object that startled me. It was a tree. It is the only tree on the whole island. It has been bent practically in half by the incessant wind, and its fronds are scrawny. "That," Colonel Mullinex pointed out, "is what we call Cocoanut Grove." Near the tree this thoughtful officer has placed a lone bench, "Honeymoon Bench."

The force that maintains Ascension is officially considered a task force; officers and men wear steel helmets, always. I cannot discuss the way the island is guarded, but every eventuality is kept in mind, even the possibility of a landing attack by Axis submarine. "Is that beach protected?" I asked innocently enough. "Well," the colonel answered, "you're standing right between two machine-gun nests, even if you can't see them."

We passed one of the hospitals, and chatted with a gang of male nurses. Once General Marshall visited this island. He asked the commanding officer if he did not want some

Wacs. "Not unless you send me a couple of thousand," the commanding officer replied.

Morale is seemingly first-class on Ascension, although it is the loneliest and most inaccessible spot any American troops are at present called upon to serve in. Measures are taken down to the most subtle detail to keep the men snappy and smiling. For instance in the remote command posts the tables are covered with a bright scarlet oilcloth, to give a touch of color. Most of the men catch something of the infectious zeal of Colonel Mullinex, their commander. He has a wonderful sense of humor. He can be serious too. He said to me, "This is the finest command any man ever had, and I wouldn't change it for anything on earth."

At about three-fifteen we drove back to our C-54; we clambered in, and strapped on our Mae Wests again. Six hours or so later we were dining in Brazil. We had crossed the Atlantic, comfortably, safely, between dawn and dusk, thanks in large part to Ascension.

I remembered what a Chinese officer had told me in Accra, "I wonder if God knew how He was helping the Allies when He dropped that island there."

Natal, Brazil, Friday, September 10.—We got in last night just in time for dinner. This is an even bigger plant than Accra. I felt my way along the crisp gravel paths between rows of bungalows. Four of us have two-decker bunks in a small room, and in contrast I remembered my handsome privacy in Accra. How spoiled one gets! Then Colonel C. C. Herrick, one of the base commanders, picked me up. He is an enormous hulk of a man, an All-American of some years back, and his energy and vigor match his size. At dinner a senior officer kept muttering, "If I have to go through this war too, and never hear so much as a firecracker fired in anger. . . ." Indeed it is remarkable how few officers ever witness action.

Up at six-fifteen. Breakfast with Colonel Herrick and

two air corps engineers, Brigadier General Franklin S. Carroll and Colonel Donald L. Putt. These two have been my companions since Accra. Brazil is very pleasant as always: cool, sunny, and packed with charm. Near the sea —Natal is of course on the tip of the "bulge" of Brazil— we saw a nest of German 88-mm guns. These were installed before the war, when Brazil was being armed—in part—by the Nazis. We cannot use these guns now because we have no ammunition to fit them. But some may turn up out of captured stores in Italy.

Colonel Herrick took us through the camp. It was faintly staggering to learn that the coffee our men drink here comes from the United States, though this country produces so much coffee the Brazilians have to burn it. It was also staggering in a different field to see how elaborate the A.T.C. installation is. It is big enough to handle a plane every three and a half minutes; it can easily "process" 3,000 passengers a day. Yesterday no fewer than 529 passengers went through Natal eastbound. In one day! Colonel Herrick surveyed the two splendid runways. An officer said, "What are we going to do with all this after the war?" The Natal staff is intensely proud not only of the murderously hard work it has put in but of its safety record. No A.T.C. ship out of Natal has ever failed to reach its destination *or* get back to base safely.

We took off in a C-46 (Curtiss Commando) at 11:34 A.M. This is the biggest two-motor plane in the world. It weighs almost 50,000 pounds. Also it is the most uncomfortable plane I have ever flown in. This was certainly not the pilot's fault but as soon as I saw him—Captain Paul S. Woolley of Eastern Air Lines—I knew he was a character, because he wore a white beret. We were slightly delayed in taking off through some paper-work error. When Woolley did lift his wheels off the ground, he flew over the dispatching tower in such a way that the whole airplane cocked a snook. I was strapped in my bucket between General Carroll and a wonderful old veteran,

Colonel Oakley G. Kelly, who made the first nonstop, dawn-to-dusk flight across the American continent, with John Macready in 1923. Both Carroll and Kelly turned slightly green as we banked vertically at seventy-five feet. So did I. "Oh well," Kelly said, "guess the pilot thinks we're a pursuit ship." Someone else said to the general, "He's doing it to impress you, sir; will you please get the hell off this ship."

We landed at Belém at 4:15 P.M. Seldom have I seen a more dashing approach to an airport. If the windows had been open (Commandos are short on windows) you could have plucked twigs off the trees. We thundered in rocking. I remembered Belém well from a trip in 1941; we drove into the town, looked at the Amazon, and shopped for alligator leather. Back to the airport in driving rain, and had dinner in what is by all odds the most charming army mess I've ever seen. The curtains were full of color; there were heaps of flowers on every table; dinner began with a tray of assorted tropical fruits that looked like something out of Gauguin.

Belém-Miami, Saturday, September 11.—This was one of the longest, most trying, and most rewarding days I ever spent. We were called at three. Captain Woolley was in a hurry. We did not get time to finish breakfast; we were in the plane by four. Carroll, Kelly, and I strapped ourselves in side by side. Next to me a frightened private could not get his belt fixed. He started to moan. We were taking off now, and in an instant the ship, with whiplash power, was hurtling through the equatorial darkness savagely. The private kept moaning. He was at least fifty. He said, "Old Lyon is never going to see Boston any more."

I said, "Who's Lyon?"

"That's me, officer."

He could not see my insignia. But it was strange to be called "officer" that way. He unstrapped himself and found a place to lie down in the rear of the plane. I don't think I've ever seen a plane so jammed. The great hull

was packed so solid with cargo that it was barely possible to crawl along the buckets and get forward. The
co-pilot had to scamper over the stuff like a goat. . . . Old
Lyon fell asleep. We looked for him again after our next
stop. He was not there. Probably he had been taken off
the ship. Maybe he was a medical case going home for
discharge. I wonder if he ever got to Boston. I hope he did.

I dipped into *War and Peace*, and dozed. I thought of
a scene last night. The intermittent tropical rain; the
plangent Brazilian darkness; the padding of bare brown
feet on moist grass; curtains gently rustling and the sound
of gurgling water—how different everything was now!
We were slashing and pounding ahead like some insane
metallic monster; we tore into the sky line an infernal
machine from Mars. Pilots may not like Commandos. But
these ships certainly fly. We bucked and pitched at something over four miles a minute. It was still dark, and at
more than 12,000 feet, sitting on a metal strip, piercingly
cold. The ship kept swaying, bouncing, and groaning, and
the violent noise shook your bones apart.

We came down sharply at eight-seven. The jungle over
British Guiana looks like the sea: a very dark blue-green,
with round nobbins of green packed close together. A very
smart colonel welcomed us at Georgetown; he wore RAF
wings as well as his U.S. insignia. We started breakfast,
but the merciless Woolley again interrupted to say we had
no time to finish. Since I was going to be in British
Guiana not more than these few minutes, I tried to see as
much as possible. The broad hard-surfaced road leads to a
beautifully kept airport. And as always I felt a sense of
admiring wonder at the efficiency and plenitude of our
equipment; I saw a crash wagon, a fire engine, and an
ambulance on the runway. "Do they take these precautions
at all Caribbean airports?" I asked innocently enough.
The colonel snapped, "They do at any airport I'm in
charge of."

We took off from Georgetown at 8:31, and arrived at

Trinidad at 10:20. This flight, and most of the flying for
the rest of the day, was of course over water. So it was
comparatively smooth. There was no nonsense about Mae
Wests. The plane may have carried them but I did not see
any. Captain Woolley made a picturesquely dramatic
landing. This is one of the best pilots I have ever flown
with. He has done more than 6,500 hours. We thought
we might try to finish our twice-interrupted breakfast.
We were now about 1,200 miles from our first unfinished
course and 400 miles from the second. Woolley said No.
The Trinidad commander asked him if he could squeeze
on two high-priority passengers. He said he could not risk
it with the load he was carrying. We taxied down the
strip and ran up. Then the door snapped open, and in
popped a man, a civilian. He had chased us down the field
in a jeep and Woolley let him stay on. We took off at
10:55.

Aside from Carroll, Kelly, and Putt most of our passengers on this trip were junior pilots going home on
leave, noncoms, and technicians. One lad wore the leather
jacket of the China service; these jackets have large
American flags woven in their backs, so that the Chinese
may recognize as a friend anybody who has a forced landing. This lad has flown the Himalayas 124 times! Yet he
could not have been more than twenty. . . . Some of us
tried to sleep; Carroll sat up with the pilot part of the
time; one gin rummy game flourished aft; Kelly and I
talked. I looked at three boys dozing on the mail sacks,
and tried to imprint the picture on my mind. They were
squeezed, back to back, so that they looked like one person
with two heads; below them a third boy was stretched
upside down. By noon we were all hungry, tired, and rest-
less. I would get up from my bucket, try to stretch, crouch
over the great mound of cargo, lean on my baggage, hoist
myself on a crate, lie down on a water tank, then unbend
and try to walk three paces on the vibrating floor.

We were flying over Puerto Rico now. And I was

mystified again by the extraordinary emptiness of the earth's surface. This island is the most crowded region, next to Java, in the world; yet we passed mile after mile without a house or sign of human habitation. Landed at Borinquen at 2:07 P.M. I knew we were in America all right. First, there were news photographers. They snapped at us as we huddled under the wing trying to avoid a sudden snarling rain. Second, there were hamburger and toasted cheese sandwiches in a dinette only a few yards from the runway. Woolley gave us half an hour to eat in. We took off again at 2:54.

We spotted a boat far below. Instantly the radio was at work reporting its position to the Navy. About a month ago Woolley saw a U-boat in approximately the same place. The technique is to pay no attention but fly right on, high and fast, and let the Navy know. The A.T.C. has been credited with sighting at least five submarines in the Caribbean area in the past few months. And Woolley pointed out a spot where one of our own ships was lost quite recently.

We were very close to home now. Everybody aboard was feeling the contagious excitement of impending arrival. We were very high and the sun seemed lower than we were; it was beginning to streak the clouds. I reflected a little on this journey which was now finally nearing its end: how it had made me love Europe again, it had taught me a little about politics and the war and much about myself; how it had strengthened me for work to come.

At 7:12 we saw a rainbow. A little later a brawny sergeant who needed a shave sighted the mainland. Someone began to shout, and an older officer had tears in his eyes. We put down at Miami at 7:23.

THE END